KARL BITTER

Karl Bitter with his oak relief panels for the organ gallery of Biltmore estate, 1895.

KARL BITTER
ARCHITECTURAL SCULPTOR 1867 - 1915

James M. Dennis

The University of Wisconsin Press

Madison, Milwaukee, &

London, 1967

Published by
The University of Wisconsin Press
Madison, Milwaukee, and London
U.S.A.: Box 1379
Madison, Wisconsin 53701
U.K.: 26-28 Hallam Street
London, W. 1

Printed in the
United States of America
By the George Banta Company, Inc.
Menasha, Wisconsin
Library of Congress Catalog
Card Number 67-20757

For
MARIE
RICHARDSON
DENNIS

Acknowledgments

THIS STUDY was begun under the guidance of Professor David Loshak, who saw me through its initial drafts with sound advice and criticism. Intensive research would have been impossible without the manuscript materials provided by Mrs. Walter Abel, New York City; Dr. Francis Bitter, Centerville, Massachusetts; and Professor John Bitter, Coral Gables, Florida. Albums and scrapbooks containing photographs were also among the materials made available to me by Karl Bitter's children; and I have thus been able to include pictures of models and clay sketches which were normally destroyed after completion of the sculpture. In some cases when a finished sculpture was later destroyed photographs are the only remaining record of the work. I wish also to acknowledge the assistance and encouragement given me by Mr. Walter Gruppe and Mrs. Margaret Witherspoon of New York City.

Important information, along with helpful photographs, was generously granted by officials of the Pennsylvania Railroad, Philadelphia; the Minneapolis Park Board of Commissioners; the Biltmore Estate, Asheville, North Carolina; and the Art Commission of New York City. The staffs of the following libraries and historical societies graciously provided original documents: Archives Division of the State Historical Society, Madison, Wisconsin; Missouri Historical Society, St. Louis; Michigan Historical Collections, University of Michigan; Fine Arts Division of the New York Public Library; and the Frick Art Reference Library, New York City.

I wish to thank Mr. William R. Dennis, Mr. David H. Elliot, Dr. James C. Butler, Dr. Richard S. Trump, Dr. Franklin M. Ludden, Mr. Norman E. Scaggs, and Mr. James T. Cook for their aid and inspiration along the way to this book. My gratitude is also due Mr. Glenn W. Jacobsen, of the University of Wisconsin History Department, for reading a large part of the final draft. No statement is sufficient to express my indebtedness to Claudia, who dedicated hours as an editor-typist on the many revisions of the manuscript from start to finish.

J. M. D.

Madison, Wisconsin
January, 1967

Contents

Illustrations

KARL BITTER

Introduction

KARL BITTER began his career in Austria during the 1880's at the end of a prolonged baroque tradition of architectural and monumental sculpture. This tradition had emerged from Italy during the second half of the sixteenth century, coming to an early fruition in the great works of Bernini. It continued north to France, Germany, and Austria where during the eighteenth century architectural sculpture underwent stylistic alterations, the main characteristics of change being the delicate touch of the rococo and its counterbalance, neoclassicism. Toward the middle of the nineteenth century such French sculptors as Rude, Carpeaux, and Barye, in concurrence with the painting style of Delacroix, applied basically baroque styles to both realistic and romantically remote subject matter. Allegory remained intact as a persistent category of sculpture, providing each generation an opportunity to employ the nude, a subject that became increasingly literal in the hands of academic modelers during the second half of the nineteenth century. Out of this trend of naturalism Rodin's work emerged as a sculptural counterpart of Impressionist painting to establish a widely emulated surface technique. Much more important for modern sculpture, however, was Rodin's re-emphasis of sculptural form: volumes, both solid and spatial, organized into a cohesive, self-contained composition.

During his career Bitter occasionally acknowledged the freely organic compositions advanced by Rodin. For the most part, however, his methods of design were in keeping with the rather pictorial devices of the academic baroque relief or with the ancient frontal orientation of the freestanding monumental figure. Consistent with the latter convention, his stylistic progress led him to a new reference for the conservative sculptor, the Greek archaic. This recently expanded classical source provided antique devices that could be alternated and sometimes combined with qualities of surface design that Bitter learned to develop from fellow Austrian sculptors, most significantly Franz Metzner. This source of inspiration originally belonged to the *Jugendstil* of the Vienna Secession, a moderate revolution against Bitter's old academy.

By 1915, the year of his premature death, signs of synthesis had begun to appear in Bitter's work. He was starting to draw together the main stylistic forces of his development; and his last figure, the nude "Abundance" on the Plaza in New York, reveals that he was working above the high competency he had maintained from the beginning.

Like most sculptors during his generation, Bitter was primarily a modeler. He worked in clay and, after the turn of the century, also used the newly invented plasteline. Unlike many conservative sculptors of the time, for example the fondly remembered Daniel Chester French, Bitter was furthermore a proficient stone-carver. He acquired this skill in Vienna while working as an apprentice on public buildings and monuments that were under construction for the Crown during the late 1880's. In the United States Bitter soon depended upon assistant carvers of his own, but he continued to do the finished carving of facial features and surface refinements.

To begin a work Bitter drew rough pencil and ink sketches, establishing the main proportions and contours of a composition. Figure drawings from life—a nude or a portrait sitter, as the case might be—then followed. Or, if a commission called for a historical figure from the past, he worked from contemporary portraits, either painted, photographed, or written. Sketches in clay or plasteline were the next step, and these were gradually built up and modeled by tool and hand to finished form. From this original figure a plaster mold would be made in which a plaster cast was produced. If satisfactory, the completed model would then be recast in bronze, or reproduced (and oftentimes mechanically enlarged with a pointing machine) in stone. Upon completion of the permanent sculpture the plaster model was most often destroyed along with the molds.

Domestic marbles and Indiana limestone were prevalent in American sculpture, but during the last ten years of his career Bitter preferred Vermont granite for his increasingly stylized, allegorical figures. For one group of flat reliefs he used an extremely resistant gray granite. He was always very conscious of permitting the permanent material to determine the composition and surface design of a work. This, in fact, became a basic topic that he pursued as archaeological research into ancient sculpture.

As a diligent professional artist concerned with the progress of architectural and monumental sculpture, Bitter succeeded not only as a sculptor but as an administrator of sculptural affairs. In this capacity he designed and directed great schemes for world's fairs demanding many contributing sculptors. Also, through the admiration of his peers, he was elected three times to preside over the recently founded National Sculpture Society and was chosen twice to serve on the Art Commission of New York City. In promoting his art no American predecessor, from Horatio Greenough and Thomas Crawford to John Quincy Adams Ward and Augustus Saint-Gaudens, had had such opportunities. The aging Ward and Saint-Gaudens recognized and respected the ability of the young immigrant to organize group efforts and carry out large programs of architectural sculpture. In spite of this success, however, Bitter became increasingly engaged in his personal artistic development. This attitude was to have a pronounced effect on his mature sculpture, on his control of its architectural setting, and on the relationship of both to the public.

Working within the quasi-renaissance that he found under way in America upon his arrival, Bitter represented toward the end of this innocent age a progressive outlook from a conservative point of view. In contrast to such academic spokesmen as the painter-critics Kenyon Cox and Edwin Blashfield, or Chicago's sculptor–art historian Lorado Taft, he was tolerant toward changes occurring outside the academy. He was interested in the *Jugendstil* and directly influenced by Secessionist sculpture and architecture. He once wrote to an artist friend in Vienna that he would even like to have been "modern" but his education and development would not allow it. He could not sympathize with the current avant-garde enthusiasm for primitive African sculpture as opposed to his own late preference for the Greek archaic.

On his trips back to Europe he did not go to Paris, and he had limited opportunity to see modern art experiments in Germany and Austria. More than likely his first substantial exposure to the avant-garde, with the possible exceptions of a few publications and Alfred Stieglitz's 291 Gallery, was the 1913 Armory Show in New York. Unfortunately, no specific response to the works he saw there is available. However, it is more than safe to assume that he would not have advocated the reductive abstractions of Brancusi, Matisse, or of Cubism and its Futurist derivatives. On the other hand, it would be interesting to know what he thought of such moderate modernists as the sculptors Maillol, Lehmbruck, and Kolbe. Judging from his involvement in Secessionist sculpture he could well have admired their work.

His opinion of the contemporary urban realists in American painting led by Robert Henri and John Sloan is also unavailable.[1] He was an immigrant with a modest background, and even a fugitive from what he considered an unjust system. However, in New York he quickly became an "uptowner" with the additional independence of a house on the New Jersey bank of the Hudson River. He never had to struggle in America as an underprivileged artist in a working class sector of the city. Immediate prosperity relieved him of tenement life, and he could assume an idealistic attitude toward poverty and its alleviation, one which was in agreement with the majority of middle class progressives during his day. A reformed political-economic system should be accompanied by a municipal face-lifting, at least on publicly owned places. If carried out in a proper classical tradition, the official setting should encourage and even inspire the individual to improve his position in the community through self-reliant means.

This was a basic attitude behind Bitter's participation in city planning. It was consistent with the City Beautiful movement advanced by Daniel H. Burnham. Wherever possible the American city should have, in addition to natural parks, a formal mall or plaza, perhaps a *corso,* and certainly a series of squares connected by boulevards creating unbroken vistas. Such would relate to a traditional baroque conception to which Bitter was conditioned as a youth in Vienna. He did not consider a city as so many practical units classified residential, commercial, industrial, or governmental with streets and railways to serve them. His attention was concentrated on urban spaces that should be aesthetically determined and architecturally controlled places of pleasure. In his mind's eye he promenaded along tree-lined thoroughfares toward a grand fountain or monument bordered by balustrades, grass, shrubbery, and flower beds, with the buildings beyond, in the background, not all over and above or continuously closing in on one's center of sight. It was an open composition, integrating architecture, monumental sculpture, foilage, green squares, and avenues that Bitter envisioned in 1898 as a master plan for Manhattan. In the face of commerce, the elevator, the elevated, and the automobile, Bitter's conception could not become a cause. In the end he could only hope to preserve some of the open areas still remaining. He would have been crushed by the high-rise confusion of glass and steel that has recently destroyed the vista once provided by lower Park Avenue. His Plaza on Fifth Avenue remains to receive the people as he thought a city should, but now it too is being encroached upon from across the street by the construction of an awesome corporation skyscraper.

The steel and glass structures of today accommodate little in the way of architectural sculpture. Concrete buildings are, on the other hand, mechanically cast into forms that might be termed sculptural. Frank Lloyd Wright eventually succeeded in designing ornament buildings that needed none of the applied ornamentation, including figural sculpture, that he employed up to the time of World War I. Conservative sculptors remain to turn out a kind of dressed-down classicism for government war memorials and a dressed-up classicism for official portraits. In modern sculpture high-relief wall hangings, freestanding compositions, and a few fountain formations are put on display. Rarely is a work conceived and carried out in conjunction with the architect as an integral part of a structure and its immediate setting. There is no demand for an architectural sculptor, creating monumental works for locations designed for such treatment. As Bitter observed in 1914, the contemporary sculptor, no longer trained "to mingle with the architect," had become primarily a "statuaire," or a producer of gallery pieces. In spite of the adoption of architectural techniques and materials into the new art of construction that much of sculpture has become since then, Bitter's observation still holds true today.

The essence of Bitter's comparatively short but highly productive career of twenty-five years was fluency, wrote Alexander Stirling Calder (see Epilogue, below). This judgment is soon shared by anyone attempting to trace all of the works, large and small, that emerged from his studio. A complete catalogue, however, is not necessary to a thorough understanding of his development as a sculptor. A readily discerned change in approach and purpose occurred between his youthful achievements of the early 1890's, and the sculpture of his final years.

To demonstrate the evolution of his mature style each of Bitter's major works will be discussed. Regrettably, several of them have suffered at the hands of progress and its destruction-engineers in recent years. In some cases the sculpture has been destroyed altogether, while in others it has either been taken down and shipped away from its original setting or has ended up in prolonged storage.

Portrait reliefs, busts, and small commemorative plaques done for friends and private patrons have a more natural tendency to disappear. Several of these are merely mentioned or roughly sketched out in Bitter's notes and letters; while a few can be seen in photographs. There may be others completely unrecorded. A good example of personal parlor sculpture is the bust of Mary Griswold Emerson (Fig. 1), wife of the writer-adventurer Edwin Emerson, who was a friend of Bitter. Presented as a classical marble bust it is also an intimate study that reflects a career-long concern, the conscientious portrayal of a personality.[2] A larger work of this nature was produced in 1904 as a high relief in pink marble of Mrs. Charles R. Crane with her son John (Fig. 2). Framed in an ornate arch of variegated marble, the composition of this portrait was "conceived in the manner of the della Robbias."[3] In his own right, however, Bitter achieved a tour de force as a masterful modeler in the intricate arrangement of hands holding grapes, and he captured a moment of maternal warmth compassionately conveyed in downturned faces.

Three works that combine small portraits with commemorative relief plaques were produced between the turn of the century and 1910. Each includes a framed low-relief portrait bust above a rectangular relief panel. The earliest of these was cast as a single tablet of bronze in 1900 to honor the memory of the Reverend Anthony Kesseler, pastor of St. Joseph's Church in New York City for over thirty years.[4] With the exception of the cameo portrait on top it was patterned after an Early Renaissance tabernacle. Its pictorial relief depicts Christ and Peter on the Sea of Galilee, an allusion to the pastor's death at sea. Four years later Bitter completed a similar plaque, measuring approximately six feet in height, to be mounted in the Court of Special Sessions in the Criminal Court Building of New

Fig. 1.—Mary Griswold Emerson, marble bust, 1911. Owned by Mrs. A. W. Penniman, Saratoga, California.

York (Fig. 3). A gift from the City Club, of which Bitter was a member, this work, now lost, commemorated Rebecca Foster. She had been called "The Tombs' Angel" for her efforts to rehabilitate delinquents at the old Tombs Prison. To represent this altruism Bitter modeled a relief showing a winged female figure gently caressing a distressed boy, and placed it under an oval portrait of Miss Foster. Both reliefs were carved in white marble while the elaborate Renaissance frame which contained them was cast in bronze.[5] In 1909 the third commemorative portrait tablet was installed as a marble relief in a simple brick memorial on the campus of Tuskeegee

Fig. 2.—Mrs. Charles R. Crane and son, John, marble relief, 1904. Crane home, Wood's Hole, Massachusetts.

Institute in Alabama. It was dedicated to William Henry Baldwin, a railroad executive turned reformer, who had supported the efforts of Booker T. Washington. To symbolize gratitude, Bitter represented a youthful Negro laborer holding olive branches up to the portrait medallion.

Since it is Bitter's major achievements as a sculptor and public figure that are of primary concern in the following chapters, they include little about his private life. In general, his writings reveal that once settled in America he lived a well-ordered, middle-class existence, especially after his marriage in 1901. His bride was Marie Schevill, born in Cincinnati of well-to-do German immigrant parents. The wedding took place in the parish house of All Souls Congregational Church in New York City, and the honeymoon was a rather strenuous two-month bicycle tour of France, Switzerland, and northern Italy. The couple returned to the groom's studio-house which he had constructed several years earlier above the Hudson River on the New Jersey Palisades in Weehawken. Steady prosperity permitted the purchase of two other dwellings during the next eight years. The first was a cottage on an island in Racquette Lake deep in the Adirondacks. In sharp contrast to this rustic retreat, the last of his few real estate investments was in a thirteen-story building of studio-apartments constructed as a cooperative on West Seventy-seventh Street in Manhattan. In 1909 its top floor was ready for the Bitters and their children, Francis, John, and Marietta. The Weehawken workshop was retained for the completion of large-scale sculpture.

Bitter proved to be a practical planner from the beginning of his career and seemed to find his way into a bustling, materialistic society with ease. His work took him from coast to coast as he carried out one project after another. During his many trips, however, he took time to enjoy the landscape and often jotted down his impressions. In the summer of 1914, for example, while on a train bound for Minneapolis, he became so enthralled with the Wisconsin countryside that he described it in German for his son Francis in a spontaneous eight verse poem.[6]

In contrast to a basic love of life, an undercurrent of melancholy is occasionally revealed in his letters. His childhood and youth in Vienna were not altogether happy, and even his eventual success in America did not erase what he termed "the tone of dark foliage against the evening sky."[7] His preference for the works of Gerhardt Hauptmann over those of other

Fig. 3.—Rebecca Salome Foster, "The Tombs' Angel," plaster model for marble and bronze relief, 1904. The location of this sculpture is not known; it was probably destroyed with the old Criminal Court Building of New York City.

contemporary playwrights is consistent with this sense of tragedy. He had the good fortune of seeing the famous Austrian actor Adolf von Sonnenthal play the lead in *Fuhrmann Henschel* on a New York stage in 1899, an emotional experience he records at length in his diary.[8] Richard Wagner was another idol, and of the many books that Bitter mentions reading, the tragic existence portrayed in Wagner's autobiography *Mein Leben* seems to have made a deep impression.[9]

At the height of his career Bitter suffered a period of prolonged depression. In March, 1914, he placed himself in the care of a psychoanalyst who operated a sanatorium in Bethel, Maine. The treatment lasted several weeks and, according to Bitter, consisted primarily of autosuggestion as a means of influencing the subconscious. He compared it to the practice of Christian Science without the "humbug." In spite of positive results he was certain he would always remain a little morose, his expressed purpose in going being to relieve his immediate "grievances against the world and social order."[10]

By Thanksgiving Day, 1914, Bitter was once again grieved, but this time by the disorder caused by war. In a letter to Hans Kestranek, his friend in Vienna, he explains his position and that of the German-American community at large. Their sympathies were understandably with Austria and Germany, and he himself was busy soliciting money and moral support for a common war effort.[11] Since he had deserted the army of his homeland in 1889 to come to America as a "citizen of the world," perhaps he felt he could in this way make up for his delinquency. Even in 1909 upon his return to Vienna to receive an amnesty he had not been very repentant. Although twenty years had passed, he still called the regime of Franz Josef "pernicious" and lamented the fact that his parents and two brothers remained in Austria.[12] On the other hand he had been welcomed to Vienna by former professors and loyal friends with a magnificent banquet at the Sachergarten, and this treatment tended to modify any hatred he had toward the city itself. On the train returning through Germany he summed up his mixed feelings by writing, "With all its charm Austria depresses me; in Germany I have less of that feeling. But when I think of America my thoughts have wings and I feel so light, so sure, so free."[13]

For a year preceding his death in April, 1915, Bitter alternated his allegiance between the Old and the New Worlds.[14] His talents, however, had been utilized almost exclusively in the United States, and it is with an international eclecticism that generally characterizes art in America that his sculpture must be identified.

I

From Vienna To the Vanderbilts

IN THE BEGINNING Karl Bitter's career as a sculptor was evenly divided between two contrasting cities. Romantic Vienna provided him tradition and training throughout the 1880's, while robust New York was the scene of his first ambitious achievements during the last decade of the century. He was born to a middle-class family in Rudolfsheim, a suburb of Vienna, on December 6, 1867, and was baptized Karl Theodore Francis Bitter in an Evangelical Church.[1] His father, Karl Johann Bitter, was a German from Karlsruhe, who had established a small business in household chemicals. His mother was the daughter of an accountant, Franz Reitter, from Vienna. Illness prevented the boy from finishing his first year of school, but reading lessons at home enabled him to rejoin his class by the third year. Report cards from the Rudolfsheim public school reveal that as a student he was just slightly better than average. His application was graded fair to good, and there were times when his attendance was rather poor. At the age of nine he entered the Gymnasium and, as Bitter later wrote, he developed an immediate dislike for the academic curriculum, especially its keystone, Latin.[2] On the other hand, he relished Germanic legends and Greek myths. He also enjoyed regular excursions through the countryside near his home, and liked reading about such adventurous travels as those of David Livingstone. It was during these boyhood years that Bitter eventually discovered an ability to draw, and when only fourteen he took it upon himself to leave the Gymnasium in order to enter the School of Applied Arts attached to the Austrian Museum of Art and Industry in Vienna.

The decision to enter art school was not only a reaction against academic education, but also a declaration of freedom from a strict and practical home life. Bitter's father was a strenuous disciplinarian who had no sympathy for either an intellectual or an artistic career. He wanted his three sons to become lawyers, and when his second-born refused to pursue this course, he was infuriated. Bitter was narrowly saved from being ejected from the household by his mother's intercession, but his father continued to insist that his son had condemned himself to the life of a worthless "Lump."[3] This accusation, however cruel, was to serve a useful purpose as a highly respected challenge that had to be met with success.

Bitter attended the School of Applied Arts from 1881 to 1884 with the initial intention of becoming a landscape painter. Nevertheless, his yearly certificates indicate that he not only attended classes in figure drawing and perspective, but also studied ornamental drawing and modeling from an instructor named August Kuehne, from whom he received his highest marks.[4] According to Bitter, he became a student of sculpture by sheer accident when he first entered the building. He was carrying a plaster reproduction of a relief by Thorwaldsen, as well as a roll of his own drawings, when an elderly porter, assuming that he wanted to attend Kuehne's class, abruptly ordered him into the appropriate studio. It was not until the term began on the following Monday that Bitter realized he had enrolled in a class of modeling. However, he was so pleased at being accepted that he made no attempt to correct the error.[5]

Although for a while his desire to paint landscapes did not wane, he was greatly influenced by the teaching of Kuehne, and it was this experience that gradually won him over to sculpture altogether. The course began with the modeling of ornaments, for which Bitter later admitted he could arouse little enthusiasm. During the second and third years he was permitted to concentrate on figures. Apparently much, if not all, of this early figure study was done from reproductions, for he recalled that at the age of sixteen he became thoroughly devoted to his work when called upon to copy Michelangelo's "Captive Slaves."[6]

In the spring of 1885 Bitter was enrolled in the Imperial Academy of Fine Arts where he attended classes through the winter of 1888.[7] The faculty of the Academy was divided into two factions. The old, conservative members remained loyal to a tradition of neoclassicism inherited from Ca-

Fig. 4.—Diana relief for W. K. Vanderbilt's Long Island home, clay model, 1893. The sculpture was destroyed with the house, by fire in 1898.

Fig. 5.—Carriage porch relief for Fifth Avenue mansion of Cornelius Vanderbilt, model for limestone, 1893. The limestone version is inside the Fifth Avenue entrance of the Sherry-Netherlands Hotel, New York City.

nova and Thorwaldsen, and the younger instructors were determined to introduce a naturalistic-baroque style that exploited an ease of contour, a richness of texture, and a greater variation of light and shadow. It was a member of the latter group, Edmund Hellmer, that Bitter chose as his teacher.[8] Vienna in the eighties also provided the student of sculpture with many opportunities to gain professional experience outside the classroom. For example, Bitter became actively engaged in the ornamentation of the monumental public buildings under construction by the Crown. His lifelong friend, Hans Kestranek, witnessed him modeling innumerable figures and their accessories from sketches given to him by established sculptors. In the studio of Duell and Friedl he helped execute the decorative sculpture on the Burgtheater, the energetic Horsebreaker groups in the Court Stables, and a large pediment for an orphanage in Innsbruck.[9] During the same period, he worked as an apprentice for a stone-carver in order to increase his ability with a chisel. Therefore, by the time he was twenty years old he was well acquainted with the techniques of the architectural sculptor. Furthermore, he had been introduced to a process of integrating a variety of media into an elaborate architectural scheme.

Two months before his twenty-first birthday Bitter's career was interrupted when he was drafted into the army. Unfortunately, he had forfeited his student classification by leaving the Gymnasium too soon, so instead of one year as a soldier he was faced with three. After serving the first of these, however, he felt justified in taking advantage of a two-month furlough as an opportunity to desert.[10] With the intention of eventually emigrating to America he fled to Germany, worked his way to Berlin, and then, with the financial aid of a Viennese friend named Rudolph Schwarz, traveled on to the port city of Bremen. On November 22, 1889, eleven days after he was to have returned to his barracks, Bitter arrived in the United States carrying a pack weighted down with tools of his trade along with a German-English dictionary and a few dollars.[11] His talent and training, however, were his most valuable possessions, and on the day after disembarking in New York he was hired by a firm of architectural decorators to model figures in clay. Only a few weeks later his work attracted the attention of the firm's most important client, Richard Morris Hunt. The architect offered to entrust Bitter with interior decorations of a mansion he had designed if the young immigrant could establish a studio of his own. Bitter eagerly accepted the opportunity, and his career as an independent sculptor was launched in a small workshop on East Thirteenth Street.[12]

New York in 1890 was an ideal place for Bitter to vindicate his choice of profession in the eyes of his father, as well as to exonerate himself following the desertion of his fatherland. With a growing population of almost two million the city was undergoing rapid construction, and with the great fortunes accumulated following the Civil War, brownstone town houses were being overshadowed by larger, more ostentatious mansions along upper Fifth Avenue. Demand for elaborate ornamentation increased accordingly, and Bitter had the advantage of being a European-trained specialist in decorative, architectural sculpture. As such he was to be the protégé of Hunt, who engaged in so many projects that only one other architect of fashionable homes, George B. Post, could take advantage of the young sculptor's amazing ability to turn out vast quantities of figures in a wide range of materials for residential interiors.

In 1891 Hunt designed a double mansion which was erected on Fifth Avenue at Sixty-fifth Street for Mrs. William Astor and her son, John Jacob. Although its façade was French Renaissance in derivation, its entrance hall assumed a German baroque appearance when Bitter added a series of half-length nude female figures to its classical walls. Carved in marble, they were attached to pilasters just beneath the vaulted ceiling, and from this location looked down upon the grand stairway. Each rose in the form of a caryatid from a cluster of drapery, but every head was free from burden, and the arms were arranged in a balanced variation of casual gestures.[13] A similar project was provided by the Collis P. Huntington residence designed by Post for the southeast corner of Fifth Avenue and Fifty-seventh Street. Its central hall was a square room with red marble paneling on the lower half which served as a background for paintings. The second story consisted of an open corridor around three sides and windows at one end. A white marble frieze between the balustrade of the corridor and the red walls below was modeled and carved by Bitter as a succession of rectangular relief panels. Each depicted a baby Bacchanalia performed by a frivolous group of *putti* frolicking about playing instruments.[14]

In addition to building Fifth Avenue mansions, the wealthy families of New York continued to compete in constructing colossal "cottages" in the

Fig. 6.—Banquet Hall fireplace, marble, Biltmore estate, Asheville, North Carolina, 1893–1895. Courtesy of Putnam Photography, Asheville, N.C.

Fig. 7.—Organ gallery, oak, Biltmore estate, Asheville, North Carolina, 1893–1895. Courtesy of Putnam Photography, Asheville, N.C.

exclusive resort town of Newport, Rhode Island. This practice also contributed to Bitter's well-being when he was commissioned by Hunt to execute sculpture for the seaside châteaux, Ochre Court and Marble House. The former was designed for the New York real estate magnate Ogden Goelet and the latter for the William K. Vanderbilts. By the time Bitter arrived from Austria, Marble House was well under construction, and to honor its architect, as well as the tradition within which he worked, Vanderbilt had Bitter do high-relief portraits of Hunt and Jules Hardouin-Mansart. Approximately life-size, the pair of figures is above the windows of the stairway mezzanine. Each holds a white medallion that enhances the mellow glow of gilt that was added to the sculpture for its location near the ceiling. Bitter was also probably responsible for the gilt wood panels of four mythological subjects carved for the Gold Room at Marble House.[15] For Vanderbilt's Long Island home, Idle Hour, Bitter modeled a high-relief figure of Diana (Fig. 4) gracefully releasing the invisible string of an imaginary bow. Although contained in a flat, classical frame, the slender nude projected far outside its picture plane, and as a sensuous study from nature was only incidentally mythological.[16]

Such domestic commissions, while rather modest in contrast to the sculpture Bitter produced for large commercial buildings through his relationship with Hunt, multiplied rapidly.[17] In fact he was soon forced to give up his cramped quarters on East Thirteenth Street and move into a larger studio on East Fifty-third Street where he and his assistants could work more comfortably. From this second location innumerable figures, freestanding and relief, continued to find their way into the town and country homes of America's culture-conscious plutocracy. The Vanderbilt family alone provided a large market for a variety of residential works.

In 1893 Post enlarged the Fifth Avenue mansion which he had designed for Cornelius Vanderbilt II ten years earlier, until it covered an entire block from West Fifty-seventh Street to West Fifty-eighth Street. Bitter was requested to execute six high-relief panels for the pedestals of the classical carriage porch on the north side of the mansion, facing the square known as the Plaza. Far removed in subject matter from the voluptuous Diana of Idle Hour, each panel consisted of a compact group of children draped in nondescript robes.[18] When the Vanderbilt mansion was razed in the 1920's to make room for Bergdorf-Goodman's, two of these panels were placed in the Fifth Avenue entrance of the Sherry-Netherlands Hotel across the street. Both extant reliefs are carved out of limestone with unadorned frames cut back to allow the bare feet of the foreground figures to overlap at the base. Neither panel is entirely clear in meaning. One shows a cluster of seven solemn adolescent boys carrying large plumes. The other, containing six musical girls (Fig. 5), is more harmonious in composition as well as content and perhaps was intended to be a welcoming feature. While their rather uniform faces might be considered Bitteresque in type, they bear a basic resemblance to the singing children of Luca della Robbia on the Cantoria in the Cathedral Museum of Florence.

The most extensive residential project that Bitter fulfilled was commissioned, paradoxically enough, by George Washington Vanderbilt, the least endowed son of William H. Vanderbilt. With the intention of using his money to construct the grandest country estate in America, Vanderbilt purchased 125,000 acres of farmlands, forests, and mountains southwest of Asheville, North Carolina. To lay out the estate, called Biltmore, he employed Frederick Law Olmsted, and to design its huge house as a French Renaissance château, he chose Richard Morris Hunt. While the exterior of the house is fairly consistent in style, the interior is less homogeneous, and Bitter provided sculpture in four different materials for three sharply contrasting settings.

The Banquet Hall, with its timber ceiling arching seventy-five feet above the floor, is the largest room in the house, and he executed a marble frieze approximately twenty-five feet long for the mantel of its triple fireplace (Fig. 6). Representing a "Return from the Chase," the narrow relief comprises a continuous array of horses, hunters, musicians, and dogs making their way through a forest toward a distant hilltop castle. The rustic romanticism of the subject is not only enhanced by medieval costumes and weapons, it is enlivened by the strenuous movements of powerful men and animals. To keep the lengthy composition in control Bitter distributed its equestrian figures in three evenly spaced groups. By means of parallel curves and diagonals, as well as a continuity of contours, he united them to their entourage. The figures wind fluently in and out of their wooded surroundings, and the trail which they follow recedes convincingly into the distance. In the lower right corner three onlookers face inward toward the principal figures, and thereby serve as a spatial *repoussoir* outside the perspective plane. At the other end of the panel, figures seem to emerge from beyond the border evoking the expectation that others will follow.

Fig. 8.—Tannhäuser, central panel of organ gallery, oak, Biltmore estate, Asheville, North Carolina, 1893–1895.

Fig. 9.—Joan of Arc and St. Louis, clay models for limestone figures, Biltmore estate, Asheville, North Carolina, 1893–1895.

Fig. 10.—Joan of Arc and St. Louis, limestone, Biltmore estate, Asheville, North Carolina, 1893–1895.

Fig. 11.—Palm Court, bronze fountain, Biltmore estate, Asheville, North Carolina, 1893–1895. Courtesy of Putnam Photography, Asheville, N.C.

Although intended to complement the vaguely medieval atmosphere of the Hall, the mantle frieze is baroque in its treatment of pictorial space and is framed by a border of purely classical motives.

Facing the fireplace from the opposite end of the Banquet Hall is an organ gallery, and Bitter was responsible for the five relief panels on its balustrade (Fig. 7). These total some forty feet from wall to wall and are carved out of individual pieces of oak. While the sixty figures involved appear to move in any direction with ease, no attempt was made to describe a recession of space illusionistically by means of low relief or inscribed lines. Instead, the blank "wall" behind is gilded to serve as a foil for the roughly whittled texture of the figures. This was apparently meant to approximate the medieval use of a gold leaf ground. However, the foreground platform gives the panels a stage-like appearance, and they are commonly referred to as scenes from Wagner's operas.[19] Since the figures of the five reliefs are obviously involved in a single episode, this is impossible. On the other hand, if the minstrel performing before the enthroned couple in the center of the compartmentalized composition (Fig. 8) is meant to be engaged in a song contest, he could very well represent Tannhäuser singing for the heart of Elisabeth, the niece of the Landgrave of Thuringia.

Two medieval warrior-saints, St. Louis and Joan of Arc, were the subjects assigned to Bitter for his final contributions to the Banquet Hall (Fig. 9). He modeled both in full battle regalia as historical heroes of the church. Joan rolls her eyes toward heaven in prayer, and St. Louis clutches a crucifix while gazing defiantly to one side. Every detail of chain mail and armor was reproduced in limestone before the romantic pair was placed above the doorway inside the hall. This location, however, was not their only destination, as another limestone edition of Bitter's clay models was placed on the exterior of the spiral staircase in front of the house (Fig. 10). Although based on the famous example in the Château de Blois, the Biltmore staircase received a more consistently Gothic treatment from top to bottom than its eclectic sixteenth-century predecessor. Thus Bitter's baroque figures stand underneath stylistically accurate late Gothic canopies when actually they might be more at home in the Renaissance setting at Blois.

Bitter was confronted with still another kind of architectural environment in producing the first fountain group of his career. This was the

Palm Court, a polygonal, glass-domed area with a sunken floor where plants and flowers raised in Biltmore's gardens and greenhouses were displayed. In contrast to the historical subjects carved for the rather rustic Banquet Hall, the figures of a nude boy and two struggling geese were designed to be cast as a bronze centerpiece for the Court (Fig. 11). Readily viewed in the round, the group has an open composition achieved by an omniaxial arrangement of wings, legs, and arms. This demanded a broad base, and to overcome the restricted surface of the pedestal Bitter introduced a rough, protruding rock form which permitted his figure to plant its feet far apart. In order to bring the top of the composition into close harmony with the bottom, the boy's arms were placed parallel to the widespread wings and straining neck of the lower bird. The texture of ruffled feathers, in turn, is repeated, and the raised neck of the captured goose resumes the verticality of the vase-shaped pedestal.

The third setting for Bitter's Biltmore sculpture is an ornate classical-baroque fireplace projecting into the library as an extension of the room's walnut-paneled walls (Fig. 12). A late seventeenth-century Italian tapestry hangs above the black marble mantel of the fireplace, and to flank its intricate frame Bitter carved two wood female figures draped in a complex of chisel-marked folds. The figure on the left more than likely represents Hestia, the goddess of the hearth, while her companion is almost certainly Demeter, goddess of the earth. As examples of ornamental sculpture in the baroque tradition, they are irregular enough to add a slight discord to the structural and pictorial design that they otherwise support. But their poses are sufficiently similar to prevent them from seriously disrupting the symmetry of that elaborate setting.

This introduction of subtle variation into a scheme that is necessarily symmetrical was repeated by Bitter in designing the andirons below. Although cast in iron and surmounted by allegorical figures of polished steel, they are apparently based on designs for bronze andirons by such early baroque sculptors from Venice as Allesandro Vittorio and Roccatagliata. However, the choice of components and their arrangement are his own. Emerging from the Vanderbilt escutcheon, two dolphins support each andiron while bordering a swag of fruit that enlarges the circular shape of a scroll-framed shell in the center. On top of this base, a small mythological relief is flanked by cornucopias as an embellishment for the pedestal of the crowning figure. The andiron on the right is dedicated to

Fig. 12.—Library fireplace, walnut, Biltmore estate, Asheville, North Carolina, 1893–1895. Courtesy of Putnam Photography, Asheville, N.C.

Fig. 13.—Andiron, iron and steel, library fireplace, Biltmore estate, Asheville, North Carolina, 1893–1895.

Venus, who glances to her right in the direction of Vulcan, her mate.[20] He is accompanied by a pair of satyrs flanking the family coat of arms below and two undraped youths who strain to look up at him from their positions on the heads of the dolphins (Fig. 13). The corresponding figures on the andiron of Venus are feminine, and, as in the case of the straining youths, the twisted pose of each nude female figure differs from that of her companion.

Biltmore was completed in 1895, and the death of Richard Morris Hunt during the same year marked the end of Bitter's prosperous apprenticeship in America. Having earned more money than was necessary for the few demands of a rather bohemian life on Fifty-third Street, he decided to build a home somewhere outside the city. He forthrightly admitted that his primary purpose was to demonstrate to his father the early success he had enjoyed as a sculptor.[21] The most impressive site he could find was on the edge of the New Jersey Palisades in Weehawken, overlooking the Hudson and the harbor beyond. He asked Frank Wallis, an architect friend, to help him design an appropriate house. Before the plans were completed, however, he celebrated his triumph in the United States more spontaneously by returning to Europe for the first time. Sailing in November, he spent most of the winter weeks in Italy where he was reunited with his family for his twenty-eighth birthday, and where he also had the opportunity to visit old friends from Vienna who had settled in Rome as art students.[22] After his return to New York in the spring, he devoted many months to his new home, which consisted not only of a house but also of a formal garden, a stable, and a large studio building. The architecture was severe in form, with the cement stucco walls of the studio rising up from the cliffs and the east side of the house mainly glass. Each building was constructed under Bitter's watchful supervision, and because of his insistence on good craftsmanship the whole complex was not completed until the end of 1897.

While the Weehawken home was made possible primarily through Bitter's immediate success in producing a wide selection of scultpure for a limited number of wealthy patrons, its studio would not be used to continue the embellishment of residential interiors for very long. In fact, with the exception of a small garden fountain that Bitter carried out one year before his death, the last of his privately commissioned ornamental works was executed before the turn of the century. In the spring of 1899 he

Fig. 14.—Fountain, plaster model for bronze fountain, Jacob Schiff home, Seabright, New Jersey, 1899. The location of the fountain is not known; it was possibly destroyed with the house.

made the model of an elongated female figure to be installed as a bronze newel post in the Fifth Avenue residence of the German-born merchant, Louis Stern.[23] Draped barely in a loincloth, the life-size figure was transformed into an Arcadian shepherdess with the aid of a hooked staff held high in one hand and a frisky lamb. A similar lighthearted quality was achieved in a bronze fountain group that he had ready for the foundry by the end of April.[24] It was commissioned for a resort home of the banker Jacob Schiff, at Seabright, New Jersey, and consisted of a nude boy and girl holding hands while dancing around a duck (Fig. 14). The raised beak of the bird functioned as a spout, and when the water was turned on, the two figures seemed to be leaning away from each other in an attempt

Fig. 15.—Fountain, plaster model for bronze version, John D. Rockefeller estate, Pocantico Hills, New York, 1914.

to avoid the spray. Both were carefully modeled as properly proportioned naturalistic forms, and the revolving composition obviously grew out of a close observation of children at play.

The universally popular theme of a barnyard animal at the mercy of a child was repeated by Bitter late in his career when, in 1914, he once again accepted a commission for a small bronze fountain. The patron was John D. Rockefeller, and the group was to be placed among numerous other relatively small-scale works by well-known American sculptors on the Pocantico Hills estate. This might be the main reason that he consented to produce a type of work he had otherwise abandoned long before. Unlike the "Boy Stealing a Goose" in the Palm Court at Biltmore, the Pocantico Hills group (Fig. 15) was located in front of an artificial waterfall as part of a garden, and was therefore designed unilaterally. Three geese and the figure of a laughing girl were faced forward with no chance of being seen from behind. In contrast to both of the earlier fountains, the base of this group was made large enough to rest firmly on the ground; and, in spite of the outward movement of the girl's foot or the outstretched wings of her companions, the composition was contained within a substantially triangular outline.

This touch of restraint may have resulted from the experience he had gained in designing increasingly monumental groups of architectural sculpture during the last half of his career. Otherwise, the Pocantico Hills fountain complied with the durable formula of ruffled feathers and frolicsome nudity employed twenty years earlier in the Palm Court at Biltmore. But mansions of the rich were not the only destinations of such ornamental sculpture, even at the beginning of Bitter's career. Flamboyant figures emerged from his first workshops to face the public from large urban buildings as well. Cast in many roles they too celebrated a concentration of wealth in an expanding economy.

II

Ornamentation For a New World Facade

DURING 1889, the same year Bitter deserted Austria for the United States, Joseph Pulitzer decided to construct the highest building in New York City to house his newspaper the *World*. For that purpose he bought the north corner of Park Row, or Newspaper Row, as it was then called. This site adjoined the entrance to the recently opened Brooklyn Bridge and was just across the street from City Hall. To design his building Pulitzer commissioned the engineer-architect George B. Post. The choice was probably influenced by Post's having designed the Times Building just one year earlier and by the architect's special interest in experimenting with steel frame construction for tall buildings. To make his new tower as impressive as possible, Pulitzer himself originated the idea of marking its entrance with a round, coarsely rusticated arch three stories high. He also insisted on surmounting the thirteen-story structure with a gold dome to contain his private offices.[1]

As was the case in most of the novel "elevator buildings," only those sides of the Pulitzer Building facing the principal thoroughfares were treated architecturally. That is, they were ornamented with customary architectural details arranged and proportioned to appear as if they were still part of a low, masonry structure. The rear wall, meanwhile, remained a blank brick surface with windows arbitrarily punched through it. A prominent part of the main, or west, façade of the Pulitzer Building consisted of a central pavilion of two-story arches, divided vertically by coupled columns, and interrupted horizontally by stringcourses. At the top of this pavilion was a pediment containing an elaborate assortment of decorative animals surrounding a terra-cotta panel bearing the owner's monogram "JP" and the date "1889." Four enormous, standing atlantes representing a Caucasian, an Indian, a Mongolian, and a Negro appeared to be supporting the pediment. Actually the sixteen-foot, undraped male figures were made of black copper.[2]

Much more visible from City Hall Park were four winged female figures of bronze placed upon a fifth-floor balustrade. Each held a torch high above her head and supported a single blanket of drapery that fell loosely around her upward-straining, half-exposed body, measuring thirteen feet from head to toe. The figures represented Art, Literature, Science, and Invention with the aid of familiar accessories. While Art naturally held a palette in one hand and knelt on a capital, Science carried a globe. A scroll lay at the feet of Literature and an open volume rested in her left arm. Invention, stated the *World,* was also accompanied by her "appropriate symbols."

A souvenir supplement to the *World,* issued on December 10, 1890, to commemorate the opening of the new building, states that John Quincy Adams Ward, Saint-Gaudens, and other leading sculptors expressed their most unreserved admiration for these figures; but there is no mention of the sculptor or sculptors who decorated the façade. Nevertheless, it is certain that at least one of the fifth-floor torchbearers was executed by the newly immigrated Karl Bitter. His lifelong friend, Hans Kestranek, reports that Bitter did an eighteen-foot figure of "Freiheit" for George B. Post's *World* Building.[3] Also, a photograph of a half-nude winged female figure lifting a torch high above her head (Fig. 16) appears in one of Bitter's personal picture albums and apparently was taken of the clay model soon after it was finished.[4] If measured from base to torch, she could have been eighteen rather than thirteen feet in height. Because of the torch held high in her right hand, Kestranek compares her with Bartholdi's Statue of Liberty. But even with a book cradled in her left arm the resemblance was limited.

Most likely meant to symbolize Literature rather than Freedom, this winged figure appeared to stride freely forward, peering downward from beneath heavy eyelids. The composition of the figure was explosive, with the burst centered upon a mask-like brooch which clasped the flowing drapery to a high belt beneath bare breasts. All of the dominant lines of

Fig. 16.—Torchbearer, model for bronze figure, Pulitzer Building, New York City, 1890. Sculpture and building destroyed.

the figure, including the contours of the wings, legs, and drapery, intersected at this point to create a radial symmetry that helped balance the figure on its narrow ledge high up on the building.

Bitter's torchbearer would have been right at home in late nineteenth-century Vienna. Instead of greeting City Hall Park in New York, she might have accompanied the lightly-draped female figure on the Hofburg that Rudolph Weyr modeled for the top of his marble fountain representing Sea Power. What is more, such a location would certainly have been longer lasting, for after 1895 photographs of the Pulitzer Building in New York guidebooks reveal empty plinths and panels where the torchbearers had originally stood.[5]

Two events occurred in February, 1890, which were to lead to larger projects for Bitter than that provided by Pulitzer. First, Richard Morris Hunt, although suffering from gout, was persuaded by his former student, George B. Post, to lead the New York contingent of architects at the Columbian Exposition in Chicago. On January 10, 1891, an advisory board of ten architectural firms, including those of both Hunt and Post, assembled in Chicago, where a prominent building of the Fair was assigned to each. As often recounted, the eastern group carried off the most highly prized assignments, namely the buildings around the Court of Honor. For instance, Post was to design the Manufactures and Liberal Arts Building, the largest and most expensive at the Exposition. It covered over thirty acres and cost one and one-half million dollars. Hunt, on the other hand, was assigned the focal point of the entire complex, the Administration Building, which was to stand at the head of the Court much as the chair of the patriarch is placed at the head of the family dining table. To supply the ornamental sculpture for their respective buildings, Hunt and Post turned to Bitter, who had been doing this kind of work for them during the past year.

The second event to bear directly on Bitter's career was the death of John Jacob Astor, grandson of the famous German-American fur merchant. Early in March his son, William Waldorf Astor, wrote to the Reverend Morgan Dix, Rector of Trinity Church. Following a suggestion once made by his father, he wished to place sets of memorial bronze doors at the main and two side entrances of the church. If this met with the approval of the vestry, Astor added, he would write to Richard Morris Hunt "to take the order."[6] Later in the month Hunt was asked to direct the designing of the doors, and as a means of locating sculptors it was decided to follow the method used for the second gates of the Florentine Baptistery. An open competition was therefore held in which any sculptor might enter by modeling a panel of a prescribed subject, in this case the Expulsion of Adam and Eve from the Garden of Eden. On March 19, 1891, New York newspapers announced that Bitter, at the age of twenty-four, had been chosen to execute the gates for the main entrance facing Broadway and Wall Street.

By this time, however, the designs for the Columbian Exposition Buildings were well under way, and by the end of the year the staff* exterior was already being applied to the superstructure of Hunt's Administration Building. For this reason Bitter put the church gates aside to concentrate on the many groups of Exposition sculpture that were being designed, modeled, enlarged, and installed under his direction. Of the two buildings placed in his hands, the Administration Building by Hunt was by far the more abundantly adorned and therefore of central concern.[7] Besides containing the administrative offices of the Fair, it was to serve as a "monumental porch" or "overture" for the visitors as they emerged from the railroad terminal located a few paces to the west. As expressed by Henry Van Brunt, another of Hunt's students who contributed a building to the Court of Honor, the Administration Building would introduce the American public to a vast new world.

"To this end the forums, basilicas and baths of the Roman Empire, the villas and gardens of the princes of the Italian Renaissance, the royal court yards of the palaces of France and Spain, must yield to the architects, 'in that new world which is the old,' their rich inheritance of ordered beauty, to make possible the creation of a bright picture of civic splendor such as this great function of modern civilization would seem to require."[8]

Unadorned, Hunt's Administration Building did not create such "a bright picture of civic splendor" but more a spirit of scholarly reserve. Its lofty dome, while not quite as large, had approximately the profile and proportions of Brunelleschi's dome for the Cathedral of Florence. However, Hunt eliminated the familiar ornate lantern of Renaissance and baroque domes, and the bare body of the building beneath was almost austere, if not severely classical. The central hall was octagonal, establishing the basic shape for the rest of the building all the way up to the oculus of the dome. To each of the narrow alternate sides of the ground plan a

* Temporary exposition buildings and sculpture before World War I were composed mainly of a material called staff. It consisted of powdered gypsum, alumina, glycerine, dextrine, and hemp, or similar fiber. Formed into any shape by the use of gelatine molds, staff objects were very light in weight and easily tinted after they were nailed in place.

square pavilion of four stories was attached. In order to conform with the other buildings surrounding the basin of the Court, these flat-roofed wings measured sixty feet from pavement to cornice, and their single colossal order—in this case, Doric—was raised upon a basement. The second order of the building was Ionic with an open colonnade or loggia on each of the cardinal faces of the octagon. The alternate sides at this level consisted of circular, domed staircase pavilions niched between heavy corner piers. From the drum of the central dome to the basement, structural ornaments were used sparingly. For example, the only volutes were those of the Ionic capitals on the second floor colonnade. Therefore, an impression of ephemeral pomp and pageantry befitting an "overture" to the White City by the Lake became the responsibility of the sculptor in embellishing the Administration Building.

To transform a sober, classical building dominated by a large dome into a festive, outgoing greeting to a World's Fair without destroying the decorum of the building was the challenge faced by Bitter. According to Van Brunt he succeeded, for the sculpture of the Administration Building was "characterized by great breadth, dignity of treatment, and by that expression of heroic power and fitness which is derived from knowing how to treat colossal subjects in a colossal way, and how to model figures so that they may assist the main architectural thought and not compete with it."[9] If viewed individually before they reached their destination it might have seemed rather farfetched on the part of Van Brunt to describe Bitter's splintered white bursts of spreading wings, raised trumpets, and outstretched arms as having a dignity of treatment that would not compete with the architecture. However, when placed on the building and seen from below as intended, the groups did become integral parts of the over-all architectural scheme (Fig. 17). As exuberant embellishments they could not be expected to sink into the surface. On the other hand, they did not destroy the self-contained contour of the building, and thereby provided a sharp contrast to the many white figures imposed upon McKim, Mead, and White's Agricultural Building.

The groups on the Administration Building were also related to one another in subject matter, although this was of secondary importance to their purely decorative function. A general allegorical program was worked out to represent man's control of nature, his institutions, and certain of his basic social values. Flanking each of the four entrances were two cleverly

Fig. 17.—Administration Building, Columbian Exposition, Chicago, 1892; Richard Morris Hunt, architect. Destroyed.

composed groups symbolizing, first, an element of nature and, second, man's control of it. For example, one entrance was embellished with "Air Uncontrolled" (Fig. 18) and "Air Controlled," while at another, "Earth Uncontrolled" (Fig. 19) was opposed to "Earth Controlled." Each "Uncontrolled" group consisted of a pyramidal pile of naturalistic nudes twisting and tumbling through either a curvilinear combination of clouds and drapery or a jagged formation of animals, rocks, and foliage. From the top of each "Controlled" group sprang the familiar, female allegorical figure that dominated so many late nineteenth-century monuments with its

Fig. 18.—"Air Uncontrolled," staff, Administration Building, Columbian Exposition, Chicago, 1892. Destroyed.

Fig. 19.—"Earth Uncontrolled," staff, Administration Building, Columbian Exposition, Chicago, 1892. Destroyed.

commanding gestures of victory. All of these groups bore an affinity to Balthasar Permoser's "Apotheosis of Prince Eugene," a vertical composition in marble completed in 1721 and eventually lodged at the Belvedere in Vienna.[10]

Serving as a finial on each corner of the building's four wings was a group of two figures—an enthroned adult accompanied by an intense child. With the aid of accessories these groups were to symbolize Abundance, Unity, Theology, Patriotism, Tradition, Charity, Joy, Liberty, Strength, Truth, Education, and Diligence. More complex groups of three animated figures were placed above, on top of the piers at either end of the colonnades. They each consisted of winged female figures holding wreaths in outstretched hands and two boys blowing long trumpets. Various objects and devices were added at random to designate which of the eight subjects of Industry, Art, Commerce, Science, War, Justice, Religion, and Peace was being represented.[11]

In style, Bitter's sculpture for the Administration Building was a product of the nineteenth-century academy. His rapid execution and flamboyant design were generated by a tradition of baroque origin that he had undoubtedly learned in Vienna. This tradition had been briefly modified by neoclassicism early in the century, only to continue during the second half of the century with the increased use of contemporary costume and a highly naturalistic description of anatomy. The latter accompanied a general return to the direct study of a live model which replaced drawing from a plaster cast. A group called "Patriotism," representative of Bitter's work on the Administration Building, included a nearly nude adolescent youth posed in an aggressive attitude and equipped with a flagstaff held high in one hand. Beside him sat a fully dressed female figure who looked into his face attentively as she sheltered his shoulder with one arm. While it was the intention of this group to display a perennial sentiment allegorically, this was not achieved through the use of timeless, classical figures. Instead, the impression was one of intimate individuality masquerading as allegory. In other words, the directly familiar competed with the symbolic, and the group thereby embodied a common characteristic of the art classified as "ideal" during this period: a confusion of the particular and the allegorical. A nineteenth-century source of this dichotomy may be found in romantic, allegorical realism displayed, for example, in Rude's high-relief groups on the Arc de Triomphe. By the end of the century juxtaposition of the real and the ideal prevailed in the French Academy. Therefore, if reduced in scale and placed in the Exposition's Palace of Fine Arts, Bitter's "Patriotism" would have been right at home in the display of over two hundred works by such contemporary French sculptors as Mercie and Barrias.

To bring to the American public a large exhibition of recent academic exercises was indeed the expressed purpose of those in charge of designing and constructing the buildings and grounds of the Columbian Exposition. Saint-Gaudens, who served as a general advisor to the chief of construction, Daniel H. Burnham, wrote that he suggested the "peristyle" of columns and statues erected at the lakeside end of the Court of Honor as well as the gigantic gilt figure of the Republic by Daniel Chester French. He furthermore considered MacMonnies' grandiose Columbian Fountain at the opposite end of the Basin "the most beautiful conception of a fountain in modern times west of the Caspian Mountains."[12]

The importance of using the Exposition to demonstrate the approved academic styles to the United States was straightforwardly expressed by Van Brunt, and his promotion for the buildings of the Exposition might have been applied to the sculpture that accompanied them. The buildings, he states, should be "a series of pure classic models . . . all set forth with the utmost amount of luxury and opulence of decoration permitted by the best usage." Above all, he hoped that their design would serve as object lessons to the profession. They should be "so impressive of the practical value of architectural scholarship and of strict subordination to the formulas of the schools, that it would serve as a timely corrective to the national tendency to experiments in design." In short, he points out that there were people in the country who were designing buildings without ever having laid eyes on a "pure classic monument," and they should be taught to respect the fixed, academic laws of design. They must learn that "true architecture cannot be based on undisciplined invention, illiterate originality, or, indeed, upon any audacity of ignorance."[13] With this as their basic practical purpose, the buildings on the Court of Honor, dominated by the Administration Building, were designed and decorated.

Bitter's own opinion of his contribution to the Columbian Exposition was recorded by his close friends and biographers, Ferdinand Schevill and Hans Kestranek. Schevill writes that "Bitter himself was wholly pleased when his groups, after making a brave show through a summer season, were 'scrapped' together with the other seven-day wonders of the brilliant White City."[14] This reaction to the Exposition is verified by Kestranek, who reports that soon after his plaster idols were destroyed Bitter smiled at the fanfare and passing enchantment that surrounded them.[15]

In October, 1892, when the construction of the Exposition had been essentially completed and the formal dedication ceremony was held, Bitter's role in the affair ended. He was then free to return to New York and take up where he had left off with the execution of the Trinity Church gates. While there is no way of knowing just how much had been accomplished on the gates by the end of 1892, it is certain that the competition relief panel of the Expulsion was completely modeled by the time Hunt's choice of Bitter was announced in March, 1891. However, since the doors were not cast in bronze until June, 1894, the bulk of the work was probably done in 1893.[16]

Actually a basic design for the gates was determined a half century earlier by the English-born architect, Richard Upjohn. He designed the church as a revival of Gothic, and its main portal became a single, pointed archway at the bottom of a spired tower. To complement the shape of this predetermined entrance Hunt was obliged to pay homage to its historical style. Such a small assignment was no problem to the historically minded architect of the William K. Vanderbilt house, and upon completion the Trinity Church gates (Fig. 20) offered at least a token payment to their setting. In spite of the unadorned *trumeau,* the canopies and pedestals containing the statuettes and the tympanum with its row of twelve apostles are Gothic in appearance. Each of the latter sits in his own niche beneath a cusped arch and a pointed gable, separated from his neighbors by miniature columns.

With the exception of these architectural details, however, the main gates of Trinity Church are not Gothic at all, but depend upon the Early Italian Renaissance for at least their basic layout. Together the doors contain six relief panels representing the Fall, Redemption, and Last Judgment of Mankind. These are framed by a border of standing prophets and saints, recumbent allegorical figures, and contemporary portrait heads. With obvious differences in number, size, and proportion, this scheme is practically identical to that of Ghiberti's second set of gates for the Baptistery in Florence.[17]

However, the individual relief panels are not based on the style of pic-

Fig. 20.—Trinity Church gates, bronze, Broadway and Wall Street, New York City, 1893–1894.

Fig. 21.—Competition panel, plaster, Trinity Church gates, New York City, 1891. Destroyed.

Fig. 22.—"Expulsion" panel, Trinity Church gates, bronze, Broadway and Wall Street, New York City, 1893.

torial relief introduced by Ghiberti and refined by Donatello. Ghiberti's reliefs were packed with hundreds of figures and objects that were described with a variety of rapidly curving folds, jagged projections, and sharp ridges. Such details as foliage, drapery, buildings, and wings were brocaded onto the surface of the bronze in linear patterns. Furthermore, a narrative of more than one event was included in a panel by Ghiberti, who also organized his crowded compositions in a succession of zones that remain essentially parallel to the picture plane. Within this scheme of space no figure was allowed to assert itself abruptly, and as a consequence a great contrast in size from figure to figure never appears in a single zone. The reliefs in bronze by Donatello became even more detailed and greatly discursive. For example, the San Lorenzo pulpit reliefs were covered with a shallow and, for the most part, uniform texture of figures and objects. Volume and depth were designated pictorially with rapid foreshortenings and linear perspective rather than by sculptural gradations in the thickness of the relief.

Unlike the bronze pictorial reliefs of the Early Renaissance, Bitter's reliefs for the Trinity Church gates are not basically linear. The figures and their settings are modeled; clouds, rocks, and foliage are briefly suggested; and little textural distinction is made from one to the other. Except for the panel representing the Annunciation, space also is not treated by Bitter in an Early Renaissance manner. The open scenes are not constructed upon vanishing lines drawn to a point on a carefully established horizon. Instead, diagonal and wide circular movements lead the eye into space and out again with an alternating rhythm. This effect of recession and return is dramatized by the use of great contrasts in the size and relief of the figures involved. Each panel contains one or two dominant figures that sometimes project forward in relief to the point of breaking out fully into the round. In contrast, as the figures and objects recede into the background they rapidly become so shallow in relief that they almost turn into two-dimensional *stiacciato*.

Bitter used this dynamic gradation of relief and proportion as a means of drawing his six panels together into one large composition. It was done by placing the dominant figures along the inside edge of each panel, that is, toward the *trumeau*. In this way the asymmetry of the individual panels lends itself to the symmetry of the doors as a whole. Such a technique of composition was obviously devised by Bitter only after he became thoroughly involved in the execution of his design. That this must have been the case may be seen by comparing the competition panel depicting the Expulsion (Fig. 21) with the panel used in its place on the completed doors (Fig. 22). The competition panel was a symmetrical composition of three equal parts. The angel stood above the very center of the panel in front of a vaguely described arched entrance to the Garden. Meanwhile, God the Father gestured from the clouds on the left to the cowering Adam and Eve, who were shown walking out of the right side with an attitude similar to that of Michelangelo's expelled Adam and Eve on the Sistine Chapel ceiling.

The permanent Expulsion panel, on the other hand, is asymmetrically balanced with a strong emphasis placed on the right or inward side of the composition. The angel and entrance have faded into the distance while a smaller figure of God has joined them to form a single unit of the design. On the other hand, Adam and Eve have maintained their original size and position, thereby becoming the dominant elements. Their significance is emphasized by the grotto-like foliage and rocks that now surround them as they descend the rough hewn steps leading from the gates of paradise into the wilderness designated by a cactus. To further buttress the right side of the panel, and to stop the outward diagonal movement of the original pair of figures, Adam has changed places with Eve. He now stands stooped and silent as he looks down at the shame-stricken Eve hiding her face on his arm. Greatly improved, the composition is made to match that of its partner on the opposite door, which depicts the "Dream of Jacob" or the eventual restoration of mankind to the paradise it lost.

The symmetrical balance of asymmetrical reliefs is continued in the central panels, where the simplicity of the "Annunciation" is paired with the "Two Marys at the Sepulchre." Of all the picture panels, the former has the most symmetrical composition, with the entrance stairway opposed to the reading table and chair from which the Virgin has fallen to her knees. Nevertheless, the inward or left side remains the dominant side as a result of the commanding figure of the Angel Gabriel. The top panels, depicting on the left the "Worship of the Church in Glory" and on the right the "Last Judgment" are closely related to each other in design. Both have many figures arranged in an upward sloping ellipse that starts with a pair of large high-relief figures placed in the lower inside corner. While the trumpeting angel, accompanied by a peaceful lion, is very similar in type to the Pulitzer Building Torchbearer, the cast-down king and his sinful companion dominate a group that is as animated and complex as the Natural Forces designed by Bitter to flank the entrances of the Columbian Exposition Administration Building.

Consistent with the earlier architectural sculpture by Bitter, the relief panels of the Trinity Church gates bear the fundamental characteristics of a baroque composition. These are asymmetrical balance, deftly modeled high relief figures, and a fluidity of inward and outward spatial movements. At the same time the panels complement their Renaissance framework by balancing symmetrically with one another. This coalition of styles is apparent throughout the portal. The ascending Christ and flanking angels represent an adaptation of the baroque to a combination Gothic and Renaissance setting. Placed directly above a plain *trumeau* that divides a pair of Renaissance doors, the figure of Christ could hardly move upward in violent *contrapposto* and swirling drapery without separating himself from the rest of the composition. Therefore, the open-armed figure rests his weight slightly on his right leg and a cluster of folded drapery falls from that hip to accent the movement.

Other full-length figures are actually freestanding statuettes on the borders of the doors. Together with the Gothic canopies and pedestals that contain them they are confined by heavy unbroken strips of molding, and out of respect for their function as the predominant parts of the vertical border they are restrained in movement. Alternating with the portrait heads, they form a cohesive decorative pattern from the top of the doors to the bottom, even though they project relief-like beyond the flat surface of the molding with a variety of stances, gestures, costumes, and accessories. The reclining allegorical figures flanking the emblems of the four evangelists on both the top and bottom of each door are more energetically baroque than any other figure outside the relief panels. Limited as they are for space inside their narrow rectangles, these figures give the impression of barely maintaining their precarious positions.

More secure, but almost as uncomfortable looking, are the twelve apostles in the tympanum (Fig. 23). Unlike the figures sitting above the lintel on the main portal of the west front of Chartres Cathedral, they squirm uneasily within the confines of their niches. They are individualized in attitude as well as age, with arms and legs assuming twelve different combinations and their comportment varying from asceticism to a down-to-earth

Fig. 23.—Tympanum, bronze, Trinity Church, Broadway and Wall Street, New York City, 1893–1894.

casualness. The latter is most noticeably represented by the apostle who sits with legs crossed, allowing his bare foot to dangle out over the *trumeau.* This touch of homely realism, along with the self-portrait that Bitter placed in the lower right corner of the portal underneath a portrait of Richard Morris Hunt, is in the Renaissance-baroque tradition of personalizing a major work of art.

The bronze gates for Trinity Church represent an art historical synthesis: a study in nineteenth-century revivals. Their architectural setting is Gothic revival in style; the organization of the doors themselves is Renaissance in origin; and the composition of the sculpture is basically baroque. This diversity, by no means unique, was consistent with the much bigger collaborations between Hunt and Bitter at Chicago and Biltmore. Altogether, within approximately four years, they carried out the romance of a make-believe château, the dramatization of a Renaissance dome, and the re-enactment of a famous episode in the history of church sculpture. To add to the variety in his workshop Bitter took on still another major project during these crowded years. It too was eclectic, but conceived in connection with a somewhat more unorthodox building, one which was to be both functional and fanciful in its expression of a full-blown industrial society.

III

Enterprising Embellishments

THE COMPLETION of a Renaissance-baroque portal for a Gothic-revival church was followed immediately in Bitter's studio by a large project of terra-cotta relief sculpture. This was executed for an extensive, two-part addition to the Pennsylvania Railroad's Broad Street Station in Philadelphia. The new building (Fig. 24) was designed in 1892 by Frank Furness, another student of Richard Morris Hunt. As demonstrated by the Broad Street Station, Furness developed, unlike George B. Post, an imaginative architecture that strayed from the scholarly boundaries staked out by his Beaux-Arts master.

The new Broad Street Station consisted of a rectangular ten-story building attached to a single-span train shed that was the largest to date. The building contained mostly office space constructed above a main hall on the first floor and a large waiting room on the second. The latter had over 8,500 square feet of floor space on a level with sixteen elevated tracks. These were spanned by a catenary roof of iron and glass, six hundred feet long by three hundred feet wide. Beneath the waiting room and behind the main hall ran an underpass that allowed Fifteenth Street to continue uninterrupted through the building.[1]

While less unique than several of his previous smaller buildings, the Broad Street Station revealed Furness' penchant for novelty. Comprising a variety of independent forms, the exterior of the main building was extremely ornate, especially above its irregularly projecting cornice. This formed a crown adorned with arcaded balustrades, a supplementary cornice, miniature columns, and triangular gable-ends filled with elaborate sculpture. The steep roof of a corner tower was in turn almost completely obscured by arcades, pointed arches, small spires, and crockets. Between the main cornice and the second story were seven identical floors of paired windows which created a uniform pattern interrupted only by the toothy projections of an occasional stringcourse of terra cotta. Slender piers, divided into five stories by evenly spaced bands of textured terra cotta, ended in two large and slightly pointed arches. The two bottom floors were distinguished from the rest by a row of pointed segmental arches and beneath them ran a porch from the Market Street, or southern, side of the building to the northern end of the Broad Street façade. In spite of its eccentricities, the new station complemented the Gothic-revival design of the original building. Furness' structures generally suggested the Gothic. Indeed, some of them could have been inspired by the published *Entretiens* of Viollet-le-Duc, who advocated the use of terra cotta on exteriors.[2]

To provide reliefs in this medium Furness chose his teacher's personal sculptor. For the two gables above the cornice Bitter designed baroque clusters of projecting figures that were somewhat inconsistent with the crockets and finials on top of their molding. However, the combination was in complete harmony with the gingerbread tower on the corner of the building. Clearly visible from the street below, the central figure in each was a female torchbearer similar in pose and drapery to the earlier example on the Pulitzer Building. In fact, since the torchbearers in New York had probably been removed by this time it is possible that Bitter decided to repeat the same figure for a location high out of reach. Because it had to be installed while the scaffolding was still in place, the sculpture on top of the building was undoubtedly the first to be finished. It may have appeared as early as autumn, 1893, while the superstructure and masonry were being completed. At any rate, Broad Street Station stood complete with all of its ornamentation by the end of 1895.[3]

In addition to the sculpture on the gables above, Bitter modeled ten terra-cotta reliefs for the dormer-like projections that pierced the cornice of the train shed on its Market Street side. Each of these panels provided an allegorical representation of a major terminal city along the Pennsylvania Line.[4] He also designed an elaborate clock which was placed above the second floor of the tower at the corner of Market and Broad streets. The timepiece was flanked by two winged female figures in heavy drapery. The eyes of one were closed to represent the drowsy contentment of Prosperity and Plenty while the other figure, wide-eyed and alert, symbolized Transportation and Commerce.[5] Underneath, Bitter included a head of Mercury, as the God of Commerce, on top of a caduceus. At night the clock face was illuminated from a glass lamp held at arm's length by a winged cherub straddling the dial. Although rather complex in composition, the supporting figures were comfortably cradled between two large segmental arches that converged at the corner. Furthermore, as ornamentation, the undulating surface of the encircling group was consistent with the broken profile of the tower roof.

Less compact than the clock, but equally varied in its gradations of relief, was the largest panel of sculpture on the exterior of the Broad Street Station (Fig. 25). This work was modeled by Bitter to fill a pointed segmental arch spanning the underpass at Fifteenth Street and Market. Composed of twelve major figures it was constructed of many interlocking pieces of terra cotta, and at the time of its erection was considered the largest panel of its kind ever fired.[6] The figures were arranged in five distinct groups. However, each contributed to a continuous curvilinear movement that rose and fell from one end of the panel to the other. The uppermost portions of the groups projected beyond the splayed molding of the arch and were thereby suspended over the street below.

Notwithstanding this outward spreading force, the pedimental composition was intimately related to the surface of the building. Four neutral areas were evenly distributed among the energetic groups to create a plane, flush with the surface of the wall above the arch. In keeping with the contrast between this flat ground and the relief that projected from it, the basically curvilinear composition also contained prominent straight lines and sharp angles emanating from the central group. Consequently, the relief panel by Bitter was consistent with the segmental arch by Furness, which was neither completely curved nor pointed, but both. Also, the top-heaviness of each group plus the use of deep dark recesses were characteristics that Bitter's sculpture shared with Furness' architecture.

In 1895 the application of terra-cotta decoration to the exterior of a large building was still considered somewhat experimental.[7] At the time Bitter also considered his use of allegory to symbolize contemporary commerce and industry as being original, and in the United States it was. At least he wanted to avoid being too literal or prosaic in his representation

Fig. 24.—Broad Street Station, Philadelphia, Pennsylvania, 1892–1895; Frank Furness, architect. Demolished in 1952.

Fig. 25.—Relief panel, terra cotta, Broad Street Station, Philadelphia, Pennsylvania, 1893–1894. Destroyed in 1952.

Fig. 26.—"Progress of Transportation," plaster, Broad Street Station, Philadelphia, Pennsylvania, 1895. This was moved to the waiting room of the new Thirtieth Street Station in 1933.

of the Pennsylvania Railroad, the subject of the Fifteenth Street panel. Concerning this subject he wrote: "I have been influenced by a desire to depart from the traditional use and wont in such cases where, as far as my experience goes, a suggestion of arrival or of departure, conveyed by simple figures at rest, or by Negroes engaged in the transportation of bales of merchandise, has been all the artist has aimed at, except perhaps in very modern instances where invention has soared to the representation of an express train, or of the interior of a Pullman palace car."[8]

Bitter's primary purpose was to symbolize steam power used for locomotion by rail, and as an abstraction such a subject could hardly be carried out in the quaint provincial manner that he criticized above. On either side of a centrally placed chariot, he presented a muscular male nude representing Man. Each figure stood in the middle of a railroad track and grasped the side of the chariot while straining to pull down a pair of rearing centaurs. These savage mythological creatures, produced by the steam billowing out from beneath the chariot, were meant to represent "the two demons Fire and Water."[9] Fire was a furious male centaur clad in a lion skin. He was bound to a female centaur identified as Water by the reeds and marsh grass encircling her loosened hair.

To fulfill his commission Bitter also wanted to suggest the outcome of placing a steam engine on a track. In doing this he made it clear that he intended to glorify the Pennsylvania Railroad as an independent American enterprise, and to idealize its effect on the growth and progress of the United States. "The European roads," he stated, "are often planned for strategic reasons, or at the nod of a ruler. The Pennsylvania system stands emphatically for the interest of the people. Following the pioneer, it is an essential auxiliary of trade and commerce, a promoter of intercourse between the sections of country which it crosses. It insures the growth of Art, Industry, and Science, and is at once a promoter and conservator of American civilization."[10]

This ideal point of view obscured the hard practical machinery of the railroad industry, which was to be further softened and refined through an association with classical mythology. In the chariot Bitter placed Mercury, "the mythological messenger and guide of Wealth and Commerce." Beside him was Minerva, the Goddess of the City. Around them were arranged the implements of Art and Industry, "showing how towns and cities have arisen in the wake of the great railroad."[11] To complete the pediment Bitter included a well-developed youth leaning against an anvil as a symbol of the Pennsylvania Railroad. A small boy decorated a shield bearing the initials of the railroad with a spray of laurel. Scattered near the two allegorical figures were such realistic accessories of railroading as car wheels and tools. In the opposite corner a nude female figure representing the City of Philadelphia was shown with a bust of William Penn, while a nude child crowned the city's coat of arms. The books, implements of art, and the owl, or bird of wisdom, accompanying them were intended to indicate the culture promoted and insured by the Pennsylvania Railroad.

Glorification of the company itself is much less emphasized in the last of Bitter's many works for the Broad Street Station. Signed and dated in 1895, it is also a large high-relief panel (Fig. 26), measuring thirty feet in length, that was quickly sketched and cast in plaster for the west wall of the waiting room behind the information desk.[12] As its subject he depicted a triumphal procession entitled "Progress of Transportation." Instead of employing classical mythology, however, he now used a variety of costumed figures to exemplify several periods of history and contrasting climates. A baroque triumph traditionally called for a central figure enthroned on a horse-drawn carriage. To comply with this convention a rather hastily modeled female figure is seated beneath a heavily draped dome ornamented with the winged wheel of progress. She personifies the Spirit or Genius of Transportation and is seen joining Asia with the Occident. A Middle Eastern patriarch is accompanied by vaguely defined Oriental figures in background relief, their umbrella being of primary concern as a compositional device. In the foreground the Western world is portrayed by a cavalier couple in the dress of seventeenth-century Europe. A loosely draped female figure stepping quickly behind the couple carries a tray of fruit at her side and was said to depict a southern European.[13]

The left third of the panel depicts the discovery and settlement of America. A Spanish horseman carrying a model of Columbus' flagship is juxtaposed with a pioneer busily managing his oxen, sheep, and covered wagon. Squeezed into the background a trader negotiates with an Indian. The four horses that pull the central carriage away from the frontier scene are guided in the foreground by a female figure in contemporary clothes, interpreted at the time as being symbolic of America. In front of the horses a group of young boys display models representing several means of transportation, including a steamboat and a locomotive. They are urged along by still another anonymous female figure. Finally, leading the whole procession, is a toddler with the model of a crude airship, a method of transportation that was still in an infant stage of development.

As in the open-air panel above Fifteenth Street, the composition of the waiting room relief tends to expand at either end beyond its frame. Also, while less distinctly divided into separate groups, the triumphal procession is united by a major curvilinear movement from end to end. This helps draw the many folds and facets of the milling figures into a cohesive whole. The impression of a somewhat shallow, but adequate, space through which the individual groups can wander is achieved by a steeply inclined ground plane and an extreme foreshortening of certain key figures. In several places rows of figures seem to recede into a background, which is actually nothing more than a modeled surface left in the rough. The spatial illusion is established by the contrast of low relief to forward projection.

In spite of this range of actual depth, the "Progress of Transportation" is more pictorial than sculptural. This results largely from the crowded figures fully dressed in period costumes and the accumulation of accessory animals and vehicles. No empty spaces like those that alternated with the radiating groups of nude figures on the outdoor panel were allowed to remain. In 1907, one observer wrote that the waiting room relief was comparable to the large paintings of the Viennese Hans Makart. Calling Bitter the Makart of sculpture, Anna Raster-Hercz stated that he was not a monumental artist in the sense of either Michelangelo or even the modern Secessionists.[14] He was, she maintained, a decorative artist and a product of the Vienna School as it was influenced by Makart in the seventies. For this reason she felt that his art was best when it was allowed to develop its "*Makartische Eigenart*" unhampered by any modern influence. Similar to Bitter's "Progress of Transportation," crowds of figures do appear in such huge paintings by Makart as the "Entry of Charles V into Antwerp" or the "Triumph of Ariadne." They are broken into figural clusters that seem to move in a number of directions independently while remaining within a rather restricted zone of space. Also, the many-shaped projections and recesses within these animated groups are interwoven by a prominent wave movement.

The opportunity to employ a much more modest, but nevertheless baroque, form of architectural sculpture soon followed the Philadelphia project. Bitter was commissioned to do three kneeling atlantean figures (Fig. 27) for another large New York office building, designed by George B. Post and erected in the year 1896. They were placed just above the main entrance of the St. Paul Building,[15] which occupied the former site of P. T. Barnum's American Museum on the east side of Broadway opposite St. Paul's Church. Carved out of Indiana limestone, the massive figures measured eight feet from the top of their pedestals to the bottom of the Corinthian entablature they supported.[16]

Bitter's atlantes were apparently the most interesting feature of the St. Paul Building. A possible exception was its height of twenty-five stories, which made it the tallest skyscraper in the world for a while. As in the case of the nearby Pulitzer Building, it was carefully designed and decorated on its two principal sides while the walls of the court and those that divided the building from the adjoining property were bare brick. According to the architect-critic, Russell Sturgis, when the building was first viewed from the south everyone threw scorn upon its ugliness, and he joined in the attack by labeling the unfinished sides "packing box walls with square holes sawed out of them."[17] Since nothing could project over the property line into the lot next door, and nothing was allowed to recede into rentable space inside, he attributed this unfortunate appearance to the business requirements of the high building.

Sturgis thought that the building would have been much better if all of its walls had remained blank and sheer, eliminating the false fronts that faced the main thoroughfares. Such simplicity would at least have been consistent in pattern all the way around. It might even have suggested some unified mode of decoration in place of the composite pilasters and heavy stringcourses applied to the principal façades. He concluded, however, that because they are governed by practical real estate requirements, big business buildings have little chance of ever being completely attractive or architecturally significant.

The atlantes did not escape Sturgis, and he criticized their location above the main entrance. His opinion may have been partially determined by a projecting cornice that originally existed underneath the crouching figures, practically concealing them from a sidewalk viewer. However, this was eventually remedied when the cornice was cut away between the figures and replaced by large consoles to support the pedestals (Fig. 28).

Fig. 27.—Atlantes, limestone, St. Paul Building, New York City, 1896. Given to the City of Indianapolis by the Western Electric Co. in 1958 when the St. Paul Building was destroyed; now in Holiday Park, Indianapolis, Indiana.

Fig. 28.—Atlantes, limestone, St. Paul Building, New York City, 1896.

The atlantes were thus more exposed to the passer-by from their location against the wall. Also to be witnessed were the important differences among the three: on the left was a figure of a Negro, in the center a Caucasian, and on the right an Oriental. For a period in which concepts of white supremacy were widely accepted and both the black and the yellow man were legally discriminated against, the equalitarianism implied by the atlantes may seem somewhat ironical. However, the central position of the white man, who pushed his head forward and used only one hand to bear his share of the burden, did actually suggest the contemporary racist point of view.

Not being identical, the muscular figures were not meant to form a completely symmetrical composition. Nevertheless, the group was evenly balanced by the outward turning heads of the Negro and the Oriental, as well as by the lowered position of their inside legs. Bitter probably worked from a live model, but at the same time he exaggerated the protrusion of individual muscles and bones to increase the notion of strain and stress. This resulted in a precise pattern of highlights and shadows, which, in addition to the consistently rough texture left by the mark of a half-inch chisel, helped to set the atlantes apart from the smooth blocks of stone that originally surrounded them.

The masculine monumentality of the figures may have been an outcome of the admiration Bitter held as a student for the sculpture of Michelangelo. The rough texture of their chiseled surface might be attributed to the widespread influence of Rodin. On the other hand, it is likely that Bitter's atlantes were direct descendants of the many such figures that appear in German baroque architecture of the early eighteenth century which, in turn, were inherited from Italian baroque sculpture. For example, the Austrian architect Fischer von Erlach often incorporated muscular male nudes into the surface decoration of his architecture. His Ministry of the Interior Building in Vienna (1711–1714) includes four of them to flank its entrance.

The arrangement of the arms and head of Bitter's central figure resembles that of the inner figures on the Ministry. Furthermore, the intrusion of drapery between the atlas and the abacus is shared by all of the figures in question, both old and new. In this respect there is also a strong resemblance between Bitter's atlantes and those executed by Pierre Puget for the door of the town hall of Toulon. However, Bitter's atlantes differ from their seventeenth- and eighteenth-century counterparts in that they are full figures and not merely half length. While the bowed head and the interlocking drapery were standard in both the German and the Italian baroque atlas, the use of a complete atlas seems to have been more prevalent in Italy. Since Bitter executed the St. Paul Building figures right after his first trip to Italy during the winter of 1896, this may account for their completeness. But this does not necessarily explain their crouching position which is rarely seen among atlantes anywhere. No doubt the size of the space and the dimensions of the architectural members around it had something to do with determining their pose and proportions.

Together with two other works of sculpture that had recently appeared on new commercial buildings in New York City, Bitter's "constructive" atlantes for the St. Paul Building were heralded by a *New York Tribune* article of May 23, 1897, as an important artistic development in the city. Architectural sculpture, according to the *Tribune,* was at last beginning to be accepted as sound business practice by the proprietors of office buildings; consequently, a common need of the people for art was finally being filled. No longer did sculpture have to be limited to a white Narcissus or a bronze portrait on a drawing room pedestal while the keystone of an arch, or some little paneling beside a doorway, was left to the mercy of a journeyman from the stoneyard. Anticipated by the placement of Saint-Gaudens' "Diana" weather vane on top of the Madison Square Garden tower, the embellishment of new buildings with sculpture was to become a standard procedure among New York owners. Far more optimistic than Russell Sturgis, the *Tribune* reporter wrote:

"If cautious proprietors hesitated, fearing that their solemnly practical buildings might be made to seem frivolous and sensational through the addition of ornaments in high relief to their vast façades, they have got over their timidity. They see now that without sculpture a new building looks somehow inferior to its neighbors. In other words, art is getting to be the fashion in ways hitherto unsuspected among shrewd builders of commercial enterprise. No longer a luxury for idle people, it is brought into the service of trade, delighting the eyes which have for years been accustomed to associating sordidly prosaic surroundings with daily labors." The article concludes that someday the traveler approaching New York's great canyons of office buildings by way of the harbor will find upon his arrival that the bases of the buildings will be as artistic and attractive as the picturesque skyline they form.

The *Tribune* prediction that it would become a standard procedure for "shrewd builders of commercial enterprise" to embellish their New York office buildings with sculpture is not demonstrated in Bitter's career. Never again would he provide sculpture for a tall building, and the main reason for this probably lies in the changes that occurred in their design. New York skyscrapers built during the first decade of the twentieth century abandoned the illogical form that such early elevator buildings as the World and the St. Paul had assumed. Instead of being treated as a conventional, low-lying masonry structure the new skyscraper was usually divided into a base, an unadorned shaft, and a cap. Along with this formula a classical simplicity replaced the ornateness of many late Victorian business buildings. Furthermore, the warning by Russell Sturgis that the tall commercial building would generally subordinate artistic considerations to real estate values proved to be at least partially correct, and a premium was often placed upon cheapness as well as height. From this point of view, sculpture, which was of questionable success on the first elevator buildings to begin with, was considered superfluous.

After furnishing the St. Paul Building with its solitary atlantes, over ten years would pass before Bitter executed sculpture for another commercial building of any kind. Then it was the classical façade of a comparatively small midwestern bank[18] that included a pediment he could fill with allegorical figures. Meanwhile, his architectural sculpture was to be produced in collaborative projects paid for by the public.

IV

Collaborations On Fifth Avenue

IN SPITE OF the limited role sculpture might play on the business building of the future, the festive spirit of Bitter's earliest architectural sculpture seems, in retrospect, to have been an appropriate outward expression of an optimistic urban-industrial growth, as well as a decorative display of the extravagant fortunes that resulted from it. Whether to celebrate the invention of the steam engine and the development of an American railroad company, or to embellish the great halls of the very rich with less symbolic scenes of hunt and play, there was actually little need to alter the style from one commission to another. Differing only in material, the composition of Bitter's sculpture for the Broad Street Station was essentially the same as that used to decorate the walls of the Biltmore Banquet Hall. Both programs included large high-relief panels populated with scores of energetic figures rapidly turned out in his Fifty-third Street workshop with the aid of many assistants. In short, Bitter's first five ambitious years in America were extremely prolific, and the style as well as the patronage of his sculpture during this time remained secure.

The end of this youthful phase in his career coincided with the death of Richard Morris Hunt in 1895, when such extensive schemes as those produced for Biltmore and the Broad Street Station disappeared from his studio. There is a clear indication, however, that he was growing weary of the huge projects anyway, and even though he considered his new studio-home above the Hudson in Weehawken as a sign of success, he also looked upon his relocation as a retreat from a frenzied way of life.[1] Schevill emphasizes that Bitter was not altogether satisfied with his career thus far, that he wanted to attain a reputation as something more than a "decorative sculptor."[2] This new ambition may have been encouraged in the late nineties when he fulfilled his first commission for a portrait monument.[3] But with regard to his architectural sculpture, the atlantes for the St. Paul Building may have become an eventual inspiration to abandon the Makartian compositions of his early ornamental work in favor of a less flamboyant style.

Actually there would be no pronounced change in the general appearance of Bitter's architectural sculpture for some time. There was, however, an abrupt shift in the origin of his commissions. After weathering a drastic decline throughout 1897 as a result of the mid-nineties depression, Bitter finally returned to a steady schedule of work following the Spanish American War.[4] However, the initial uniformity of patronage that he had known throughout his association with Hunt no longer existed. As indicated at the end of Chapter I, commissions for residential interiors and grounds all but ceased for the remainder of his career with only an incidental decorative figure, an isolated relief panel, and one small garden fountain. In the place of wealthy patrons seeking such private ornamentation Bitter discovered the original American patron for architectural sculpture: the government.

Since early in the nineteenth century when Benjamin Latrobe sent to Italy for the first sculptors to decorate the United States Capitol Building, the federal government had been the central source of public funds for architectural sculpture. However, toward the end of the century, as the individual state, county, and municipal governments constructed larger and more elaborate public buildings, the demand for locally commissioned work became more widely distributed. For example, the need for a new court building in New York City was created when the State Constitution of 1894 established the Appellate Division of the New York Supreme Court in the First Judicial Department. The east side of Madison Square at the corner of Twenty-fifth Street was chosen as the site for the building, and in 1896 the Justices of the Appellate Division approved the plans of James Brown Lord, a Princeton graduate who had established a reputation mainly as a residential architect. For the court building Lord designed a long, three-floor structure which is basically Beaux-Arts in style, with columned porches on its two exposed sides and an attic story above a prominent

Fig. 29.—Appellate Court Building, marble, Madison Square, New York City, 1896–1899.

cornice. He also proposed that the exterior of the building be generously ornamented with sculpture. Consequently, when it was completed, roughly a fourth of the total cost had been allocated for this purpose.[5]

The sculptural scheme was conceived by the architect himself and he enjoyed complete control over the artists who carried it out.[6] Consisting of twelve statues, four full-length caryatids, two allegorical groups, and a small pediment, the sculpture was intended to represent the universal acceptance of law and its basic benefits to mankind. The freestanding marble figures placed prominently on the attic balustrade are imaginary portraits of both oriental and occidental lawmakers accompanied by a group representing Justice and another representing Peace. On January 25, 1899, Bitter signed a contract to execute the latter group, and by the end of June the model was inspected for the last time by Lord, who pronounced it complete.[7]

In accepting the commission for the Peace group Bitter was participating in the first collaboration of New York sculptors that served to promote their new organization, the National Sculpture Society. Each of the fourteen sculptors who contributed to the court building was a member of the Society, and the sculpture was divided evenly among them. Bitter's three-figure group (Fig. 29) was designed to crown the narrow Madison

Fig. 30.—Karl Bitter's studio, 1899.

Square façade as a triangular apex for the symmetrical composition of sculpture above the main cornice on that side of the building. Four caryatids, representing the seasons, were executed for the attic story by Thomas Shields Clarke, who was primarily a painter, not a sculptor. A statue of Confucius, or Chinese Law, placed to the right of Bitter's group, was modeled by the French-born and European-trained Philip Martiny. Finally, the statue of Moses, representing Hebraic Law, was the first work by William Couper after his return from twenty years in Florence.[8]

The marble figures that evolved from this strange international mixture demonstrate the oneness of taste and treatment in sculpture that existed throughout the Western world at the end of the nineteenth century. Even though they vary in function and subject, the caryatids, the portrait statues, and the allegorical group all consist of the same basic stylistic ingredients. Each is caught up in a baroque abundance of cascading drapery, and the allegorical figures, including the caryatids, combine the universality of abstract symbols with the familiarity of the naturalistic, academic nude.

As may be seen in the photograph of Bitter's studio (Fig. 30) taken at the time he was working on the Peace group, the central figure was based on the "Aphrodite of Melos," of which a small-scale reproduction is visible in the background. An earlier design for the figure of Peace is also seen as a plaster model directly behind Bitter. It did not have the bent right leg or the upright head that he adopted for the final clay model by reversing the *contrapposto* of his famous Hellenistic prototype. This source of inspiration is actually concealed from anyone viewing the full-scale marble version from the street below because Bitter drew the relaxed foot back from its original forward position and added drapery to the torso as well as dancing arms and hands. The seated female figure, which leans on a cornucopia and holds a sphere emblematic of wisdom and wealth, may also have been inspired by the Aphrodite. However, it appears that Bitter was more precise in rendering the details of her torso. The heads of both female figures, moreover, are not derived from an ideal type of Hellenistic sculpture but conform more closely to a late nineteenth-century canon of idealized feminine beauty. As for the male figure leaning on the fasces as a symbol of strength, it is typical of the slender, but properly proportioned, naturalistic nude in fashion for public allegorical figures of America and Europe.

Just what Bitter had to do with designing the pedestals for his group is uncertain, but in contrast to the group called "Justice" by Daniel Chester French on top of the Twenty-fifth Street façade of the court building, his composition is as closely integrated with the architecture underneath as freestanding sculpture of this style could be. French's figures perch fully exposed on a square block of marble illogically placed over the solitary pediment of the building. Bitter's group, on the other hand, is locked in place by two paneled plinths that also terminate the vertical lines formed by the colossal Corinthian columns and the caryatids. This verticality was wisely adopted by Bitter and continued in his design through the fasces and the cornucopia, to be thrust even higher by the raised arms of his central figure. As a countermovement, the inside legs of the seated figures, together with the drapery which spills over the pedestal blocks, anchor the triangular composition of the group to the solid balustrade, rather than resisting its architectural support as the cross-legged figures by French unfortunately do.

Madison Square would continue to be the scene of collaboration among

National Sculpture Society members throughout the late summer months of 1899. The new project, while more spontaneous and less substantial than the court building, was also financed by public funds. The occasion for the project was the return of Admiral Dewey from his celebrated victory at Manila. At the suggestion of Charles R. Lamb, one of its original architect-members, the Society decided to take advantage of the official reception planned by the city and offered its services to Mayor Van Wyck as an opportunity to promote an interest in public sculpture.[9] After considering a number of suggestions, a committee appointed by the mayor to take charge of the affair approved the Society's plan to erect a triumphal arch on Fifth Avenue at Twenty-fourth Street through which the hero and his procession would parade.

Lamb designed an arch with the main proportions of the Arch of Titus, but with transverse arches through the pillars in addition to the major opening.[10] A "colonnade," extending along either side of Fifth Avenue southward to Twenty-third Street and northward to Twenty-fifth Street, consisted of paired columns. In front of each pair and poised on a globe, a winged victory bearing the name of a ship from the victorious fleet extended a crown of laurel over the heads of the marchers. To make the ends of the colonnades more impressive three columns with colossal groups of sculpture were placed on either side of the avenue. The arch itself was enriched with sculpture glorifying the United States as a powerful maritime nation. High-relief groups on the piers included such subjects as "Patriotism, or The Call to Arms," "Triumph, or The Victors Return," and "Progress of Civilization." Standing in front of the attic story, above eight attached Corinthian columns, were portrait statues of American naval heroes. Finally, to crown the triumphal arch, an exact copy of the "Winged Nike of Samothrace," refurbished with head and arms, was placed in an ocean-born chariot drawn by five sea horses and a couple of tritons as an allegorization of "Victory at Sea."

An excuse for such straightforward plagiarism might be found in the fact that from the day late in July when the plans for the ostentatiously ornamented arch were accepted and appropriated for by the city, only six weeks remained to carry them out in time for the Dewey reception.[11] To accomplish this, all but one of the sculptors represented on the Appellate Division Court Building took part in producing the figures out of staff, the transitory material used for the whole structure. For much of the preliminary work the basement of Madison Square Garden was put at their disposal. During the last two weeks, with growing crowds of spectators watching the progress both day and night, the arch and its colonnades were assembled just in time for the scaffolding to be removed on the evening before the parade.[12] Because of his experience in turning out large involved schemes of decorative architectural sculpture at a rapid pace, including the huge groups in staff for the Administration Building of the Columbian Exposition, Bitter was a logical choice to supervise the enlargement and assembly of sculpture at the site of the Dewey Arch. Otherwise, his share in the arch consisted of designing one of the four main groups applied to its piers.

The group by Bitter was entitled "War" or "The Combat" and comprised a winged female figure above a projecting cluster of battle-worn American seamen. All the large groups of sculpture on the Dewey Arch seemed to sprout and spill from the surface of their classical support. Bitter's high relief was no exception, and in this respect it was similar to his natural element groups flanking the entrances to the Administration Building. The allegorical figure for the arch, however, became a helmeted goddess of war holding a spear and a shield emblazoned with a screaming mask, which made up for her own innocent expression. She also appeared to be riding the crest of a wave with her long gown half-obliterated by a swirl of spray that served as a link with the "real" world below. At this lower level Bitter represented, with a minimum of accessories and details, a naval gun crew in action. The men, gathered around an armor-plated cannon, looked out toward a distant target upon which they had presumably just fired. Actually, the composition was designed to face the oncoming procession at the moment of entrance into the arch, and it is to Bitter's credit that his was the only one of the four pier groups that did this.[13] However, as may be seen in the clay model of the arch (Fig. 31), the basic design for the sculpture was determined in the beginning by the composition of the structure as a whole. All four pier groups consisted of the same general elements—a winged female figure above an anecdotal group. Consequently the relief for the Dewey Arch was the only work of Bitter's career in which the allegorical and the anecdotal appear so close together as to form a single group. But in this instance it was strictly ceremonial and short-lived.[14]

Following the brief encounter on Madison Square with America's chau-

Fig. 31.—Dewey triumphal arch, staff, Madison Square, New York City, 1899. Destroyed. Courtesy of State Historical Society of Wisconsin.

vinistic pride in being a new world power, Bitter returned to his studio where still another project for the City of New York was waiting to be finished. As part of the current extension and elaboration of the Metropolitan Museum of Art, this project was also a sign of the nation's growth, but in a healthier direction. To house the museum's ever-increasing collection, the third, or East Wing, was under construction and Bitter was responsible for providing sculpture to ornament its Fifth Avenue façade. The municipal government had appropriated a million dollars for the wing as early as 1895. Richard Morris Hunt, a trustee of the museum from the time of its incorporation, was not only asked to design the new extension but to lay out a general scheme that could be followed in all subsequent additions until the entire area set aside for the museum was covered. Following Hunt's death that same year, the long-term project was turned over to his son Richard Howland Hunt, and George B. Post became consulting architect. Exactly when Bitter was brought in to participate is not certain, but it is likely that his connection with Hunt must have had something to do with his being commissioned.[15]

As the elder Hunt planned the façade of the East Wing, it was to include a large amount of sculpture. Four allegorical groups representing the great periods of art—Ancient, Medieval, Renaissance, and Modern—were to be placed on the attic story of the central pavilion. Niches were provided between the paired columns, directly underneath the principal groups, to contain marble reproductions of statues that would exemplify each of the periods.[16] In addition, keystone heads for the three great arches were to be accompanied in the spandrels by six medallion portraits of famous artists, and two full-length caryatids were designated for the second story of each wing on the façade. To continue the general theme of the central pavilion, these four figures were to represent painting, sculpture, architecture, and music.

According to Hunt's directions the large groups for the attic story were to be assigned by the National Sculpture Society to different sculptors. However, mainly because of insufficient funds, this was never carried out and the rough blocks of stone which had been set in place for carving remain untouched.[17] Only the keystones, medallions, and caryatids commissioned to Bitter were finished.

The East Wing of the Metropolitan Museum of Art is another offspring of the Beaux-Arts architecture that Hunt and his circle generated in Chicago in 1893. As in the case of the Appellate Division Supreme Court Building, which is also of that derivation, its sculptural decoration was dictated in detail by the architect. Therefore, with the exception of a major modification in the caryatids, Bitter simply filled Hunt's order. The model for the keystones which he sent to the architect's office in February, 1899,[18] was essentially the same helmeted female head already specified in the original elevations of the building.[19] This also applies to the medallions which portray Bramante, Michelangelo, Raphael, Dürer, Rembrandt, and Velasquez. Neither their use nor their form was Bitter's idea. With regard to the caryatids, however, he apparently complied only with the sex and symbolism prescribed by Hunt, for by the time the limestone figures (Fig. 32) were placed on the building they just vaguely resembled the conventional caryatids which originally appeared in the architect's drawing.[20] Instead of remaining underneath the entablature, Bitter's figures were brought out into the open, and the pilaster-like panels, to which they are barely attached, appear to be supporting members of the exterior masonry construction. In other words, the caryatids as designed by Bitter became less structure-oriented than is implied by the categorical term used to describe them.

The composition of these so-called caryatids is basically baroque with prominent classical overtones. The pose of each is the familiar S-curve stance inherited from Greek sculpture and used repeatedly since the Renaissance. More specifically, the outflung hip, the exposed thigh, and the rather self-conscious gestures of the arms and hands leading up to the bowed head recall a number of female figures of the late sixteenth century.[21] If Bitter's figures representing the fine arts are to be associated with any one man's work, an appropriate choice might be Giambologna, who actually made several allegorical figures of this type. For example, Bitter's "Music" (Fig. 33) on the outside panel of the north wing is similar to the figure of "Charity" that Giambologna executed as one of a series for the Grimaldi Chapel.[22] Both figures rest on their right legs and the protruding thigh of each is connected with an outward curving hip by a diagonal roll of clustered folds across the lower abdomen. Bitter also followed the sixteenth-century tendency toward the sensual by exposing just enough flesh in strategically chosen areas to emphasize further the female form underneath loose-fitting drapery. With that, however, the resemblance to Mannerism ceases.

Fig. 32.—"Architecture" and "Music," limestone, on Fifth Avenue façade of Metropolitan Museum, New York City, 1899.

Fig. 33.—"Music," clay model for limestone figure on Metropolitan Museum.

Bitter was, after all, designing his figures to fit a given panel and they could not be elongated to the extent of conflicting with those proportions calculated to contain them. What is more, a general design was to be consistently repeated for each identical setting. Not only were both pairs arranged so that the mass of each figure stands on the leg nearest its partner in caryatid fashion, but the corresponding arms were more or less matched in position and the two heads turned toward one another. Thus, while the four figures of the Metropolitan Museum are not proper caryatids, neither are they freestanding figures in the round, and the form they assumed was determined as much by the architectural framework to which they were committed as by any single type or style of figure from the past.

The Metropolitan Museum wing was intended to be one of several collaborations among members of a newly developed community of New York sculptors and architects. That it was not to be the last joint effort was indicated immediately by a similar project started before the turn of the century in the drafting room of McKim, Mead, and White. The Borough of Brooklyn was to have a museum of its own and an ambitious design called for eighty 12-foot-high figures along the cornice of the building's four façades.[23] This grand scheme of sculpture was meant to represent the arts and sciences of the various ancient and modern civilizations that were to be exhibited in the museum. Only half of the building was actually constructed, and to make certain that its forty figures would be uniform in style, an exhibition of quarter-size models was finally held in the Vanderbilt Gallery of the Fine Arts Building on Fifty-seventh Street in November, 1907. This gave the director of sculpture, Daniel Chester French, and the architects an opportunity to weed out any figures "which threatened to make breaks in the general scheme."[24]

Bitter had modeled four figures, representing the ancient philosophy, art, religion, and law of China. They were accepted and carved to full scale for the east pavilion of the building's north façade. Soft Indiana limestone permitted naturalistic features as well as deep drapery folds, which were made to match the heavy robes of the three dozen other figures standing on the cornice. Under such controlled conditions the many participating sculptors could hardly pursue individual styles, and Bitter's contributions likewise comply with the specified form. But no matter how involved he became in such conformity he never doubted the social significance of public sculpture, especially allegorical figures. Nor did this restrictive collaboration of applied figures have any apparent effect on his personal conception of sculpture as something integral with architectural structures and spaces. Quite the contrary, those concerns were to remain preoccupations of his independent work throughout the decade and a half allotted to him in the new century.

V

Portrait Monuments & Elegiac Memorials

THE FIRST YEARS of Bitter's career were taken up by the production of sculpture that had one basic purpose, to embellish a building. Most often this entailed the execution of many different kinds of figures for large programs of either allegorical or historical subjects. During this period, however, he was not called upon to produce a portrait statue, the standard commission for sculptors at the time. One reason for this may have been that several American sculptors were already well established in the trade of portraiture, and those individuals or institutions wanting a portrait were more likely to approach such well-known statue-makers as Augustus Saint-Gaudens, John Quincy Adams Ward, or Daniel Chester French. On the other hand, Bitter's workshop was so occupied with huge projects, such as Biltmore, that possibly no time could have been found to do a portrait statue. It was, however, while he was completing the sculpture for George Vanderbilt's mansion in Asheville that he received his first portrait commission. This was to be of Dr. William Pepper (1843–1898), a famous medical researcher and diagnostician, who had served as provost of the University of Pennsylvania from 1881 to 1894. Under Pepper's direction the university experienced an era of rapid expansion, and upon his retirement a group of friends decided to have a monument made as a means of commemorating his good work.

The portrayal in bronze of men who had figured prominently in the history of American educational institutions was a fairly well established custom by 1895. Ten years earlier, William Wetmore Story completed a full-standing portrait of Dr. Joseph Henry, a leading scientist at the College of New Jersey and the director of the Smithsonian Institution. At approximately the same time, French executed a heroic, idealized portrait statue of John Harvard for Harvard University, and in 1889, Saint-Gaudens did a high-relief portrait of Dr. James McCosh, who, as president of the College of New Jersey, led the way to its transformation into Princeton University.

As does French's John Harvard, Bitter's William Pepper (Fig. 34) sits in a large armchair that was placed on top of a stone pedestal. The use of such a pose and position for portrait statues was to become common among American sculptors and could already be seen in Ward's Horace Greeley of 1890, as well as in the Harvard by French. Also, Saint-Gaudens was working on his seated portrait of Peter Cooper when Bitter's Pepper monument was in process. Since the officially seated or enthroned figure has an unavoidable frontality, such monuments are usually placed close to a building and often right against one of its walls. Sometimes they become terminal features of a road, walk, or stairway. The figures of French and Saint-Gaudens sit with their backs turned to prominent façades. Saint-Gaudens went so far as to have his Cooper enshrined beneath an Ionic entablature, thereby restricting the figure even more to a frontal approach.

Whether Bitter knew from the beginning where the site for his first portrait monument would be is not certain. Pepper had been instrumental in establishing and building the new University Museum of Science and Art, and for this reason it was appropriate that the statue be placed somewhere on its grounds. The location finally chosen was in the center of a formally terraced plot at the northwest corner of the museum.[1] Since the new building was not opened until December, 1899, this site may not have been decided upon until after Bitter had completed the portrait in 1895, and perhaps not even until after the figure was cast in bronze one year later. That this may have been the case is well established in that Bitter waited until 1899 before beginning work on the pedestal, which was completed in the middle of April. Two months later he went to Philadelphia to "inspect" the site for the monument.[2]

Had Bitter been aware of the site all along, it would seem somewhat strange that he, a sculptor experienced in relating his work to architecture, should have relegated a figure seated in an armchair to the center of an open place. The back of the chair is of little interest to the observer and for this reason Pepper could never be a completely successful figure in the round. It is possible that the type and location of the monument were strictly dictated by the committee of sponsors or that some initial, more suitable, site was abandoned.

Whatever may have been the case, the composition of the monument shows signs of an attempt to make it as much sculpture in the round as is possible for such a seated figure. First, the base of the chair was not filled in or in any way covered up except, of course, in the front. An open space was left underneath the figure which allows the long academic robe to be seen as it falls behind the man's legs. Furthermore, the full sleeves of the robe cascade over each arm rest and flow back until they slightly overlap the rear of the chair, thus helping to soften the transition from the back of the composition to the front. To encourage a forward direction the figure was forced into a slumping position with head tilted and legs pushed out to the edge of the pedestal. The pedestal, designed four years later, was equipped with an object of interest on all four sides. Lettered bronze plaques, framed by a scroll, were placed on both the front and the back, while bronze relief panels, each containing an allegorical female figure and an inscription, were applied to either side.

In keeping with the baroque character of his early style, Bitter used the robe of his figure to open up the composition and to modify any stiff, upright angularity that might result from an overly dominant chair. Large folds of drapery push out from the seat of the chair and succeed in practically concealing it altogether when viewed from the front. The composition is also thrown off symmetrical balance by the tilt of the head toward the right and by the rhythmic arrangement of the hands and feet. The right hand is raised and clenched while the foot below it is pulled back and pointed inward. On the left side just the opposite is true; the opened hand is forced down on the thigh and the foot is pushed forward.

Unlike the seated statues of Saint-Gaudens, the Pepper statue does not give the impression of being forever enthroned and all powerful. Quite the contrary, the pose is one of momentary meditation and suspended motion. In representing his subject in this attitude of animated reflection, Bitter apparently succeeded in interpreting the man's personality quite accurately; for it was said that Pepper had an almost Napoleonic power of doing two or more things at once.[3] While he was an active administrator and even a shrewd manipulator of power who accomplished many practi-

Fig. 34.—William Pepper monument, bronze, University of Pennsylvania, Philadelphia, 1895–1899.

cal things, he was also admired as a deep-thinking theorist and researcher in his field. Bitter sketched his likeness from life, and the features and expression of the man as he saw them resemble those of the precisely realistic painting of Pepper by G. W. Pettit which hangs in the university's College Hall. The one apparent difference is in the age of the subject, the face by Bitter being older and more careworn.

Of all the portrait monuments that Bitter did in his career, including both those in the round and those in relief, this first, a seated bronze statue of a university president, was to be one of the very few that he would do of a living subject. Commemorative monuments in the United States are usually erected as memorials to either long-departed national heroes or recently deceased local leaders, and rarely is the subject of a memorial still alive at the time it is commissioned. Approximately fifteen years were to pass before Bitter would portray another living person for this purpose. In the meantime, all of his major portrait monuments represented heroes of an earlier era in American history.

The first of these to be erected was an equestrian portrait statue of the German-American Civil War general, Franz Sigel, which was completed in 1907. Prior to the Sigel, however, he designed two monuments that were never executed. These portrayed two other foreign-born military heroes of the United States, Marquis de Lafayette and Baron von Steuben. In 1898, approximately $100,000 was raised to erect a memorial statue of Lafayette in the Place du Carrousel, within the court of the Tuileries at the Louvre. It was to be dedicated during the Paris Exposition in 1900. Slightly less than half of the fund was contributed by the public school children of America; a small amount was appropriated by the State of New York; and the other half was raised by Congress through the sale of fifty thousand specially coined Lafayette dollars. All of the money was turned over to a Lafayette Memorial Commission which was given the responsibility of arranging for the memorial's design.[4]

Early in the year 1899, Bitter submitted a design of his own for the Paris monument following an unsuccessful collective effort. Sometime during the previous autumn, the Lafayette Memorial Commission had consulted him concerning the project, and it was decided that he should work out a design in collaboration with another sculptor and an architect. Bitter recommended Paul W. Bartlett and Henry F. Hornbostel for the respective positions, and the three of them went to Washington in December to present their preliminary designs and sketches to the commission.[5] A photograph of an ink-and-wash sketch of their proposed Lafayette monument appears in a scrapbook-diary Bitter kept at the time, and beneath the picture is written "submitted in Washington Dec., 1898." It shows a tall pylon with two equestrian figures flanked by spread eagles at its base and a group of three draped female figures on its top. A balustrade projects from either side of the pylon and steps extend in a half-circle out in front of the monument.

By the middle of Feburary, 1899, the first sketch of the monument had been developed into a model and was approved by the American jury made up of John Quincy Adams Ward, John La Farge, and George B. Post. Another photograph in Bitter's scrapbook-diary labeled "Lafayette design shortly before submitted to American jury" shows the architecture of the model as being essentially the same as that of the first sketch with only the steps and the balustrade having been modified. However, the group on top now consisted of a winged nude male figure standing between two seated half-draped female figures. Only one equestrian figure remained at the base and the eagles were replaced by early-adolescent nudes surrounded by foliage.

During the several weeks of work on the model the collaboration did not prove to be congenial. At the end of January, Bitter records difficulties with Hornbostel, whom he calls conceited, and later accuses both collaborators of being unfaithful.[6] When the model was shown to the jury on February 7, Hornbostel had painted the group on top a stone color instead of a bronze for which it had been composed by Bitter. The conflict came to a climax ten days later when Hornbostel informed Bitter by telephone that the Paris jury had not accepted their design and that he and Bartlett had already started a new one. While visiting Bartlett's studio the next day, Bitter was accused of not treating the monument in an artistic way but more as a mere job, and that ended the short-lived collaboration.[7]

Bitter was determined to submit his own design, and with the permission of Ward, Post, and La Farge, he asked Richard Howland Hunt to assist him with the architecture. Exactly how much assistance he received from his new collaborator is questionable. While Bitter started on the new design immediately, he wrote that Hunt was indifferent toward the project and he was not certain whether he would receive any help from him at all.[8] That he actually worked out the design on his own is substantiated by

Fig. 35.—Plaster model for LaFayette monument competition, designed for the Place du Carrousel, Paris, France, 1899. Destroyed.

the model (Fig. 35), which when finished at the end of March, turned out to be a refined version of a sketch Bitter had made immediately after breaking relations with his first collaborators.[9]

In contrast to the Pepper monument, Bitter's design for the Lafayette monument was more of an architectural than a sculptural solution. A bronze portrait of the hero standing in front of a chair was to occupy a stone pedestal in the middle of a circle half enclosed by an exedra. By this means, the figure would not have been left alone in a wide, open, empty space, but would have been virtually surrounded by an architectural setting. The choice of an exedra was possibly inspired by Daniel Chester French's Hunt Memorial on Fifth Avenue in New York. Since both Lafayette and Hunt represented a close association between America and France, Bitter perhaps thought that a monument to the former, intended for Paris, could legitimately resemble the one to the latter, already existing in New York City. At any rate, the architecture of both conformed to the classicistic style promoted by the Academy in France during the nineteenth century, and the New York monument was thus a suitable tribute to the leading American advocate of the Beaux-Arts tradition. However, in contrast to the Hunt Memorial, the Lafayette monument by Bitter was designed for a large open square contained by the newest wings of the

Louvre, and it was doubtlessly this site that determined the major differences between the proposed monument and its Fifth Avenue predecessor.

Since it was not to serve as a shelter in which to stop and rest alongside a street, the Lafayette monument was expanded to become a complete circle that could be entered from either wing of the exedra by climbing four low steps. The entablature was high enough to allow for free passage and the pronounced verticality of the Ionic columns and terminal pillars was accentuated by two finial vases. An aggressive group of sculpture went over the central bay depicting an eagle flanked by American and French escutcheons. Close attention was to be drawn to the featured figure by pairs of cherubs turning to look toward Lafayette from their pedestals at either end of the exedra. The animated figures, the rusticated stone, and the fragmented balustrade might have successfully complemented Lefuel's baroque façades facing the Place du Carrousel. This, however, they would never be able to achieve, for Bitter's model of a large exedra encircling a portrait statue failed to win the competition. In April, 1899, the American jury decided in favor of the design by Bartlett which was simply an equestrian statue of Lafayette and much less of an architectural composition than the monument conceived by Bitter.

Such a choice was not unusual in the United States, where, at least after the Civil War, the popular idea of a portrait monument was a statue on a pedestal. Battlefields and village squares are full of lonely figures which are barely related to their casual surroundings and rarely designed as part of a larger architectural setting. In the extreme, such repositories of monuments as Gettysburg National Park have much in common with most urban cemeteries.

In designing his Pepper monument, for the University of Pennsylvania, Bitter also shared in this failure to plan architecturally, but it was a mistake that he would never repeat. The Lafayette model provided such a predominant architectural framework that the portrait statue itself practically joined the subordinate groups as adjuncts to the architecture. Even though this scheme failed to gain him the opportunity to be permanently represented in Paris, it set a precedent that was to last throughout his career. Whenever he was called upon to execute a complete portrait monument thereafter, not only was the portrait figure itself intimately related to an architectural structure, but it tended to be practically dominated by it.

In other words, his predilection for an architectural composition employing sculpture as an integral part of the scheme was always maintained as far as possible. Thus, Bitter set out to prove himself an architectural sculptor, while portraiture per se remained a secondary concern.

As is discussed in chapters to follow, this basic change in attitude concerning the primary purpose of his profession brought Bitter into the public place, and it was there, in the interest of the growing American city, that the most significant cultural achievements of his career developed. This does not mean, however, that he was to ignore the personal patronage of the wealthy altogether. In addition to a great number of public portrait monuments, Bitter did periodically agree to embellish privately commissioned memorials with elegiac figures; but since they were usually destined for a graveside, their location was at least semipublic.

The first work by Bitter that may be considered an elegiac memorial was actually not a freestanding structure enshrouded by the intimacy of a family circle, but was constructed as a functional part of a church in full view of succeeding congregations. It consists of a pulpit and choir rail (Fig. 36) presented in 1900 by Sarah R. Cornell to the All Angels' Church of New York City in memory of her husband and two sons.[10] A band of approximately thirty-five angels was modeled by Bitter and carved in limestone as eleven separate panels measuring two and one-half feet in height. Starting at the right side of the choir the figures mournfully play instruments as they file toward the focal point of the memorial, while those mounting the steps and encircling the pulpit look down from their lofty location as they tug nervously at garlands of flowers. The pulpit is borne on the back of an atlas designed as a bearded prophet, and crowning the round wooden roof above is the large figure of a trumpeting angel carved out of walnut. While the interior of the church is Gothic in detail, Bitter's panels are incrusted with a broken texture of interweaving forms that again suggest a baroque composition. The individual figures, however, are so contemporary in type that at least those on the choir rail (Fig. 37) could very well have accompanied the eight maidens tending the oars of Frederick MacMonnies' ship-shaped fountain at the Columbian Exposition without seeming out of place. Lithe and slender, they are draped in clusters of curvilinear folds; and the irregular creases that flow freely from their arms and legs have a scumbled appearance, even though carved in stone. The heads bear a family resemblance to those of the sever-

Fig. 36.—All Angels' Church, choir rail and pulpit of limestone and walnut, West Eightieth Street, New York City, 1900.

Fig. 37.—Choir rail, detail of model for limestone relief in All Angels' Church, West Eightieth Street, New York City, 1900.

al relief figures done earlier for the Vanderbilt residences and represent an idealistic convention that Bitter adopted and repeated throughout the nineties.

The first graveside composition by Bitter (Fig. 38) was dedicated to the memory of John Erastus Hubbard, a prominent businessman and philanthropist of Montpelier, Vermont.[11] Arrangements for commemorating the bachelor with a memorial were made in the summer of 1901 by Senator William Paul Dillingham, and by the end of the following spring Bitter had finished the project.[12] Having asked his Viennese friend, Hans Kestranek, to design a rectangular exedra of granite, he simply attached a bronze figure to its side, thereby transforming what might have remained a mere marker into a memorial. Although similar to the interpretation of grief achieved by Saint-Gaudens for the well-known Adams Memorial in Washington, Bitter's figure is that of a youth. Upon first glance he appears to be

Fig. 38.—Hubbard memorial, bronze figure and granite exedra, Green Mount Cemetery, Montpelier, Vermont, 1902. Photograph by Robert Lizzari.

writhing in anguish. Actually the figure itself is rather quiet in pose while most of the movement results from the animated shroud draped around it. This billows out to the side only to be pulled tightly around the plaintive upturned face before falling loosely to the pedestal. An unbroken serpentine curve, which starts at the feet and winds its way through clutching fingers to the head, draws the composition together and assists in suggesting the spiritual content of the subject. Bitter's early experience in copying the "Dying Slave" by Michelangelo may have influenced the facial expression of his first funereal figure. However, the attitude as a whole was apparently inspired by the lines from Bryant's "Thanatopsis" inscribed on the granite support:

> . . . sustained and soothed
> By an unfaltering trust, approach thy grave,
> Like one who wraps the drapery of his couch
> About him and lies down to pleasant dreams.

Before the Montpelier commission was completed Bitter started to design another memorial in which the sculptural and architectural components would not be conceived separately and then attached to one another. Instead they would be treated as one and the same, thus fused as a single structure. Erected in the summer of 1904, the new memorial (Fig. 39) marks the grave of Henry Villard, the German-American journalist and railroad financier, buried four years earlier on top of a hill in Sleepy Hollow Cemetery overlooking the Hudson. A thick hedge of hemlock encloses the picturesque site, and Bitter's composition is approached from the west by climbing a brief set of stairs in line with the short axis of the rectangular ground plan. As a naturalistic nude the allegorical figure of Labor, dominating the memorial with its height of approximately eight feet, is hardly unusual for the period. During and after his years in Paris George Grey Barnard, for example, had depicted essentially the same muscular youth in several energetic poses, while Bitter himself had already used this type on the base of the Vulcan andiron at Biltmore (Fig. 13).

However, Bitter wrote that he was determined to make this work "modern" in style;[13] and he turned to the contemporary *art nouveau* movement of design for inspiration. As a result, his memorial became a large freestanding adaptation of a basically two-dimensional motive. Its graceful shape might have originated as a border on a book cover, or perhaps it was borrowed from something as small as a piece of jewelry. Whatever happened to be his immediate source, the three slightly flattened curves of the panel and the practically indiscernible narrowing of its width from base to arch were stock-in-trade of the *art nouveau* designer. Even the stylized trees which Bitter coupled on either side as a means of joining the front with the back typify the *art nouveau* penchant for adopting elongated plant forms as ornamental devices.

Although the figure is contained as part of the flesh-tinted marble, and the head emerges from a rough-textured surface in the accepted Rodinesque manner (Fig. 40), the over-all effect is almost as pictorial as it is sculptural. The curvilinear contour, the flanking trees, the signs of the zo-

Fig. 39.—Villard memorial, marble, Sleepy Hollow Cemetery, Tarrytown, New York, 1902–1904.

Fig. 40.—Villard memorial, detail, marble, Sleepy Hollow Cemetery, Tarrytown, New York, 1902–1904.

diac etched on the concave arch, as well as the diligent detailing of Labor at rest with his tools, are responsible for this. Consequently, the Villard Memorial lacks the architectural orientation that Bitter was to achieve in his public portrait monuments; and as a decorative relief, it could very well have been destined for a wall of the Villard home rather than for the family burial ground.

Of course, the possibility of achieving architecture with portrait monuments varied with the patronage. Sometimes sponsors of a monument, instead of relying upon the discretion of the sculptor, would designate specifically what kind should be erected. This could lead to difficulties with private patrons who refused to be persuaded otherwise by the artist under commission, but there was still less room for negotiation when the patron was the United States Government and the erection of a specific type of monument was called for by an act of Congress. Such an enactment led Bitter to design another ill-fated model for a monument to a foreign-born American military hero.

On February 27, 1903, a bill was signed by President Roosevelt providing for the erection of two statues in Washington, D.C. One was to the memory of Brigadier General Count Pulaski, and the other was to be dedicated to General Baron von Steuben of the Continental Army. Fifty thousand dollars apiece was appropriated "for the purpose of procuring and erecting said statue with a suitable pedestal."[14] To direct the expenditures and select the site, a commission was created for each monument. In the case of the Steuben statue the commission was composed of the Secretary of War, the Chairman of the Committee on the Library of the Senate, and his counterpart from the House of Representatives. Finally, in July, 1905, competition was invited for the Steuben statue and in October Bitter was one of six sculptors who submitted models.[15] In December the commission selected three of the models and requested their sculptors to prepare larger ones for final consideration. Only Bitter and German-born Albert Jaegers entered the second competition, and in May, 1906, the commission chose the design by Jaegers. Bitter was extremely disappointed by the outcome of this competition, the second two-man contest he had failed to win. He sincerely believed that his design was good and that the commission of politicians had made the wrong choice.[16]

Jaeger's monument was erected in 1910 on the northwest corner of Lafayette Park, joining the statues of Lafayette, Rochambeau, and Kosciusko in this attractive area across the street from the White House. The Steuben statue is a bronze figure of the Baron placed on top of a severe granite shaft.[17] This is flanked by two bronze allegorical groups composed of paired nude figures and their accessories. As the sculpture stands out in sharp contrast to the color and contour of the stoney shaft, it is the most dominant aspect of Jaeger's monument. In fact, the architecture and the sculpture appear to have been conceived as two separate and distinct elements which were nonchalantly brought together as a matter of mere convenience. The nudes and the heavily-caped Baron are not closely related to the granite shaft and its adjoining pedestals. That any other support might do was demonstrated when a replica of the portrait was given to Germany and placed on another stock pedestal in Potsdam without any attempt to unite them as a single scheme. The only indication that the Washington shaft and the Potsdam pedestal were meant to support the same figure of Baron von Steuben is the bronze lettering which identifies the monuments. Like many other contemporary statue-makers, Jaegers apparently considered the sculpture to be his primary obligation while its architectural setting was only of incidental concern.

Bitter, on the other hand, obviously interested in both aspects of a portrait monument, placed a strong emphasis on architecture as a means of providing a proper foil to his sculpture. Therefore, in contrast to the monument by Jaegers, Bitter's model (Fig. 41) for the Steuben competition presented a statue and a "suitable pedestal" joined as complementary units. This does not necessarily mean that his portrait figure of Steuben could not have been placed somewhere else. It does mean, however, that the pedestal was designed for this specific figure and could not have served as a suitable support for any other portrait without undergoing major alterations.

The portrait which Bitter sketched for the top of his pedestal was a little over one-third the total height of the monument and relatively small in proportion to the over-all dimensions of the design. Steuben was not represented as an extremely heroic-looking military figure but rather as a casually dressed gentleman leaning on a walking stick. While his feet were placed wide apart and in line with each other, his hands were symmetrically opposed, one clutching the top of his walking stick and the other gripping the hilt of his sword. The basic shape and balanced position of the fists were repeated on the pedestal by the ornamental helmets applied to the top of its narrow, alternate sides and again by the heads of the lions protruding below. The triangle created by the man's head and hands was also restated on a larger scale by the pyramidal ascent of the pedestal to the boots of the figure.

The pedestal was divided into two parts roughly comparable to a large baroque terminal vase independently supported in the middle of a broad platform. Where the curved vase-like form met the angular base an indentation was created which Bitter filled with supplementary sculpture. The figures of two lounging lions seemed to inhabit the pedestal. In front a portrait medallion, framed by a garland of foliage, was supported by a simple block decorated with the same triangular *guttae* that fell from the corner helmets above.

Fig. 41.—Plaster model for Steuben monument competition, designed for LaFayette Park, Washington, D.C., 1905–1906. Destroyed.

Thus, confronted with the legislated limitations of a statue on a pedestal, Bitter designed the latter as an imposing part of his model for the Steuben monument. To create an architectural support that would complement the portrait figure thematically, as well as structurally, he incorporated supplementary sculpture into the architecture itself. In this way he overcame the customary unimportance of the pedestal to the composition as a whole and at the same time demonstrated his interest in the subordination of portrait sculpture to a larger architectural conception.

The care which Bitter took in choosing and, as far as possible, controlling the immediate surroundings of his monuments is exemplified in his one equestrian portrait statue (Fig. 42). The subject is Franz Sigel, who escaped from Germany after the unsuccessful Revolution of 1848 and

Fig. 42.—Franz Sigel monument, bronze, West 106th Street and Riverside Drive, New York City, 1904–1907.

Fig. 43.—Franz Sigel monument, bronze, West 106th Street and Riverside Drive, New York City, 1904–1907.

later fought as a Union general in the American Civil War. Upon the death of General Sigel in August, 1902, several plans were proposed within the German-American community to erect monuments in his memory in cities throughout the country.[18] The most ambitious of these plans was introduced in New York City by a Sigel monument committee which included Carl Schurz. Through public subscription and private solicitation the New York group had raised over $4,000 by the time it met in the Schurz home just two months after Sigel's death.[19] By the beginning of 1904 the goal of $15,000 was almost realized and Bitter was commissioned to execute a monument within three years.[20] In March, 1907, the committee visited his studio to view the finished model which was then cast in bronze and soon erected.[21]

Bitter was certainly cognizant of the inherent design limitations of the equestrian portrait statue when he selected a rather unorthodox location for his General Sigel.[22] Instead of placing the equestrian statue in an open square, he chose the top of a wide flight of stairs descending from the end of West 106th Street to the sidewalk of Riverside Drive. The pedestal projects beyond the edge of the top step and rests on a second block of stone which was brought out flush with the riser of the fifth step down. In this way the pedestal seems to emerge from the steps as the continuation of a single structure. To enhance this close association the grooves that are cut into the banisters are the same depth and width as those on the base of the pedestal.

While the location of the statue is indeed dramatic, the horse is a study of restrained motion. From the sidewalk below it seems to be standing perfectly still and no sudden movement disturbs the clear-cut monumentality of the stairway and the statue as a total composition. The horse is placed on all four hoofs with its head pulled down to face the observer who ascends the stairs in front. But legs and tail are also set at the same angle, and together they establish a succession of parallel diagonal lines that at least suggest forward motion. In fact, as one climbs toward the statue the impression of perfect calm that a view from below creates suddenly disappears, and a close observation reveals a forceful play of tension between man and horse (Fig. 43). Bitter was an accomplished horseman and consequently familiar with the subtle maneuvers involved in riding. For his Sigel monument he chose to depict an instant of restraint anticipating movement by having the rider rein in his mount just as the animal is about to start forward. The horse's lower jaw is pulled back, the head is brought down, and the neck is arched; but the hoofs have not had time to move.[23] Sigel, who was a small man with a slight build, sits erect in the saddle automatically forcing his horse to stand for a moment while he surveys the valley beyond.

The Sigel monument was obviously tailored to fit a specific site, and in turn its design must have been conditioned by the general character of the area surrounding it. The statue was meant to be viewed either from a vehicle moving along Riverside Drive below or by pedestrians walking along the sidewalk or climbing the stairway. When seen from the lower street level the equestrian figure thus stands quietly upon its plain stair-born pedestal complementing the gentle curves of the solid stone banisters. In contrast to the ornate façades of an apartment building on the corner of 106th Street, the composition of the man on his horse maintains the monumentality of the architecture beneath it. Even without this busy background an extremely vigorous pose would not have worked as well with the peculiar position of the pedestal. A platform high above a flight of stairs would be a rather precarious perch for a quick-strutting horse. In keeping with this location Bitter managed to hold the horse of General Sigel in check, and not one hoof is raised to threaten the balance between the design of the statue and the solid simplicity of its stairway support. Nevertheless, he did not pass up the chance to portray the violence of a spirited stallion resisting the control of its rider, and the notion of complete calm that one receives from a distant glance is abruptly changed upon close inspection. After all, as will be witnessed in a large, wildly rearing horse modeled for the Pan-American Exposition in Buffalo, Bitter was imbued enough by his schooling in Vienna for the excitement of its baroque tradition to last beyond his youth.

VI

Fair Weather Sculpture

BITTER'S early association with Richard Morris Hunt was to have at least one lasting effect on his career. Having produced such an enormous amount of decorative, architectural sculpture during his first years in America, he became well known for his ability to organize and administer extensive projects. This fame was to be furthered immediately following the turn of the century when America, anxious to display its "material progress," was the scene of two more international fairs, and Bitter was named director of sculpture for both. The first, the Pan-American Exposition, was held in Buffalo in 1901. Planned in the tradition of the nineteenth-century European exposition, it did not commemorate any specific historical event. Pan-American primarily in name only, its main purpose was to display the abundance of natural resources in the United States and to dramatize their use in the development of her industry.

In spite of its emphasis on modern technology, however, the Pan-American Exposition was for the most part architecturally conservative. As explained by John M. Carrere, Chairman of the Board of Architects responsible for designing the buildings and grounds, the basic idea was to create a picturesque ensemble on a formal ground plan.[1] This resulted in a strictly symmetrical shape with outlines resembling a huge church, including a long nave, transept, and choir. To project what was advertised as Spanish American, long lines of arcades, richly detailed openings, complex spires, pastel-colored walls, and red tile roofs with overhanging eaves replaced the white columns, cornices, balustrades, and flat roofs of the Columbian Exposition. Nevertheless, there were still enough classical forms in evidence to fully justify a classification of the general style as "a free treatment of the Renaissance."[2] The architects' plan also specified how much sculpture should be used as well as the location and relative size of allegorical groups, statues, and fountains. It did not, however, determine the subject or design of the sculpture and the National Sculpture Society was asked to choose one of its members who could come up with a suitable scheme for the empty pedestals and bare buildings. Bitter was unanimously elected to assume the responsibility.[3]

In organizing the sculpture for the Pan-American Exposition, Bitter insisted that the ideas it expressed and the subjects it represented should be related intimately to the purpose and theme of the exhibits. He wrote that the arrangement of the buildings supplied "the natural basis for a scheme of sculpture" and if the two were carefully juxtaposed they could be considered "the phraseology of the sermon that was to be delivered."[4] Starting with the Esplanade, or "transept" of the church-like ground plan, the buildings of its west wing were devoted to forestry, mining, and other natural resources; thus, the theme of the sculpture in this corner of the Exposition became Nature. The opposite wing of the Esplanade was dominated by the United States Government Building and its sculpture was devoted to Man. The main court, that is the "nave" of the plan, which was called the Court of Fountains, was flanked by the largest buildings of the Exposition, and these included Machinery, Transportation, Manufactures, and Electricity.[5] For that reason, Bitter decided to represent the Genius of Man and his development of Art, Science, and Industry as the theme of this third and largest group of sculpture.

Not only did Bitter originate the general scheme of sculpture but he also worked out the subjects for each subordinate group. A "Fountain of Nature" in the west wing of the Esplanade featured a female figure supported on a globe by allegorical figures depicting the four elements. Ceres and Kronos occupied smaller fountains on either side while Mineral, Vegetable, and Animal Wealth were the subjects of six large pedestals placed around the broad basin of the central fountain. At the opposite end of the Esplanade an identical arrangement featured a "Fountain of Man," with a double-faced, double-bodied figure on top to suggest the mystery of the psyche. This peculiar work by Charles Grafly was supported by five nude figures representing the senses, while groups of figures crouching beneath them expressed such human characteristics as love, hate, courage, and cowardice. For the two smaller fountains Bitter chose Hercules and Prometheus as related mythological subjects. The large pedestals encircling the basin held groups depicting three ages of man's social evolution: for the Savage Age, an abduction scene and war dance; for the Age of Despotism, four male figures representing the masses pulling a chariot of state with Truth and Justice chained behind; and for the Age of Enlightenment, groups representing religion, education, and the family.[6]

A didactic use of allegory and mythology was continued into the nave-like Court of Fountains meant to correspond with the flanking buildings devoted to technological advance. Around the edge of a very long basin, several groups of sculpture representing human emotions and the intellect were accompanied respectively by the "Birth of Venus" and the "Birth of Athena." Art, Science, Manufacturing, and Agriculture were honored on outlying pedestals of the same scheme. For the very center of the Exposition, where the Court of Fountains and the Esplanade joined, Bitter appropriately chose to embellish a circular basin with a fountain depicting Abundance.[7]

The focal point of the Exposition, however, was a glorification of the dynamo in the form of an Electric Tower. Erected at the northern end of the Court of Fountains it was illuminated at night by forty thousand incandescent electric lamps arranged in lacy patterns of varied colors. Although resembling Stanford White's Spanish-inspired tower for Madison Square Garden to the point of having a nude goddess on top, the Electric Tower was not part of a building but was joined to a curving colonnade that bordered a large reflecting pool. Along with the water, cascading from a niche in the base of the Tower at the rate of eleven thousand gallons per minute, the power was supplied by the Niagara. The sculpture that Bitter planned to accompany the already lavish ornamentation represented man's mastery and use of the Great Lakes. Each lake was represented by a group displayed in a niche on one of the piers at either end of the colonnade. For the base of the Tower itself, George Grey Barnard contributed two more groups depicting the "Great Waters in the Time of the Indian" and the "Great Waters in the Time of the White Man."

In contrast to his performance at the Columbian Exposition Bitter executed few works of sculpture at the Pan-American. For a keystone above the central niche of the Electric Tower he designed an unusual female head representing light. For a frieze high up on the tower he provided the figure of a child which was duplicated as a pattern and joined at the corners by gilded eagles. Between the keystone and the frieze, an escutcheon containing the device of the Exposition, a map of North and South America, also came out of his workshop.

In addition to this accessory sculpture for the Tower, Bitter's most prominent work was executed for the Triumphal Causeway (Fig. 44), a monumental entrance at the opposite end of the Court of Fountains. Designed by John Carrere, the Causeway crossed a narrow body of water separating the exposition grounds from Delaware Park to the south.[8] To balance the Electric Tower, the Causeway was punctuated by four giant pylons that were most likely inspired by similar structures at the Paris Exposition of 1900. Each consisted of a rusticated base, a square shaft with Corinthian pilasters, a prominent cornice, and an attic story with a flamboyant equestrian figure on top. The sculpture of the Causeway as a whole was "an apotheosis of national pride" and included groups in niches representing such stately virtues as Benevolence and Patriotism.[9] The pylons also had single pedestals connected to them that accommodated freestanding compositions depicting either Trophies of Power or Trophies of Peace. From each pedestal a heavy buttress curved upward to a high relief designed by Bitter. As duplicated four times over, it consisted of two loosely gowned female figures, emblematic of North and South America, that seemed to be dancing ecstatically around an elaborate shield of the United States (Fig. 45).

Of even greater prominence were four casts of an equestrian standard-bearer (Fig. 46) which Bitter modeled for the pyramidal pedestals surmounting the pylons. Standing one hundred and sixteen feet above the water, each figure was forty-six feet in height, and faced toward the outside corner of its pylon. The double theme of Peace and Power was carried out here on top with the nude riders wielding either a shield or a lyre. In both cases, the standard-bearers were said to express "the triumphant struggle of the people of the United States to free themselves from the institutions of despotic ages and governments."[10]

Bitter was proud of his first freestanding equestrian figure and boasted that the thirty-foot horse was the largest ever made as a piece of sculpture.[11] The main components of the composition were carefully bal-

Fig. 44.—Triumphal Causeway, Pan-American Exposition, Buffalo, New York, 1901. Destroyed.

Fig. 45 (above).—Relief for pylons on Triumphal Causeway, model for staff, Pan-American Exposition, Buffalo, New York, 1901. Destroyed.

Fig. 46 (right).—Standard-bearer, clay model for staff figure on Triumphal Causeway, Pan-American Exposition, Buffalo, New York, 1901. Destroyed.

anced above the hindquarters of the horse, which were merged with a gnarled vine that helped serve as a supporting base. The naturalistic figure of a youth wearing only a Greek helmet and a tattered loincloth glared over the right shoulder of his mount toward the ground, while the head and hoofs of the horse twisted around in the opposite direction. These counterthrusts were repeated by the flag and shield, which together created a triangular framework brought to a climax at the point of the standard. Such sculpture could be declared a true descendant of the baroque in style and spirit.

At the same time the Pan-American Exposition was taking place in Buffalo, plans were already under way for the St. Louis World's Fair. Under the leadership of former Missouri Governor D. R. Francis, it was envisioned as the largest international exposition held anywhere thus far. Following the method used at Chicago and Buffalo, the St. Louis Fair was financed in three equal funds: by the municipal government, through public subscription, and from a federal appropriation. The total amount to be secured was fixed by a special St. Louis committee at fifteen million dollars, the sum paid to France by the United States for the Louisiana Territory.[12] The Act of Congress appropriating its share of the money provided "for celebrating the one hundreth anniversary of the purchase of the Louisiana Territory by the United States, by holding an international exhibition of arts, industries, manufactures and the products of the soil, mine, forest and sea. . . ."[13] In August, 1901, the President issued a proclamation addressed to all nations, inviting them to participate, and approximately forty agreed to be represented by buildings and exhibits.[14] The desire of St. Louis to surpass all previous expositions was demonstrated immediately by the size of the site it provided for that purpose. The western half of Forest Park, a heavily wooded and rolling area of 1,240 acres, known locally as "The Wilderness," was cleared for the fairgrounds. When completed, the buildings of the St. Louis World's Fair actually did cover more ground than did those of the Columbian Exposition, the Paris Exposition of 1900, and the Pan-American Exposition combined.[15]

While not as festively uninhibited, the architectural style of the St. Louis World's Fair was obviously influenced by the Paris Exposition. In fact, the designing of the featured buildings and central ground plan was under the direction of E. L. Masqueray, a French-born architect trained at the Ecole des Beaux-Arts and winner of the Prix de Rome.[16] This direct connection with Paris only underlined the overriding influence of the French Academy on public architecture in America at the time. From it the steel-framed and glass-roofed exposition palaces of St. Louis were embellished with ornamental classical motives. Large semicircular arches buttressed by decorative piers, for example, were copied from the Paris Exposition of 1900 and added to the colonnades, cornices, balustrades, and triumphal arches inherited from the Columbian Exposition.

For the main portion of the St. Louis Fair the ground plan assumed the shape of a fan, with cascades, lagoons, and a large central basin providing the outlines in which the most prominent buildings were placed. The focal point was a circular, domed Festival Hall, designed by Cass Gilbert. It was erected on top of a hill as the centerpiece of an imposing semicircular colonnade by Masqueray, called the Terrace of the States. At the ends of the colonnade, round restaurant pavilions were also covered with domes to echo that of the Festival Hall. To complete the composition, the face of the hillside was terraced and a series of three cascades tumbled from the colonnade into the key-shaped grand basin. This also furnished the water for the narrow lagoons that ran down the middle of the avenues between the exhibition buildings.[17]

Before any construction could be carried very far a scheme of sculpture that would join the buildings with the grounds had to be laid out. Once again Bitter was summoned to assume this responsibility. His appointment as chief of sculpture came rather late and unexpectedly when F. Wellington Ruckstuhl was forced to resign in December, 1902, after holding the position for only three months.[18] Regardless of the short notice, or of any delay involved, Bitter contracted to design the entire scheme. He also had to allot the work to a variety of sculptors, pass upon their individual performances, and supervise the enlargement and placement of each group. Since there were some 250 groups and over 1500 single figures to be completed and installed within a matter of months, this was no small task. To accommodate the many sculptors from New York, Bitter set up an enlarging shop in Weehawken, and fifty-four carloads of full-scale sculpture in staff were shipped from there to St. Louis. The huge Education Building was used as a workshop on the Exposition grounds where the work was delayed even further when the Plasterers' Union demanded a greater part in the fabrication of the figures. Bitter was able to persuade the men differently and an all-out strike was avoided. When completed, the cost of providing the sculpture totaled $511,000.[19]

Unlike his plan for the Pan-American Exposition, Bitter's program of sculpture for the St. Louis World's Fair placed little emphasis upon industrial progress or the exploitation of natural resources. Instead, the primary purpose of the sculpture was to celebrate and commend America's Manifest Destiny encouraged by the acquisition of the Louisiana Territory a century before.[20] Confronted with a theme of historical consequence, Bitter was under pressure to stress the anecdotal in the form of portraiture and local color, but he managed to make ample provisions for allegorical and mythological sculpture as well.[21] These more abstract subjects were concentrated at the southern end of the grand basin, where the sculpture of the Festival Hall, Colonnade of States, and the cascades was treated as "a jubilant termination" of all the sculpture in the Fair.[22]

The highest group of this composition was a florid cluster of twelve figures depicting Apollo and the Muses mounted above the entablature of the Festival Hall. In a very large niche directly underneath the Apollo, a complex entanglement of figures framed the waterfall of the central cascade, which in turn was flanked by pedestals of ornate sculpture descending to the basin below. Figures of Liberty, Justice, and Truth were the most prominent of those in the niche, and they were carefully related in proportion and position to the fountains of figures placed over the other two cascades. These symbolized the Atlantic and Pacific, respectively, the idea being that such virtues as liberty and justice were secure between the two oceans. The thirteen states and the Indian Territory that evolved from the Louisiana Purchase were also represented as allegorical figures and placed on pedestals in the circular bays of the Colonnade.

As Bitter explained his entire scheme, the allegorical sculpture was used in connection with structures dedicated to "a more ideal mission," while the historical subjects were grouped with the buildings devoted to "the more material side" of the Exposition.[23] The two types were here and there intermingled on a single monument. For example, an imposing work entitled "Apotheosis of St. Louis," designed by Charles H. Niehaus for the entrance to the Fair, featured a huge equestrian statue of Louis IX. Its pedestal was embellished with a female figure and two winged youths, symbolizing the City of St. Louis and its Guiding Spirits.

Fig. 47.—Louisiana Purchase monument, staff, St. Louis World's Fair, 1904. Destroyed.

Fig. 48.—"Peace," model for staff figure on Louisiana Purchase monument, St. Louis World's Fair, 1904. Destroyed.

A similar combination appeared in the sculpture that Bitter himself contributed to the Fair. Less prominent than the standard-bearers at Buffalo, it was nevertheless executed as part of the Louisiana Purchase monument, a central attraction designed by Masqueray for a gathering place known as the Plaza of St. Louis at the north end of the grand basin (Fig. 47). The monument was not much more than a smooth cylindrical shaft, approximately one hundred feet high, with the entasis of a classical column. It rested on a round base, carried a sphere on top, and was repeated in much smaller scale along either side of the grand basin as decorative posts. The sphere surmounting the monument was actually a globe bearing the signs of the zodiac, and Bitter modeled four robust nude figures to sit underneath as the cardinal points of the compass. He also designed a crowned figure of Peace (Fig. 48) to alight on top of the globe with windblown drapery and an upraised hand bearing the conventional olive branch.

Below, on the base of the monument, the Mississippi and Missouri rivers were each represented as a nude female figure riding the prow of an ancient boat. The featured group of the monument, however, was historical, not allegorical. It depicted the meeting of Monroe, Livingston, and Marbois to sign the Louisiana Purchase Treaty. In order to balance the speaker's rostrum built into the northern side of the monument, this anecdotal high relief was at least twice life-size and located on a platform facing the grand basin. When in full use, therefore, the base of the Louisiana Purchase monument became a busy scene of dark-suited orators accompanied by gigantic bleach-white figures of staff. Through this composition of black and white occurred a juxtaposition of the visionary past and the envisioned future. While the sculpture was a plaster portrayal of a promise-laden past, the words spoken from the rostrum were no doubt dominated by pride-ridden projections of a great American century. This visual reminiscence of a formative period in the country's history and the optimistic anticipation of its future were brought together throughout the largest of world's fair as one big, grand and glorious generalization of greatness.

Although the decorative sculpture for an exposition is ephemeral, the atmosphere in which it is done could very likely have a prolonged effect on a sculptor's work. At least there is some indication of a sustained expositional spirit in the first collaborative project of architectural sculpture in which Bitter participated after the St. Louis World's Fair. In 1906 the plans for a new United States Customs House were completed by Cass Gilbert, one of the leading architects of the St. Louis Fair, and its construction in downtown New York, between Bowling Green and Battery Park, was started in the same year. True to the classical Beaux-Arts formula the building consists of a rusticated basement, colossal Corinthian columns, a prominent cornice, attic story, balustrade, and a somewhat less common mansard roof. The stone of its seven stories is Maine granite, and the major, or north, façade is embellished with marble sculpture which

Fig. 49.—Clay sketch for granite relief, Customs House, New York City, 1907.

helps to identify the function of the building and distinguishes it from a courthouse or a bank. On the attic story twelve statues with elaborately carved period costumes represent ancient as well as modern seafaring powers, while the four pedestals in front of the first floor hold fanciful groups by Daniel Chester French representing Africa, America, Asia, and Europe. Each one of the latter consists of the familiar French female accompanied by subordinate figures and such accessories as lions, eagles, skulls, and a sphinx.

Bitter's contribution to the collaborative embellishment of the Customs House is a high-relief group (Fig. 49) crowning the façade. Its subject, an ornamental shield of the United States supported by two energetic female figures, is identical to that of the relief Bitter designed for the pylons of the Triumphal Causeway at the Pan-American Exposition. However,

Fig. 50.—Granite relief, Customs House, New York City, 1907.

the composition of this later version was derived from a definite prototype —the group on top of Nicola Salvi's Trevi Fountain in Rome. As does the example of eighteenth-century architectural sculpture, Bitter's Customs House group interrupts the balustrade (Fig. 50). It is thereby closely related to the paired figures of the attic story below. But unlike the Trevi Fountain group, the composition by Bitter is not contained as a rectangular shape, and in place of the complicated papal device above the escutcheon in Rome, a spread eagle perches on its top.

Of greater significance is the difference between the winged female figures of the two works. In contrast to the corpulent baroque angels of the Trevi Fountain, Bitter's figures are slender, thinly draped nudes that appear to be studies of a live model. Although one holds a sword and the other a fasces as symbols of force and strength, neither looks very powerful and both are equipped with the innocent, finely featured face that appears repeatedly at the turn of the century as an American ideal of feminine beauty. In short, while Bitter borrowed a traditional heraldic decoration from baroque architecture, he adapted it to a public building in New York City by introducing contemporary symbolic and stylistic conventions.

The Customs House marks the end of a phase in Bitter's architectural sculpture that is characterized by a succession of single allegorical figures and assorted groups for public buildings and ceremonial monuments. Many of these from the time of the Appellate Division Supreme Court Building were produced as part of a perennial collaboration among members of the National Sculpture Society, and very often the subject and type, if not the style, of this sculpture were prescribed by the architect in charge. The planning and supervision of sculpture for two international expositions was as close as Bitter came to repeating the tremendous production of his first five years in America. But even though his individual commissions became much more modest in scope, the style of his architectural sculpture from the late nineties through 1906 remained fairly consistent with that of the early years. At the same time there is also no significant stylistic difference between the public architectural sculpture of this second phase and the sculpture that Bitter provided for the estates, and subsequently for the grave-sites, of the wealthy. However, a pronounced change in style was on the way, and a new direction for Bitter's architectural sculpture was already appearing by the time his baroque-inspired group was hoisted to the top of the United States Customs House in the summer of 1907.

VII

Classicistic Checks On a Changing Style

BITTER had been in the United States fifteen years when he wrote to Hans Kestranek in Vienna a brief critique on the contemporary condition of American architecture. He stated, "The many young architects that were drawn to Paris have forced a certain warmed-over Ecole des Beaux-Arts atmosphere upon the taste of this country which reveals indeed much knowledge but absolutely no individuality. In addition, McKim, Mead, and White have developed their own school which takes pleasure in copying good, old examples and promises to remain under the influence of the Italian Renaissance. Everything else is nipped in the bud by these two classes of architecture."[1] Such a progressive reaction to the academic could have been conditioned by the buildings Bitter had admired in Chicago, Buffalo, and St. Louis by Louis Sullivan, whom he met in 1903.[2]

No matter how critical Bitter may have been at times toward existing American architecture, his career as an architectural sculptor in America depended largely on the continued construction of public buildings in an academic, classicistic style. Sullivan, after all, had not followed his one-time master, Frank Furness, in using large amounts of sculpture to accompany his florid ornamentation, and Frank Lloyd Wright was in accord with the European Secessionists in allowing only limited accommodation for figural sculpture on his early major buildings. In fact, after the Imperial Hotel Wright's more ambitious projects were increasingly initiated as ornament-designs that allowed for less and less applied decoration of any kind.

There was good reason why most American architectural sculpture remained the handmaiden of a classicistic building. The academic architects at the helm of American architecture were the one dependable source of commissions for sculptors. Bitter spoke of the relationship as an "ancient alliance," and the Architectural League of New York, as well as the Society of Beaux-Arts Architects, saw to it that their allies in the National Sculpture Society remained loyal. Speakers were exchanged, mutual exhibitions held, and even a school for decorative sculptors was established to make sure the supply would last.[3] Of equal importance, an intermittent, international fair provided an opportunity for the alliance to become firmly entrenched. If a sculptor grew tired of this arrangement he might carve up mountains as Gutzon Borglum did, design an enormous monument dedicated to peace, but never to be erected, like that of George Grey Barnard, or abandon public monumental sculpture altogether to follow the avant-garde sculptors in producing gallery pieces. Since none of these alternatives suited Bitter, any decisive change in style or technique that might come about in his architectural sculpture would first appear inside a classical pediment, on top of a classical entablature, or between classical columns.

In the autumn of 1906, Bitter maintained his association with the old guard of America's academic architects when he was commissioned to provide sculpture for a bank building designed by one of his original architect-clients, George B. Post. The building was to house the Cleveland Trust Company in Cleveland, Ohio, as a three-story white granite structure containing a rotunda surmounted by a double, glass dome. In order to accommodate such internal spaciousness, the walls were brought out to the edge of a relatively small corner lot. This, in turn, limited the projection of the classical temple fronts applied to the Euclid Avenue and Ninth Street façades to only one column's width beyond the surface of the building. With the exception of floral swags between the Corinthian capitals and acanthus wreaths along the frieze above, the pediments of the two streetside façades received the only applied ornamentation. Both were assigned to Bitter, but since the Ninth Street pediment was reserved for a company coat of arms only the principal pediment (Fig. 51) facing Euclid Avenue was considered worthy of full sculptural treatment. In May, 1907, the blocks of granite were set in place for carving,[4] and on New Year's

Fig. 51.—Cleveland Trust Company, granite, Euclid Avenue and Ninth Street, Cleveland, Ohio, 1906–1907.

Day, 1908, the building, complete with sculpture, was honored with its first public showing.

To commemorate its new home the Cleveland Trust Company published a booklet, and in it Bitter explained the subject of his pediment. The seven figures allegorize Land and Water, "the mainsprings of wealth," as well as Banking, "the interchange of resources and the accumulation of wealth." The latter is glorified in the form of an enthroned figure flanked by two "altars" laden with fruit. These Bitter interpreted as "symbols of the country and the industry of its inhabitants that makes a flourishing banking business possible." The three figures to the left of the central composition represent the occupations of the land, that is, Industrial Labor, Agriculture, and Mining; while the threesome to the right symbolizes the importance of water for Commerce, Navigation, and Fishing. The extreme ends of the pediment are occupied by fish and fowl, which further carry out the division of the composition into Land and Water.[5]

Although a scheme of sculpture glorifying the banking business is not far removed in subject from a sculptural apotheosis for the railroad industry, Bitter's Cleveland Trust pediment, when compared with the pediment he did twelve years earlier for the Broad Street Station in Philadelphia (Fig. 25), shows a marked change in composition, technique, and style. First of all, there is a great contrast in materials between the two, and a design for granite is almost certain to be different from one for terra cotta. An explosive composition of undulating surfaces and innumerable minor facets that cause a shifting pattern of light and shadow is much more readily modeled in soft clay than chiseled in hard granite. This does not necessarily mean that a work in granite should be any less detailed, however, and Bitter's later pediment includes many subordinate accessories. The figures are also accurate approximations from nature and in certain aspects of anatomy are less generalized than those on the Broad Street Station. Even the drapery of the Land and Water groups is carved in folds irregular enough to suggest the movement of a pliable, woven material. On the other hand, the waves and leaves in the Cleveland Trust pediment are much more stylized and precisely patterned than any equivalent details in the Broad Street Station pediment.

This distinction, however, is overshadowed by more basic differences between the two compositions. In contrast to the five curvilinear clusters that radiated from the center of the arched pediment above Fifteenth Street in Philadelphia, the later composition maintains a regular rhythm of mainly vertical forms from end to end. The corner figures of Mining and Fishing are less prominently diagonal, as half-length figures emerging from the ground and sea, respectively, than they might have been as full-length figures. Furthermore, any deviation from the over-all vertical order of the composition is held in check by a careful alignment of the heads in parallel relationship with the raking cornices.

Although a composition for a classical pediment, Bitter's sculpture for the Cleveland Trust Bank is a compact, cohesive group with all of its figures and their accessories physically joined. Such well-known Greek pediments as those from the Temple of Aphaia at Aegina, from the Temple of Zeus at Olympia, or from the Parthenon consist mainly of separate, freestanding figures. These are each necessarily posed to fit a compressed, triangular space, but they are not joined as attached parts of a panel in the form of a relief.

The few permanent American pediments that preceded the Cleveland Trust composition follow the classical precedent of separated figures with only partial success. The first, Thomas Crawford's pediment for the Senate Wing of the United States Capitol Building, is a loosely organized collection of illogically proportioned figures and objects strung together like so many items on a shelf. Another, rather modest example was executed approximately forty years later by Bitter himself for the Bank of Pittsburgh building, erected in 1895. A George B. Post design, the building was dominated by a classicistic temple façade, and to accompany a city emblem centered in its pediment, Bitter added four seated male figures. As allegorical nudes with symbolic accessories they were divided in theme between commerce and industry, and though pleasantly related in proportion as well as position to the triangular space, they were just casually integrated as a group.[6] A more impressive pediment was achieved with numerous figures by Paul Bartlett and John Quincy Adams Ward in 1904. Entitled "The Balance of Trade," it surmounts the temple façade of George B. Post's New York Stock Exchange and is far better organized than Crawford's premature endeavor in Washington, D.C. Nevertheless, the end figures rather obviously crawl in order to fit into the acute angle to which they are confined and the female figures of the intermediate groups, between the center and the ends, are not properly proportioned to their male companions.

Bitter furnished the Cleveland Trust Company with its allegorical pediment soon after Bartlett and Ward completed their embellishment of the Stock Exchange. Unlike his predecessors, however, he composed a triangular group in high and low relief as if it were carved from a single block of granite. Even such neutral, open areas equivalent to those on his early, pedimental, relief panel for the Broad Street Station were now embossed with details. But instead of using standard classical motives to match those bordering the figures, Bitter devised his own decorative leaf pattern. A major contradiction between the sculpture and its architectural setting is avoided, however, by the design of the enthroned female figure in the center, the natural focal point of the composition.

Approximately twelve feet in height, this heroic, fully draped figure is unlike any earlier figure by Bitter. It conforms to the perfect symmetry of accompanying oak leaves patterned in low relief as well as to the altars and armrests that flank it. Even the little finger of each hand touches the front of its rectangular armrest in the same way and on the identical spot as its opposite. In contrast to the irregular drapery of its seminude retinue, the drapery of the featured figure falls quietly in precise, parallel folds. A uniform, zigzag pattern appears along the edge of the loosely falling sleeves. It vanishes behind balanced folds that arch over the knees, only to appear again in a series of angles down the middle of the full-length chiton. The head, with its sexless, oval face, is as formalized as either the drapery or the pose. There is no suggestion of a contemporary ideal type, nor do the features express the individuality of a live model. Instead, the long narrow nose, the prominent blank and bulging eyes, and the full lips are of a classical derivation. This impression is substantiated by the border of uniform curls between the brow and the close-fitting hood.

These characteristics, however, belong to different periods of classical art, and it is therefore unlikely that Bitter could have located all of them in any one example of Greek or Roman sculpture. The strict symmetry, the patterned hair, and the zigzag folds in the drapery suggest Greek archaic sculpture. The face, however, with its emphatic gaze, originates from a later period. In other words, the featured figure of the Cleveland Trust

Fig. 52.—First National Bank, granite, Euclid Avenue, Cleveland, Ohio, 1908; J. Milton Dyer, architect. Demolished in 1920.

Fig. 53.—West relief panel, "Agriculture," granite, First National Bank, Cleveland, Ohio, 1908. Destroyed.

Fig. 54.—East relief panel, "Knowledge," granite, First National Bank, Cleveland, Ohio, 1908. Destroyed.

Fig. 55.—Central relief panel, "Commerce," granite, First National Bank, Cleveland, Ohio, 1908. Destroyed.

pediment is too perfectly classical to be archaeologically valid, and represents, instead, Bitter's academic conception of an ideal classical type. At the same time, in conjunction with the precisely patterned areas of high and low relief, the central figure represents a significant change in Bitter's style. The exuberant, basically naturalistic, baroque figures of the Pulitzer Building, the Broad Street Station, and the Customs House have now given way to a much more sober architectural sculpture.

During the summer of 1907, while the Cleveland Trust pediment was still being carved, Bitter negotiated with a local architect, J. Milton Dyer, to do the sculpture on another Euclid Avenue bank. At that time Dyer was designing a new building for the First National Bank to face south from the middle of a block near the public square. Bitter described the young architect as a "typical Beaux-Arts man,"[7] and the entire structure bore out this opinion. In sharp contrast to the dark, nineteenth-century, brick buildings on either side, the white granite façade (Fig. 52) was dominated by four colossal Corinthian columns resting on low bases and supporting the inevitable entablature with a bold cornice topped by a balustrade. The architect's elevation also designated a group of sculpture composed of an oval device, upon which was perched a spread eagle flanked by two lounging female figures. The drawing duplicated this design above the entrance and over the two ground floor windows.[8]

After reaching a financial agreement with Dyer,[9] Bitter worked on the sculpture during the winter and spring of 1908. But instead of providing an ordinary decorative device that might be applied arbitrarily to almost any classicistic façade, Bitter developed a scheme of three matching, yet individual, groups. Each consisted of a vertical relief panel measuring about five and one-half feet by two feet, flanked by a pair of allegorical figures seated in spaces approximately four feet square. As a subject for the group above the west window, Bitter chose Agriculture (Fig. 53). Each of the two seated figures was carved with a sheaf of wheat over his shoulder, and the low-relief nude in the central panel balanced a sickle in his hands. Over the east window Knowledge was symbolized, and the seated figures in this group (Fig. 54) held books, while the nude in the middle, representing Science, measured a sphere with dividers. Commerce and Abundance were reserved for the entrance, where a winged male was flanked by the only female figures of the scheme and they supported cornucopias (Fig. 55).[10]

That Bitter's architectural sculpture underwent a decisive change in style beginning in 1907 was more prominently demonstrated in the First National Bank sculpture than in the Cleveland Trust pediment. This change becomes especially pronounced when the three groups are considered against a conventional academic solution. The latter was provided a few years earlier in a small allegorical work that Bitter contracted to do for the top of the entrance to the Chamber of Commerce on Liberty Street in downtown New York City. His solution then merely was to flank an ornate escutcheon with reclining figures depicting Mercury and Ceres in a standard composition similar to that originally suggested for the First National Bank by Dyer.[11]

Independent of the Cleveland architect, Bitter tailored for the First National Bank a unique architectural group to fit the areas encompassed by the huge attached columns and the openings of the first and second floors. Resembling an elongated keystone, the vertical relief panel in the center of the group connected the lintel below with the window sill above and at the same time established a frontal, or forward, plane for the composition. From the frame of this panel the square spaces occupied by the large allegorical figures receded into the thick walls of the building in a succession of narrow rectangular grooves and moldings. The window sill crossed over the space as another lintel to which the heads of the large figures were adjoined. However, neither the design of the headgear nor the way in which it was attached to the unornamented sill suggested a classical caryatid. Nothing resembling an abacus was used between the head and the sill, and the decorative design of the cube-shaped headgear included no ancient motives. Also, the figures did not give the impression of supporting any weight, even though they conformed rigidly to the right angles of their architectural setting. In fact, since their legs vanished underneath drapery over the corners of the door or window frames, they practically failed to become full figures.

The architectural treatment of the First National Bank groups did not prevent Bitter from maintaining some degree of naturalism. In addition to the small, low-relief nudes, the generalized torsos, arms, and hands of the large figures conformed to carefully studied anatomy. But the stern, almost sinister faces were less anatomical. Where their structural planes joined, they were not rounded off to suggest fleshy forms. Instead, angular ridges and sharply defined shadows established an area of transition between round, muscular shoulders and geometric headwear, the latter seeming almost as much a part of the building as of the figures. A similar combination of architectural stylization and naturalistic description appeared in the drapery. It turned and twisted in irregular creases, but these were carved as overlapping strips with square profiles rather than round, clothlike projections. The books, sheaves of wheat, and cornucopias were also abstracted into plain, geometric forms to match the design of the blockish heads.

Comparison can be made between the figures of the First National Bank

Fig. 56.—Fountain relief, bronze, Woodland Cemetery, Dayton, Ohio, 1909.

façade and reliefs executed in the same period by Franz Metzner, a Secessionist sculptor from Vienna. One of his most ambitious projects was the interior sculpture for the Haus Rheingold, Bruno Schmitz's beer hall and restaurant in Berlin.[12] Both its *Mahagoni-Saal* and *Steinsaal* included paired relief figures composed within rectangular spaces and worked out to plain, borderless edges. With a tendency toward contortion, heads were bowed at times acutely and attenuated bodies became angular in design. As such they resembled caryatids or atlantes to about the same extent as Bitter's more conventionally proportioned figures. Surface anatomy was generalized and articulated by Metzner into pronounced patterns. At the same time a smooth finish softened the play of light and shadow from one section to the next. When drapery was included it was form-fitting and did not interfere with the stylized nudity. While Bitter did not revisit Berlin until 1909, he certainly must have been familiar with Metzner's sculpture through German art periodicals. At any rate, an affinity between the changes in his architectural sculpture and the style of Metzner's appeared in the First National Bank figures. It increases in subsequent works, but always in accordance with an old commitment to naturalism and in conjunction with his newly developed interest in early ancient Greek sculpture.

A change in style for allegorical figures was not to be reserved entirely for large-scaled prominence along busy streets. In 1909 Bitter modeled a modest relief cast in bronze for a small classical fountain of pink marble. It was constructed to welcome visitors inside the main gate of Woodland Cemetery in Dayton, Ohio (Fig. 56). Kneeling in perfect symmetry, a pair of nude children flank a tablet inscribed with a message to the "God of the open air." The figures hold a swag of uniform blossoms between them and together they form an angular composition in front of an irregular leaf pattern. After the panel was cast in bronze Bitter installed the original plaster model above the fireplace of a cabin he had built several years before as a summer home. The relief was thereby removed from its solemn, ceremonial function and re-used as an embellishment for a rustic family retreat on an island in Racquette Lake deep in the Adirondack Mountains.

The architectural sculpture, large and small, that Bitter created in Ohio for very conventional, academic structures was a shift in style far from revolutionary. He did not abandon the naturalistic nude of the nineteenth century altogether. However, his figures became more generalized than before, and heads, drapery, and symbolic accessories were designed as precise, geometric forms. Poses were also directly determined by the immediate architectural framework, which he may have helped arrange as an integral composition. This is more than a mere possibility in the case of the First National Bank where the figures were predominantly rectilinear, blending into their segment of the façade. Less derivative from ancient classical sculpture than the enthroned figure of the Cleveland Trust pediment, they nevertheless furthered its monumentality and widened its break from Bitter's early, baroque-conditioned embellishments. Such change in style was part of a fairly widespread development among moderate sculptors in Europe. The Secessionists of Vienna, particularly Franz Metzner, were stressing a new conciseness and clarity in their highly generalized, and often precisely patterned figures. As will be discussed, Bitter admired Metzner and was to indicate that Vienna served as a source of inspiration alongside Athens. But it was to the latter city that he turned in seeking out a direction for his next large-scaled, architectural project.

VIII

Wisconsin Capitol Sculpture

WHILE BITTER was in Europe during the early summer weeks of 1906 a competition of five architectural firms was concluded and the winning design for a new Wisconsin state capitol building was announced.[1] Daniel H. Burnham had been hired by the State to make the final judgment, and his choice of George B. Post & Son was to be a favorable one for Bitter. With regard to sculpture for the exterior of the building, Burnham recommended that "no free portrait figure should be used upon or close to the building; only purely architectural ones should be allowed; every one used should be made and placed because the architecture demands it."[2] From this point of view, the most obvious accommodation for sculpture was of course the pediments of the Roman temple porticoes applied to the building's four wings (Fig. 57). The west and east wings were the first to be completed, and Bitter was commissioned to provide the pediments of both with sculpture. This might have been the extent of his contribution to the building if Burnham had not also criticized the competition design by Post. In the initial drawings Post indicated four prominent *tourelles* resting on the podium or terrace at the base of the dome. These would have overlooked the corner pavilions between the wings. Burnham thought they were too large and wrote that they should be modified.[3] As a result of this advice, the *tourelles* were eventually omitted altogether and replaced by four large groups of sculpture designed by Bitter.

Although the east pediment was actually carved before any other sculp-

Fig. 57.—Wisconsin state capitol, Madison, north view; George B. Post, architect. Courtesy of State Historical Society of Wisconsin.

Fig. 58.—West pediment, sketch (*right*) and plaster model (*below*) for granite relief, Wisconsin state capitol, Madison, 1906–1911.

ture on the new capitol building, Bitter started with the west, and a sketch for this pediment was approved by Post as early as August, 1906.[4] Two and one-half years later the plaster model (Fig. 58) was exhibited at the Architectural League in New York City, and in March, 1909, it was shipped to Madison for display in the rotunda of the old capitol building.[5] In the meantime Bitter prepared a sketch for the east pediment, and by February, 1909, it was also transformed into a finished model. Since the exterior of the building was to be constructed entirely of white Bethel granite, the stones for the sculpture had to wait their turn at the quarry in Vermont.[6] The granite company decided to prepare the east pediment first, but a delay in shipment prevented the Italian carvers hired by Bitter from beginning until July, when the proper stones were finally set in place. The crew was supervised by John Grignola, a carver who served as Bitter's assistant for many years. That Bitter also kept a close watch on the work was demonstrated by the instructions he continually gave to his field boss. For example, after the east pediment was under way, he decided to change the position of several figures, thus causing a major adjustment in its carving.[7]

In such a large project involving so many people, other strictly practical problems tended to postpone the completion of the sculpture. At one point a whole block of granite fell out of place. Also, as the Wisconsin winter set in, the carvers not only demanded that the scaffolding be enclosed but that it be furnished with a stove.[8] By the end of winter, however, the east pediment was essentially completed and in March Bitter added the last refinements with his own chisel. A series of misunderstandings with the granite company caused a longer delay in carving the west pediment, and any hope of completing it by summer was abandoned. As the stones gradually arrived one by one they were placed on a banker, rather than being set into the pediment as before, and the pointing was done in a shed built on the ground. All of the necessary stones had not been quarried when in April, 1910, Bitter took his family to Austria for a long visit with his elderly mother. However, upon his return in early autumn, the sculpture was completely roughed out and ready to be hoisted to the pediment. This was finally accomplished in the middle of November, and the carving continued through December. When at last the final retouching was done, Bitter began the New Year of 1911 by destroying the plaster model.

Since the west wing of the capitol building was constructed to house the Assembly, the governmental body most representative of local activities, Bitter decided that the natural resources of the state would be an appropriate subject for its pediment (Fig. 58).[9] In the center of the composition he represented Wisconsin as a standing female figure that "unfolds her beauty and her wealth" by drawing back her veil. The compact groups on either side, to which the figure of Wisconsin is intimately related, portray agriculture, the state's most important economic activity. On the right side a man and his son lead a horse and a goat through a heavy stand of grain. A mother and daughter, accompanied by an ox and a ram, stride in the opposite direction. In the left corner of the pediment sits a half-draped male figure holding an axe, representing forestry, while an Indian hunter reaches for his dog. At the other end a nude male figure kneels to haul in a fishing net. He is paired with a partially draped female figure holding a bowl of fish and leaning on a vase that overflows with water, a reference to Wisconsin's many lakes and rivers. Finally, in the corner lurks a badger, the state totem.

Although the central, female figure of the west pediment honors a community rather than a private institution, the rest of the figures portray the primary economic pursuits of a state, subjects very similar to those of the Cleveland Trust pediment. The west pediment resembles the earlier work in its composition also. Numerous components are again physically attached as one solid relief rather than remaining separate and distinct. In this way, the figures, while composed within the framework of the pediment, were also well displayed as an independent, unframed group. In fact, the high-relief composition was seen to better advantage without the extra large modillions and dentils that surround it in place on the building.

Following the precedent established by the Cleveland Trust pediment and the First National Bank groups, the west pediment is also a combination of naturalism, classicism, and precisely patterned stylization. The featured figure is almost perfectly symmetrical, and the innumerable folds of her widespread drapery fall with rigid regularity. On the other hand, the flattened, zigzag edges suggested in the drapery of the Cleveland Trust figure were abandoned for a less orderly succession of rapid curves. The head of the Wisconsin figure is obviously based on Greek sculpture of the late archaic period. More specifically it resembles the Ionic type exemplified by the marble statues of maidens discovered on the Athenian Acropolis in the late 1880's.

The long neck of Bitter's figure supports an oval face which, in turn, is partially framed by the conventionalized curls of tightly waved hair. Three long curly strands fall forward from behind each ear to merge with the vertical drapery folds over the breasts. The almond shaped eyes and heavy lids, as well as the diadem, are also features that appear on the female votive figures from the Acropolis. To serve as a transition from the classical archaism at the apex of the composition to the earthy naturalism on either side, Bitter covered the shoulders of his two large domestic animals with garlands of uniform leaf patterns and braided the horse's mane into an unusual geometric design. The hair of the human figures is also formalized in contrast to the individualized faces and naturalistic bodies that it crowns. Finally, as further indication of this continued concern for accurate description, Bitter requested the Capitol Commission to supply him with a live badger for his last model.[10]

Bitter's use of human figures, animals, and plant life as one continuous relief was immediately influential in the design of pediments in the United States. Paul Bartlett, his old acquaintance and onetime collaborator, adopted this form in a pediment for the House Portico of the United States Capitol Building. Bartlett began this project in 1909 and could easily have seen the model of Bitter's west pediment while it was being exhibited at the Architectural League of New York during February. However, he did not imitate Bitter's figural style, and the lava-like fluidity of his clay-modeled group stands in contrast to the clearly defined composition of rounded contours, diagonals, and vertical lines that overlooks the State Street corner of the public square in Madison. The Washington pediment, moreover, does not contain the precisely patterned details that Bitter designed to be carved from granite.

The east pediment (Fig. 59) of the Wisconsin capitol is less regional in subject than the west. Its figures represent the theory and practice of law, an appropriate two-part theme for a wing built to house the State Supreme Court. According to Bitter, he interpreted the legal world "on lines distinctly American," by placing a female figure in the center to represent Liberty.[11] Liberty carries a torch in her right hand to provide light for Justice seen holding a set of scales, her standard symbol. Directly opposite Justice, in an identical pose, sits Truth. With a mirror held high in one

Fig. 59.—East pediment, granite relief, Wisconsin state capitol, Madison, 1906–1909.

hand, she acknowledges the protecting shield of Liberty with the other. This central group of three allegorical figures is encircled by a classical stone bench that separates them from the rest of the composition. Closely associated with the seated figures, however, are two pairs of figures bearing documentary sources of law. A bearded old man and a boy present the Decalogue, while two female figures, "Anglo-Saxon in type," display the Magna Charta. To complete the pediment, it was Bitter's intention to represent the hereditary or instinctive ideas of right that live from one generation to the next as well as the detailed codification of these ideas. Therefore, the group on the far left consists of "a mother imbuing her children with the first, primitive ideas of right and wrong," while the group at the opposite end is composed of two students of applied law.[12]

Although the composition of Bitter's east pediment is divided into five distinct groups, it remains a relief of closely clustered forms. The most detached of the figures is Liberty, brought into asymmetrical relief against a circular expanse of stylized shrubbery and a heavily draped shield. This addition of widely spread accessories tends to flatten the figure visually while it fills what would otherwise be a neutral area. The drapery of all three central figures is as complex and formalized as that of the featured figure in the west pediment. It falls in close vertical folds with the bottom edges emphasized by a sinuous line. The curvilinear contours of the entire design, rising and falling from end to end, appear at first glance to revert to the style of Bitter's early relief panels, such as those done for the Broad Street Station and Biltmore. However, an open, free-flowing baroque composition is prevented in this case by the classical pediment, and the orderly arrangement of heads in front of the prominent dentils carries out the strict symmetry established in the seated figures of Truth and Justice. In the subordinate groups Bitter remained consistently true to nature and for the little girl in the family circle he portrayed his own daughter.

In the autumn of 1910, after returning from his summer in Europe, and before the west pediment was completely carved, he started to design the four groups to be placed around the colonnaded drum of the capitol dome. By March, 1911, two of the models were practically finished and he wrote Kestranek on March 11 that he was under pressure to finish all of them as quickly as possible. A month earlier he had notified Lew Porter, the Secretary of the Wisconsin State Capitol Commission, about the subject matter of the groups. First, he explained that he did not expect to "label" each group with a distinct name but that leading motives "would express as far as the architectural requirements will permit, certain features which go to make up the characteristics of a state."[13]

Two groups of male figures were to suggest Strength and Wisdom, respectively. By Strength, Bitter not only meant military strength, but more basically "the virility, manhood, and physical force which is evident in the industries of the state, the muscle and sinew which is one of the chief requirements of a people that shall be called progressive." The group (Fig. 60) placed on the southwest side of the drum consists of a Roman warrior armed with sword and shield; a bearded Hercules with a club, cestus, and decorative lion skin; plus a figure of Labor with a mallet and a large gear. In Wisdom Bitter intended to refer to "the prudent mind which guides the powerful arm . . . a wisdom that is based upon the experience of the past and is fostered by institutions of learning." This group (Fig. 61), comprising a youth holding a sphere, an elderly philosopher, and a student with an open book on his lap, is on the opposite side of the dome from Strength.

The two remaining groups are the feminine subjects Faith and Abundance. In choosing Faith, Bitter said he wished to point to "the religious life of the community," but intended in the broadest sense "to cover the existence of a soul." The standing figure (Fig. 62) faces southeast with her head resting quietly on her folded hands, while the other figures, sitting with their eyes closed in meditation, touch their fingertips to their breasts. The fourth group, Abundance (Fig. 63), was to represent "that hope of success which is the stimulus for the wealth of a people and the basis of its earthly welfare." Located on the northwest side of the drum, the featured figure is accompanied by a vase overflowing with fruit. She also has coins in her outstretched hand to complement the cornucopias held by the seated figures below.

In spite of his eloquent explanations, there is nothing especially original about Bitter's choice of subject matter. Such optimistic ideals were simply fashionable bywords from the province of public allegory and appeared repeatedly in contemporary mural paintings as well as in sculpture. But the subjects of the groups were secondary in importance to their more tangible architectural function. This was clearly stated as a closing remark in Bitter's letter to the Capitol Commission. He wrote, "Of course you will understand that it will be impossible for most people to read off these pre-

Fig. 60.—"Strength," granite, Wisconsin state capitol, Madison, 1910–1912.

cise sentiments in the architectural granite statues and ornamentation, which will be placed upon the building, not as an assemblage of art objects, but as organic parts of the structure."

To accommodate each group of three figures, a large pedestal, approximately fifteen feet wide, was designed to extend as a platform from the base of the dome underneath the colonnade (Fig. 64). On top of this was placed a smaller pedestal to receive the central figure which is about twelve feet high. As a means of bringing the triangular composition into relief-like proximity with the surface of the building, the intercolumniation behind each group was filled in until the two flanking columns became attached rather than freestanding. In other words, the square paneling, stringcourse, and arch of the sculptural bays were brought out a few feet from those of the empty bays. The four windows affected were replaced by masonry to provide a solid backdrop for the figures and their accessories.

Before starting the figures Bitter insisted that they "should be very simple and classical"[14] in order to achieve their essentially architectural purpose. Thus he devised a style dependent upon Greek sculpture of the late archaic period. Since classical archaistic motives had appeared in his pediments as early as 1907, this period of ancient art was not altogether strange territory for him. He had already ventured quite far into it when he borrowed a type of Ionic head from the Athenian Acropolis for the featured female figure in the west pediment of the capitol building. But now he was beginning to develop an architectural sculpture that was even more explicitly built upon an inspiration provided by the Greek archaic.

Thoroughly photographed and widely publicized archaeological discoveries of Greek archaic sculpture provided convenient source material for anyone interested in analyzing or even imitating its early fifth-century phase. However, in May, 1910, during his first lengthy stay in Austria after receiving an amnesty, Bitter traveled to Greece "in order to make professional studies."[15] Upon touring the Acropolis Museum in Athens he wrote to Mrs. Bitter, who stayed in Vienna with the children, how excited he was to see ancient works in the original. "There are magnificent things there, technically perfect works whose production one cannot see on a plaster cast . . . and I saw in complete reality what I for so long believed I was acquainted with from pictures."[16] Just a few months before his departure for Europe he had already written about the "peculiarly beautiful

Fig. 61.—"Wisdom," granite, Wisconsin state capitol, Madison, 1910–1912.

Fig. 62.—"Faith," granite, Wisconsin state capitol, Madison, 1910–1912.

style of Greek Archaic sculpture,"[17] and his first work upon returning to the United States—the four Wisconsin capitol groups—gave concrete expression to this enthusiasm.

The figures are replete with the surface mannerisms of archaic sculpture, but like the archaistic works produced by Neo-Attic Roman sculptors during the first century B.C., they also contain characteristics of their own time and place. Dressed in full-length chitons that fall in ornamental patterns of flat linear folds, the female figures are much more archaistic in appearance than the half-draped males. A very fine and slightly raised band is carved at wide intervals to describe tightly stretched cloth, and a zigzag as well as a sinuous edge carries it out as a robe. Heads are oval with features correspondingly geometric. The brows of each face are delineated with sharp ridges that arch over the eyes and continue to the nostrils, leaving the nose a flat, rectangular surface. Every coiffure is parted in the middle, ornamented with a circlet, and tightly curled to fall symmetrically along both sides of the forehead as a decorative border.

Not all heads and faces, however, are strictly archaistic. For example, the hair of the seated figures in the Abundance group is a leaf-and-grape motive matching the precisely carved cornucopias that overflow alongside. Such details are drawn with wide lines cut deeply into the granite. This same technique is used on the berry-and-leaf swags that are merged with the highly conventionalized wings of a spread eagle in the center of each base. The front of the pedestal behind the eagle is also embellished, by a banner of stars and stripes draped with rectangular clusters of fruit clasped in the center by a shell.

Only the hair and certain parts of the drapery in the male groups resemble Greek archaic sculpture. While the partially nude bodies, as well as the faces, are generalized in structure, Bitter was too much in the habit of portraying a naturalistic nude from live models to tolerate all the anatomical inaccuracies of archaic sculpture. Noses, fingers, muscles, and bones are not rounded off and smoothly finished, but they are properly proportioned and joined. The expressions assumed by the male faces are too varied and, upon final analysis, life-like, to be truly archaistic. The eyes sink into deep sockets and the mouths are all too solemn to come anywhere near approximating an archaic smile. Finally, the poses of all the figures, male and female, are flexible. The standing figures are for the most part relaxed in appearance while the seated figures, although posed as strictly

Fig. 63.—"Abundance," granite, Wisconsin state capitol, Madison, 1910–1912.

Fig. 64.—"Abundance," clay sketch and mock-up for granite group, Wisconsin state capitol, Madison, 1911.

symmetrical pairs, move their arms and hands as no archaic figure would.[18]

Nevertheless, Bitter helped make his architectural granite groups "simple and classical" by adopting Greek archaic characteristics of design. In addition, he devised his own precisely patterned accessories, and marked out the structure of the figures in distinct, clearly articulated areas. As a result, each group becomes a composition of precise, but playful, shadows that run up and down as wavy dark lines, encircle clustered spots of sunlit granite, or serve as a scalloped fringe at the bottom of a garment.

Through this surface vitality the large forms of the generalized figures prevail, permitting a monumentality to win out against ornateness. Regardless of the state-prescribed symbolism, which goes unrecognized without the aid of a Capitol Guide Book, Bitter's compositions demonstrate his concern for achieving an architectural style. For these large groups he drew upon newly discovered ancient sources. Other figures from this period of his career, for example those that graced the First National Bank in Cleveland, showed an affinity with current architectural sculpture produced from the Secessionist movement of Austria. In either case, among America's conservative sculptors, Bitter promoted a moderate evolutionary shift away from the academic naturalism of the late nineteenth century.[19]

IX

Sculptural Accessories To Justice, Education And Death

THE ARCHITECTURAL advance that Bitter made in the sculpture of the two Cleveland banks and the Wisconsin capitol building did not end above the square in Madison. It was to continue as a major modification of his early baroque naturalism with a stylization inspired by the Greek archaic and encouraged by recent Secessionist sculpture. These influences remained together in the allegorical figures that he designed for public monuments during the last years of his career. For these monuments he not only provided the sculpture, but in each project the architecture and its setting were also to come under his control. Before these last efforts at monumentality were under way, however, Bitter was again engaged in the multiplication of America's portrait statuary. Although he found little artistic satisfaction in portraiture, he was a professional in search of commissions, and public as well as private funds were available for such sculpture before any other. Among the wealthy there also remained a dwindling demand for elegiac, graveside sculpture, and he was to contribute two more works to this traditional category in 1912 and 1914.

Bitter assumed the responsibility of supervising a program of portrait sculpture for the exterior of just one major public building. The new Cuyahoga County Courthouse, built in Cleveland, Ohio, in 1911, was designed in the same academic, expositional style as the two Euclid Avenue banks nearby. Unlike the bankers, however, the county judges insisted on history in their sculpture, and the figures they ordered for the courthouse were to portray famous men in the development of law. Five million dollars were allocated for the large, three-story building. Much of this was spent for a granite façade that follows the familiar French baroque formula of a rusticated basement, colossal fluted columns, a balustrade above the cornice, and a pediment over the attic story of the central pavilion. Of the total cost, the rather modest sum of fifty thousand dollars was set aside for sculpture.[1] This amount, however, was flexible and may have been increased; for when it was completed the building displayed ten large freestanding marble figures on its cornice and two heroic seated figures in bronze at each of its main entrances.

Since the courthouse was a public project, the building specifications were published in detail, including instructions for the production of the sculpture. In fact, they went so far as to order that all modeling was to be done in Cleveland under the personal supervision of the Building Commission.[2] While this requirement was apparently by-passed, a specification that all of the carved figures were to be first cast in plaster of Paris and that these full-scale models were to be installed for inspection on the building was adhered to. On July 15, 1909, Bitter was in Cleveland to supervise the placement of the trial figures on the cornice, an operation carried out under the watchful eye of the Building Commission, the architects, and the local press.[3] The height of nine and one-half feet for each figure had been recommended by Bitter and was endorsed after the dry run. Pedestals were then placed on the main cornice of the north and south façades, where the figures were to stand as decorative additions to the building's two central pavilions. (Fig. 65). No architectural ornaments were applied above the cornice, and plain panels were included on the attic story to frame the heavily draped figures in line with the huge freestanding Ionic columns below.

Each of the ten carved portrait figures represents an important episode in the evolution of the Anglo-American legal system. The four marble statues on the central pavilion of the north façade depict ancient sources of this system: Moses, the moral code or Biblical law; Justinian, civil law; Alfred the Great, English common law; and Pope Gregory IX, canon law. On the central pavilion of the main façade six marble figures depict the development of law on English soil. From left to right, Stephen Langton represents the Magna Charta; Simon de Montfort, the institution of the House of Commons; Edward I, the legal reforms during his reign, includ-

Fig. 65.—Cuyahoga County Courthouse, marble sculpture, Cleveland, Ohio, 1909–1911.

ing the establishment of equity; John Hampden, the Petition of Right in the struggle between Parliament and the Crown; John Somers, the Declaration of Right; and William Murray, Earl of Mansfield, the adaptation of common law to mercantile pursuits and its extension by judicial decisions. The sculptor of the first two figures was Herbert Adams. Daniel Chester French did the two central figures, and the pair of figures on the right depicting Somers and Lord Mansfield are the work of Bitter.[4]

Simple compositional devices were used to help draw the six English figures together as a symmetrical group. The fairly uniform fall of heavy drapery is perhaps the most obvious of these, but a subtle relationship of quiet gestures is also effective. Each of the two figures at either end raises an arm nearest his partner and the same reciprocal movement is seen in the central pair. Bitter made certain that his eighteenth-century Englishmen (Figs. 66 and 67) were intimately associated with one another. Lord

Fig. 67.—Lord Mansfield, model for marble figure, Cuyahoga County Courthouse, Cleveland, Ohio, 1909.

Fig. 66.—John Somers, model for marble figure, Cuyahoga County Courthouse, Cleveland, Ohio, 1909.

Mansfield steps to the corner of his pedestal toward John Somers, who returns the gesture with a high-heeled slipper poised over the outside corner of his pedestal. The two bewigged jurists, ostentatious in the legal robes of their period, are posed in rhythmical, almost dance-like attitudes that are very nearly mirror images of each other.

Somers and Mansfield were the first of only four portrait statues by Bitter to be carried out in marble, and they were the only ones to be placed high up on a building. Since they were originally modeled for plaster casts set in place for the approval of the architects and building commissioners, they could have been subsequently remolded in bronze, as most freestanding portrait statues are. However, these particular figures were to stand in a row along a cornice and tradition prescribed that they be carved from stone. Although difficult to see in detail from the street, the intricacies of eighteenth-century robes and wigs are precisely described in marble. Bitter may have been encouraged to make his figures ornate by the very lack of ornamentation on the bare granite wall immediately behind them. But the choice of English innovators of justice instead of nude allegorical figures was apparently that of the Common Pleas judges who held the final decision-making power in designing and decorating the building.

No matter what determined the design of his Somers and Mansfield, Bitter was not very enthusiastic about their completion by the time they were cast in plaster for the trial installation. On that day (July 15, 1909) he wrote to his wife: "I think I characterize the situation best if I say that I didn't feel that these old English gentlemen were the most important things in my life, but they ought to have been for the time being at least." That a period portrait high above the ground was not satisfying to him was expressed again a few months later. He had been commissioned to execute a statue of Henry Hudson for the top of a colossal fluted column. It was erected in the center of a small park just north of New York City's Spuyten Duyvil Creek, the place where Hudson supposedly first landed. A model was completed but Bitter lost whatever enthusiasm he had for the project and never put the figure into permanent form.[5] Regarding this unfinished work he wrote to his friend Kestranek (Jan. 2, 1910): "It is of no importance. A statue on top of a column, anything else is of very much more interest to me."

Bitter's lack of interest in the carved portrait statues for the Cuyahoga County Courthouse may have been caused in part by a greater concern for

Fig. 68.—Cuyahoga County Courthouse, bronze figures of Jefferson and Hamilton, Cleveland, Ohio, 1909–1911.

the other two works he did for the front of the building. These are the heroic, bronze figures of Jefferson and Hamilton, measuring about eight feet from base to top, that sit on either side of the broad stairway leading to the main entrance (Fig. 68). In connection with the general theme of the building's sculpture the presence of Jefferson represents the Declaration of Independence while Hamilton is meant to commemorate the Federal Constitution. Although the figures are separated by several yards, Bitter used a device similar to that introduced in the composition of his Somers and Mansfield to bring the two together as a pair. That is, the foot nearest the figure opposite is pushed out so far that it slightly overlaps the inside corner of its pedestal. This helps to create a symmetry that is strengthened by the inward-turning pose of both Hamilton and Jefferson

Fig. 69.—Jefferson, model for bronze figure, Cuyahoga County Courthouse, Cleveland, Ohio, 1909–1911.

Fig. 70.—Hamilton, model for bronze figure, Cuyahoga County Courthouse, Cleveland, Ohio, 1909-1911.

who look toward the observer as he reaches the center of the first step from the sidewalk. The two armless chairs on top of polished limestone block pedestals are identical, and the clothes of the figures are essentially the same except for the shoes. Hamilton wears a light slipper tied with a ribbon while Jefferson wears a heavy square-toed shoe that buckles over a prominent tongue.

This minor variation in the costumes of Jefferson and Hamilton reflects a larger contrast in the two personalities as they were interpreted by Bitter. An avid reader of history and biography, Bitter investigated any historical subject that he was called upon to do and was apparently familiar with the popular images that these two American heroes had acquired from the early years of the republic.[6] Thus, while his Jefferson (Fig. 69) has a massive and generally rustic appearance, his Hamilton (Fig. 70) is seen as an aggressive young aristocrat. With both hands occupied, Hamilton sits upright, free from the back of his chair. His head is thrown back and he peers through narrow eyes down the length of his somewhat aquiline nose with an expression of impatient condescension. Jefferson, on the other hand, seems to be lost in contemplation and his posture is consequently relaxed. A number of crumpled papers hang loosely from his right hand, while his left arm rests heavily on the back of the chair. The empty hand falls in idle suspension, becoming, nevertheless, a prominent part of the composition. With head tilted forward he looks out of rather phlegmatic, unfocused eyes beneath the low, straight brows that were Jefferson's. Finally, while the jaw is firmly set, there is a slight suggestion of a smile.

As if to underline the differences he portrayed between Jefferson and Hamilton, Bitter varied the extent to which he finished the modeling of the two figures. The hair, facial features, vest, and hat of Hamilton are all precisely described and the knee-length trousers are tightly fitted over smooth, silk-surfaced legs. No detail, including the long row of lapel buttons, is the least bit undefined and even the coat falls down over the chair in crisp, orderly folds. As for the surface of the bronze, only a carefully refined ripple remains to suggest the texture of modeled clay. In the statue of Jefferson, however, one finds a much less formally finished work. The greater number of folds in the cloth, skin, and hair are more casually suggested while the larger, relatively unwrinkled, surfaces also bear the parallel strokes of the clay modeler's tool. As a result the light of the sun casts a texture of small uneven shadows over the sagging coat, vest, and stockings worn by Jefferson.

This subtle differentiation of two historical images in bronze demonstrates the sympathy and interest Bitter could apply to public portraiture. True, the figures resemble the official heroic portraits that were multiplying rapidly in the parks and squares of a growing urban America. Especially the imperial thrones and the period costumes were standard accessories of a conventional historicism. But in spite of these inherited qualifications and with respect for the officially prescribed façade in the background, Bitter's treatment of pose, expression, and surface saves both of his paired figures from positions of elevated austerity above the street. He at least brought them within range of direct identification for the people.

Less accessible to the public at large and more modest in scope than the Cleveland sculpture are the portraits of three university presidents that Bitter executed as commemorative campus monuments. Two of these academic portraits were of presidents at the University of Michigan. They were modeled in high relief and installed as bronze panels on opposite walls in the main entrance hall of the Alumni Memorial Building, which was designed as an art gallery and dedicated in the spring of 1910. The first portrait panel to be completed for the hall, that of President James Burrill Angell (Fig. 71), was unveiled one month after the dedication of the building.

As was possible for the portrait statue of William Pepper fourteen years earlier, Bitter was able to sketch the recently retired President Angell from life. The first sitting was in May, 1909, at Angell's Ann Arbor home, and Bitter wrote enthusiastically about it to his wife. He was delighted to have the opportunity to do a portrait of another intelligent man for a public monument, even if the building that was to house it was "not too beautiful" (letter of May 5). In November of the same year Bitter was still working on the portrait[7] and by the end of January, 1910, the finished model was ready for casting in bronze.[8] Unlike the Pepper monument, the Angell relief portrait panel was not paid for by a group of admiring friends but by one man, Arthur Hill, a wealthy lumberman from Saginaw, who was an alumnus and regent of the university as well as one of its most generous benefactors.[9] He provided five thousand dollars for the Angell relief but unfortunately died before Bitter could complete it.

Fig. 71.—James Angell, model for bronze relief, Alumni Memorial Building, University of Michigan, Ann Arbor, 1909–1910.

Fig. 72.—James Angell relief, pen and ink sketch, dated May 6, 1909.

From the day he started this work Bitter designed it as a pictorial composition in an architectural frame that was to be fitted into a bare wall. His initial conception appears as a quick pen-and-ink sketch in a letter home dated May 6, 1909 (Fig. 72). It shows the elderly administrator sitting in his academic robes at a large desk covered with papers and books. Around the figure and its accessories in this first sketch, Bitter indicated a frame that is similar to that of the finished panel. Although minor alterations were made in the basic design of the panel when it was gradually worked out in clay, the frame and its contents were adjusted together as two parts of a single composition (Fig. 73). In other words, the "picture" was not merely framed when finished but the two parts were designed simultaneously. As the work progressed, the figure of President Angell was turned around to face the entrance of the hall and was increased in relative size to fill almost half the panel. The frame, in turn, while retaining its segmental arch from beginning to end, was denied its original horizontal proportions, was made square and then finally vertical in shape. The finished panel, including the frame, is approximately five feet by seven

Fig. 73.—James Angell, clay sketch for bronze relief, Alumni Memorial Building, University of Michigan, Ann Arbor, 1909.

feet and the relief is about one foot deep from its forwardmost projection to the slightly raised inscription.

The development of decorative motives for the frame may be seen by comparing the sketch in clay (Fig. 73) with the finished work (Fig. 71). The acanthus leaf consoles appear in both, but the florid pattern of the earlier arch became much simplified in the final design. A neat arrangement of ancient Greek devices was worked out, with an ogee molding on top, an egg-and-dart range underneath, and two lines of the bead and reel for a frieze. Rather unusual bordering pilasters, composed of a Roman capital design above a soft relief pattern of leaves and berries, replace the harshly fluted pilasters of the sketch.

Although his life as journalist, diplomat, and university president was varied, Angell is not recorded to have been exceptionally aggressive. On the contrary it is reported that he was a rather retiring person with a conservative manner that was even called bland.[10] During negotiations he would seek a middle road, and his many years as the head of a state university were characterized by only gradual changes in the curriculum and hardly any increase in the physical facilities of the different departments. He was of medium height, wore a Horace Greeley beard from his youthful years as a journalist, grew heavy in his old age, was noticeably myopic, and as a result of an early affliction in the throat, spoke very softly. To make his portrait coincide with the broad outline of his subject's personality Bitter chose a pose far removed from that of his William Pepper. In contrast to the dynamic attitude of his predecessor in Philadelphia, President Angell is placed well back in his straight chair, has both feet firmly planted on the floor, and appears to be unconsciously thumbing through a few papers with one hand while he holds his eyeglasses in the other.

While still working on the Angell relief portrait Bitter described his figure as "ceremonious" and wrote of the "full vestments" in which he posed the elderly administrator, as if it were his intention to emphasize the authority of the man's office over and above his individual personality.[11] President Angell is almost completely covered with the official costume of his profession. That Bitter calculated this to be a formal portrait of an administrator, one who reigned as a university president for almost forty years, is also suggested by the large desk with which the man is so closely associated. If any given moment were intended, it could be a time of relaxed reflection just before the performance of another ceremonial duty.

The formality of this official portrait evolved through frame and figure from the rough sketch to the finished version. To be sure, some small details are left imperfect enough to suggest modeling in clay. Even broad surfaces bear a slight, plastic texture. However, the work as a whole has been carried to an academic level of completion. The linear edges and contours of the drapery, paper, and furniture are even more precisely ruled and rendered than the architectural frame itself. Heads and hands, as well as robe and desk, emphasize surface finish in high relief.

When Bitter started the relief portrait of President Angell he wrote that he did not want to make his panel look like one by Saint-Gaudens.[12] A few months later (on Nov. 17, 1909) he explained to his friend Kestranek that portraits were in great demand in the United States and that the competition was very stiff, especially with the disciples of Saint-Gaudens, who were doing a large portion of them. These two statements indicate the lasting influence of the late American master. It was so widespread that a somewhat narrow notion of what a relief portrait should be existed in the American mind. In spite of any desire he may have had to the contrary, the two relief portrait panels that Bitter did for the Alumni Memorial Building in Ann Arbor do resemble the work of his famous predecessor, and this probably was exactly what his Michigan patrons expected of him.

Of the two panels, the second actually bears a closer resemblance to a specific work by Saint-Gaudens. By coincidence the Angell panel has an arched, classical frame similar to the one used by Saint-Gaudens for his Shaw Memorial in Boston. But Bitter's portrait relief of Henry Philip Tappan (Fig. 74), the first president of the university, could have been directly influenced by the bronze memorial relief of Princeton University's Dr. James McCosh which Saint-Gaudens executed in 1889.[13] Although of different proportions, the two panels are alike in shape, and the poses of their respective figures have much in common. Each rests his right foot over the front edge of the platform upon which he stands, and the panel includes a raised inscription plus a single accessory.

Unlike either McCosh or Angell, Tappan had long since died by the time his portrait was finally executed as a public monument in 1912.[14] Be-

Fig. 74.—Henry Tappan, bronze relief, Alumni Memorial Building, University of Michigan, Ann Arbor, 1912.

fore becoming the first president of the University of Michigan in 1852 he earned an international reputation as a philosopher and theologian through his publications on the question of the freedom of the will. In spite of this prominence, his progressive demands on the state legislature and his liberal opinions about what a college education should be soon brought him into conflict with a conservative board of regents and he was asked to resign after serving nine years as president. In keeping with his assertiveness, Tappan was a man of striking appearance who carried a massive head and shoulders on a six-foot frame.[15]

To emphasize the dynamic spirit and commanding stature of his subject, Bitter made his life-size figure so high in relief that it practically projects into the round from its narrow concave setting. Nothing is allowed to interfere with the prominence of the figure. Only one string of bead and reel serves as a frame for the panel, which is eight feet in height. As in other portrait figures by Bitter, his Tappan presents a duality of motion and rest. In this case it actually divides the figure down the center. When viewed from the right side both feet are seen flat on the ground as the arm falls quietly against the straight-hanging coat. The figure of Tappan seems to be standing perfectly still. However, from the opposite side his projecting leg alone can be seen and he appears to be pushing a walking stick against the ground as a man does when striding forward.

Bitter introduced a large mastiff as an accessory figure, and through its close association the dog complements the force and energy of the man. Originally the animal appeared to be walking alongside, which encouraged the sensation of forward movement, but in the finished panel Bitter stopped the dog in its tracks.[16] The two heads face out in the same direction and are roughly equal in size. The bluff expression of the man is repeated by the dog, whose jowls and ears also approximate the growth of hair around his master's face.

As the Jefferson in Cleveland contrasts in surface finish to that of its companion statue of Hamilton, Bitter's Tappan is much less refined than the relief of President Angell on the opposite wall. In each of the Ann Arbor reliefs, the figure and its framed panel give the impression of having evolved concurrently from one piece of material. The rough-edged footing above the base of the Tappan relief looks as if it were left over when the niche was hollowed out around the figure. Once again Bitter allowed details of clothing, hair, and flesh to remain in the rough, and, more evident than before, the brush-like marks made by a tool working rapidly over soft clay are reproduced in the bronze version. Bitter compared modeling to painting and maintained that a good sense of color was important to his method of working. He wrote: "When I model planes and curves in clay, then I search for color relationships. The form usually must subordinate itself to this pleasure of color, that is, those shadings that I regard as color."[17]

Why Bitter would very carefully complete one portrait monument in a precise fashion and then have the next portrait cast with an obvious roughness is open to speculation. Perhaps he considered a "painterly" texture more suitable for a less formal representation of a down-to-earth subject, the man and his dog. In the Tappan panel, unlike the Angell relief panel, the subject's official connection with the academic world is only incidentally identified by a modest inscription. Also, in a way similar to the Cleveland Jefferson, he was spared the fixed statuesque attitude that his position in life might have prescribed. Neither being abstracted into an aloof monumental symbol of impersonal authority, Jefferson and Tappan were interpreted by Bitter as private personalities. Consequently, they evoke an intimate sympathy in the observer rather than a distant veneration, and the surface imperfections of modeled clay seem consistent with this end.

A personal relationship between the figure and the observer is similarly established by the casual pose and the roughly modeled surface of Bitter's last portrait monument of a university president. The subject, Andrew D. White, cofounder and first president of Cornell University, was eighty years old when he came to the sculptor's studio in November, 1912. A little more than a week of daily sittings was time enough to complete a small model, but the full-size statue in bronze was not placed on the Cornell campus and dedicated until after Bitter's death in 1915 (Fig. 75). A man seated in a large ornamental armchair on top of a pedestal was indeed a familiar formula for a portrait monument. However, Bitter once again refrained from enthroning his much honored subject in a rigid frontal pose and very objectively described a bearded old man sitting with one leg crossed comfortably over the other. The prominent features of the large, almost scraggly, head are briefly but accurately recounted and the swollen knuckles of the stiffened hands are as obvious as the high-topped boot that projects over the pedestal.

Fig. 75.—Andrew D. White, bronze, Cornell University, Ithaca, New York, 1912–1915.

Bitter was deeply impressed with the public career and extensive knowledge of President White.[18] He might have conceivably been tempted to produce an idealized image of the man who had served not only as an academic administrator but as historian, progressive educator, and diplomat as well. The time was ripe for the creation of monumental apotheoses of the great, as may be witnessed in the Lincoln monuments that followed the precedent set by Saint-Gaudens. However, the kindhearted old gentleman who had seen to it that Ezra Cornell's university would provide a liberal education for the many and later had worked for world peace at the Hague Conference by urging the establishment of an international court of justice, was not to be glorified in a flawless, formally finished statue. It is as if in Bitter's opinion a great man who had attained his prominence by representing the urgent needs of mankind should be portrayed in a straightforward style that would not strive for polished perfection but would openly exploit the imperfect and the unfinished.

Enthusiastic though Bitter might become over the career of a great man whom he was engaged to portray for a public monument, he nevertheless expressed distaste for doing portraits of contemporary figures. On January 2, 1910, for example, he wrote a long letter to Kestranek in which he discussed his basic interests in art and described his current works. He ended with the complaint that the labors of an artist seldom make the artist himself happy, especially if he must work on portrait commissions of "rectors and politicians."

At the time of this letter to Vienna, Bitter was completing the relief of President Angell, and the latest portrait from his studio to be erected was a statue of Senator Matthew S. Quay.[19] Quay, who died in 1904, had wielded an absolute mastery over the Republican party in Pennsylvania and was very much revered by the industrialists of America for his constant efforts to maintain a high protectionist tariff. As a consequence, Bitter was highly paid for his portrait, which is a freestanding figure slightly over life-size carved from white marble. It stands on a pedestal placed in a niche above the stairway of the Pennsylvania capitol building rotunda, all of which are constructed out of the same pallid stone. The expression of the man is as stark as his surroundings, and every detail of head, hands, and business suit is precisely cut and smoothly finished. Two years later Bitter was commissioned to do a similar portrait of John F. Dryden, who died in 1911 after serving as president of his family's firm, the Prudential

Life Insurance Company, and as a senator from New Jersey. Once again, Bitter complained about his lack of interest in the contemporary, clothed figure and this time turned the portrait over to his student-assistant, Karl Gruppe, who worked out the model under Bitter's guidance.[20]

Allegorical sculpture provided a release from such labor, and Bitter could take comfort in the nude figure even if it were at times modest in scale and destined to be removed from public view. Ironically one of his most sensitively conceived figures is in fact kept under lock and key inside an elegiac memorial near New York City. A small bronze, it is part of the sculpture for a mausoleum raised to three children of the Prehn family of Passaic, New Jersey. The white marble structure (Fig. 76), designed by the classicist, Henry Bacon, was based on a favorite model among American academic architects, the choragic monument of Lysikrates. Upon seeing Bacon's design Bitter wrote that he considered the memorial complete without the addition of sculpture.[21] Nevertheless, he worked out a scheme that includes the bronze figure as well as a series of six reliefs, and these were in place by the summer of 1912.[22]

The relief panels were designed to fit between the pilasters of the cylindrical structure, directly beneath the entablature. Each contains three mournful infants walking counterclockwise and carrying a garland of leaves (Fig. 77). Although high in relief, the figures were not permitted to project beyond their curved frames. Modeled and cast before being carved, they retain the pliable appearance of clay, especially in their disheveled hair and fragments of drapery. The small background holes are drilled all the way through the stone and approximate the tesserae used by Donatello on the relief panels for the Cantoria in the Cathedral Museum in Florence. While emotional, the mood of Bitter's children is, however, diametrically opposed to that of Donatello's wildly dancing groups. Otherwise, the Early Renaissance work probably served as a source of composition to the same extent that Luca della Robbia's Cantoria apparently inspired the limestone reliefs for the Cornelius Vanderbilt mansion twenty years before.

The bronze figure (Fig. 78) for the Prehn Mausoleum is probably the most poignant interpretation of deep-seated emotion that Bitter ever did. Referred to as "Faded Flowers,"[23] it represents Sorrow as a nude child, sitting with her feet tucked beneath her hips, watching with bowed head as the loose petals of a bouquet fall from her upturned hands. Unfortu-

Fig. 76.—Prehn mausoleum, marble, Cedar Lawn Cemetery, Paterson, New Jersey, 1911-1912; Henry Bacon, architect.

Fig. 77.—Prehn mausoleum, detail, Cedar Lawn Cemetery, Paterson, New Jersey, 1911–1912.

nately, this small figure kneels on a pedestal inside the mausoleum and is therefore concealed from view. Whenever the door is opened, however, a similarity of treatment between the reliefs above and the figure within is revealed, all being originally clay-modeled, a technique interchangeably reproduced in soft stone or bronze.

A life-size kneeling figure on a simple square pedestal was carved from marble and erected in Forest Hills Cemetery, Utica, New York, in the spring of 1914 as Bitter's last elegiac memorial (Fig. 79). To commemorate the wife of John G. Kasson the figure was conceived as a female personification of the Soul, accompanied by the inscription FEAR NOT THE NIGHT, THY SOUL IS AWAKE WITH THE STARS. The gesture of arms crossing over the head might be another surviving trace of Bitter's student experience with Michelangelo's "Dying Slave." The uneven drapery suggests the rough, impressionistic finish popularized by Rodin. However, the surface of the memorial is consistently carried to completion, while the torso and legs are seen to exist as cohesive forms beneath the shroud. Unlike the Rockefeller Fountain of the same time, the Kasson Memorial is a

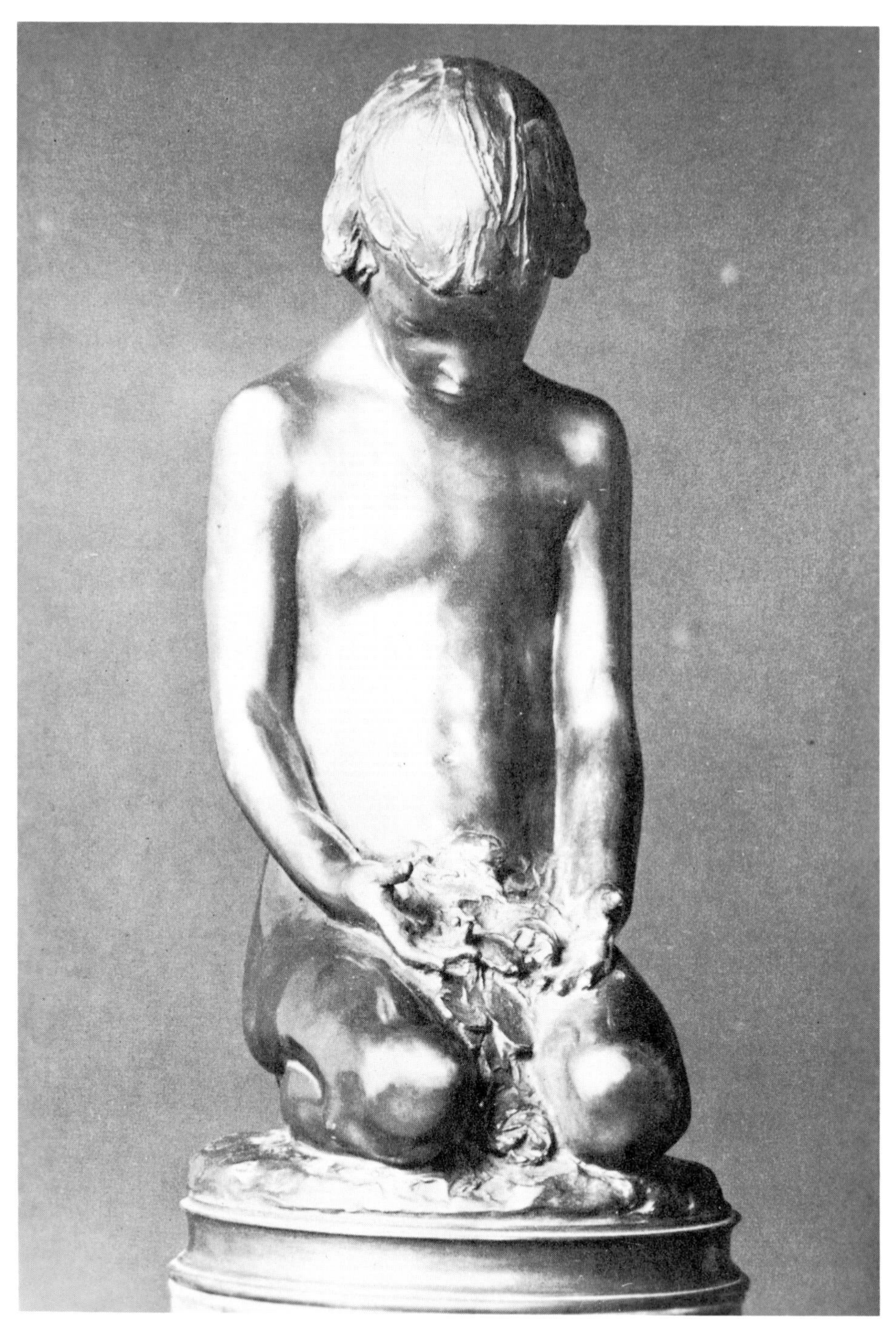

Fig. 78.—"Faded Flowers," bronze, Prehn mausoleum, Cedar Lawn Cemetery, Paterson, New Jersey, 1911–1912.

Fig. 79.—Kasson memorial, marble, Forest Hills Cemetery, Utica, New York, 1914.

concise composition held within the area of a block as designated by the pedestal. A fixed frontality is avoided by a dramatic, upward-turning movement with vine-like folds rising from the pedestal to accentuate the action.

Thus, as an example of ornamental sculpture, this memorial remains a direct descendant of the many energetic figures populating Bitter's early residential compositions. Whether intended for a stairway, an organ gallery, or a fireplace, these were designed mainly as accessories to structures over which he had little if any influence. As discussed in following chapters, it was the public portrait monument that provided Bitter an opportunity to regulate the immediate architectural setting in conjunction with his most experimental sculpture. In the summer of 1909 he had become actively engaged in the preliminary planning of an ambitious scheme for St. Louis that was to involve sculpture, architecture, and landscaping. Although the sculpture ended up exclusively historical portraiture, the new project as a whole provided him an opportunity to demonstrate his comprehension of large-scale public planning and organization, a talent not ordinarily required from the American sculptor.

X

The First Jefferson Memorial

THE DISSATISFACTION that Bitter expressed during the last years of his life with portraiture per se, and with the contemporary figure in particular, was not alleviated by allegorical figures alone but also by public portrait monuments that permitted the planning of an architectural setting. While he had an unfulfilled opportunity to control the immediate surroundings of his projected Lafayette monument for Paris and was privileged to choose his own site for the Sigel monument, it was not until the last five years of his career that he was able to take an active part in the over-all architectural design of a permanent public monument.

Bitter's first real opportunity to participate in the designing of an architectural setting for a major portrait monument came as a result of the position he held in the Louisiana Purchase Exposition of 1904. Under the terms of the appropriations made by Congress and the City of St. Louis for the Exposition, both were to receive a share of any surplus money. Each amount was to equal that returned to the stockholders of the Exposition Company when the World's Fair came to an end. Since the surplus amounted to approximately one-half million dollars, it was obvious that to divide one-third of this among the 15,000 stockholders would result in individual sums too small to warrant the return. Therefore, the directors of the company, under the leadership of former Missouri Governor D. R. Francis, proposed that the money be spent to perpetuate the purpose of the Exposition which was, of course, to commemorate the Lousiana Purchase.[1]

Since there was no monument of consequence anywhere in the country dedicated to Thomas Jefferson, it was furthermore decided that this was an excellent opportunity to pay permanent tribute to the President who was chiefly responsible for the acquisition of the large region between the Mississippi River and the Rocky Mountains. Under the persuasion of Francis, the Sixtieth Congress authorized the Exposition Company to expend $150,000 of the amount due the government for the erection of a monument to Thomas Jefferson in St. Louis. Following this action by Congress, the Board of Public Improvements of St. Louis stipulated that as a part of the plan to restore the site of the Exposition, the monument should be placed in Forest Park and $200,000 was allocated for that purpose. The company, in turn, added its share of the surplus money to the fund and placed the responsibility of designing the monument in the hands of a commission composed of the architect Isaac S. Taylor, Director of Works for the Louisiana Purchase Exposition; George F. Kessler, who was its landscape architect; and Karl Bitter, chief of sculpture.[2]

In the summer of 1909 this three-man commission met in St. Louis to work out preliminary plans for the Jefferson monument. In a letter to his wife Bitter wrote that Taylor had come up with a satisfactory scheme for the monument which he could completely endorse. He apparently was surprised at the ability of Taylor as an architect, for he wrote, "We made some slight modifications and adopted it and I did so without any special thumbscrew on my conscience. His scheme, architecturally, satisfies me completely—don't know where he got it; it may be his."[3]

Upon returning to New York Bitter sent a report of the conference to Francis which reveals more explicitly why he was enthusiastic about the first plans. Not only was the monument conceived as a work of architecture, but it was also to include an elaborate arrangement of landscaping and open-air sculpture. Taylor's idea was to erect a "classic temple" to enclose a statue of Jefferson which, Bitter wrote, "seemed to cover so fully the spirit in which this monument shall be erected." The statue was to be carved from marble because "the impression created by a single, heroic marble statue under a dome is always reverence inspiring and decidedly more impressive than the silhouette of a black bronze figure seen against the sky."[4]

The site chosen for the temple was at the foot of a hill in the center of the park, between a carriage road and a bay of the park lake. On the other side of the carriage road, in an axis created by the temple and a shelter house recently erected on top of the hill, the commission proposed to build a semicircular terrace with an ornamental retaining wall. On it would be placed a bronze relief derived from the large plaster "Signing of the Louisiana Purchase Treaty" that Bitter had executed for the base of the Louisiana Purchase monument at the Exposition. To accompany the revised relief, Bitter suggested a series of panels that would portray the historical figures produced by the Louisiana region, reflecting the growth of its states and communities. From this first terrace, two series of steps were to ascend through a "proper arrangement of landscape gardening" to a second terrace embellished by fountains. More stairways were to lead to the shelter house "from which a splendid view can be had over this monumental panorama which covers over two thousand feet in length and breadth."[5]

In late September the executive committee of the Exposition Company considered the recommendations of the commission and through a letter written by Francis expressed admiration for the plan. There was general assent to the site for the monument, but the committee was not certain if the best results could be achieved by an "architectural canopy." It also wanted to know if "imposing fountains or cascade effects" could not be introduced.[6] In short, the executive committee was obviously concerned about the austerity of a temple for the Jefferson statue and seemed to be more in favor of an outdoor display that would continue the festive character of the Exposition.

During the next year, however, this initial response to the preliminary plans for the monument was completely disregarded. Instead of becoming more imposing, the Jefferson monument, while retaining its temple-like quality, became very practical. By the end of 1910, the proposed location on the shore of the park lake had been abandoned. Instead of a hillside terrace, complete with relief sculpture, plans were made for a library to house the records of the World's Fair plus a historical museum of the Louisiana Territory. These were to be constructed as wings to the temple enshrining the statue. The new site for this monument-building was on the park side of Lindell Boulevard facing DeBaliviere Avenue to the north, exactly where the entrance to the Fair had been.

In December, 1910, a committee of local architects, all of whom had served on the commission of architects for the Exposition, was invited to view the new plans and make suggestions.[7] Ironically enough, the architects responded to the practical monument-building in the same way that the executive committee had reacted to the original plans of a year before. They felt that the monument would not be "ornamental" enough. In a rather ambiguous report the architects insisted that Taylor's design was almost wholly utilitarian in character with nothing that suggested a commemorative monument. The monument, they claimed, would be mistaken for a municipal or commercial building of some sort. They recommended a more "monumental" design that any ordinary spectator could distinguish at a glance as a memorial to some important person or event.[8]

It was Bitter who, in answer to the criticism of the consulting architects, wrote a long, cleverly constructed letter to Francis which defended the proposed design of the monument-building.[9] He maintained that a central motive in the form of a dome and an archway between two utilitarian wings would serve not only as a proper receptacle for the Jefferson statue but also as a monumental gate to Forest Park. In Bitter's opinion the architects' commission did not find fault with the proposed plans legitimately. Indeed, the two wings that transformed a temple into a useful building had to have a utilitarian appearance for they "cannot and should not belie their purpose, to wit: that they are actually municipal museums of historic relics and documents." But, at the same time, an effective monument to Jefferson could be provided by a "colossal statue upon an elaborate pedestal." This would have such a prominent position in the structure as to make it evident, even from a distance, that this was no ordinary building, but that it "encloses shrinelike something of unusual importance."

Bitter was repulsed by a suggestion that a large obelisk or shaft be used in place of the monument and entrance dome. "It is a commonly accepted fact that a shaft or obelisk of considerable height is a Terminal rather than an Entrance. It serves best at the end of a formal avenue or elongated park, upon a rise or elevation of the ground, or it is also well introduced at the intersection of several roadways or arteries, or possibly as a solitary object in a wide and unobstructed open plain. But its use has never been considered proper as an 'Initiation' or Entrance feature because it does not lead into something, but leads up to itself." Bitter warned Francis that he must be prepared for such criticism as that of the architects, "without which no great thing as yet has come to light" and advised him not to be misled, "especially not by the numerous, well-meant suggestions that are bound to rain upon any monument commission and are likely to dim its clear vision."

Bitter could not see how a structure with an entrance conceived as a triumphal arch could possibly lack a monumental aspect, especially when it would contain a statue that, in addition to being accented by a dome, would stand out boldly against the verdure of the park. Even if the design had faults, he cautioned, solutions could not be found by upsetting several years' thought and labor and throwing to the wind the conclusions reached so far. "The desired result," he wrote in the letter to Francis, "can be accomplished by changing the architectural expression which our accepted ideas have found in Mr. Taylor's design and this surely can be done without the throes of a rebirth."

That it was not only the "architectural expression" about which Bitter was concerned is frankly brought out at the end of the letter. The report of the architects also threatened Bitter's commission, and to lose the opportunity of producing a monument of such national importance would have been a great disappointment. He had already completed a preliminary sketch of the Jefferson statue and his long reply to the architects was intended to defend it against "immature interjections."

Bitter's counterattack in this wintertime skirmish saved the monument plans from major alteration, and his victory was crowned in May, 1911, with a contract. According to the agreement he was to furnish all of the sculpture attached to the monument-building. This included not only a heroic-sized portrait statue of Jefferson but also a remodeled, bronze casting of the Exposition relief, "The Signing of the Louisiana Purchase Treaty," plus a decorative eagle to be duplicated in stone for the cornices above the front and rear entrance porticoes. In addition to all of the materials for the sculpture and its pedestals, Bitter was to furnish its transportation and setting. Upon completion of this work he would receive a total of $25,000.[10] The contract was awarded to him after he had exhibited and explained his plaster sketch of Jefferson to the executive committee.[11] This first sketch then served as the basis for a scale model which was used as a guide when he finally started to complete the full-scale figure in clay toward the end of 1912. In January, 1913, the clay figure was cast in plaster, and in the middle of April he went to St. Louis to chisel the features of his marble Jefferson in time for its unveiling on the thirtieth.[12]

The sculpture furnished by Bitter for the Jefferson monument in St.

Fig. 80.—Jefferson memorial, Missouri Historical Society, Forest Park, St. Louis, Missouri, 1911–1913; Isaac S. Taylor, architect.

Louis is not as extensive or elaborate as he had originally hoped. But it is intimately related to the theme, function, and design of the monument-building over which he had a large share of control from beginning to end. As Bitter argued in his reply to local criticism, the core of the building (Fig. 80) serves as a monumental gateway to Forest Park and at the same time through its massive, classical construction enshrines the featured figure in a temple. In keeping with this latter function, the unfluted Ionic columns of the identical porticoes are repeated on the inside to form a peristyle around the statue of Jefferson (Fig. 81). Facing north, away from the park, the nine-foot portrait is carved from light pink Tennessee marble and sits on top of a plain polished pedestal underneath a shallow dome decorated with colored tiles. The vaulted entrance hall, including the rotunda, is seventy feet long, and since it is open at both ends, its statue of Jefferson is neither outside nor entirely inside.

Bitter's Jefferson for the St. Louis monument is different in conception from his earlier portrait statue in Cleveland (Fig. 69). There are several possible reasons for this. First of all, the completely open-air figure is cast in bronze while the enshrined figure is carved from marble. This difference in permanent material might have influenced him to change the

Fig. 81.—Jefferson memorial, marble, Missouri Historical Society, Forest Park, St. Louis, Missouri, 1912–1913.

character of the original design in clay, though not necessarily. More important, the locations of the two seated statues are dissimilar, and because Bitter was so much concerned with the relationship between his portrait figures and their immediate architectural surroundings, this factor undoubtedly determined some of the major changes he made from one work to the other. The Cleveland Jefferson is placed to one side of a very wide stairway and is paired with a contemporary companion. Together they form a symmetrical composition, and as a means of drawing them together Bitter turned each one in his chair to face the spectator standing at the center of the bottom step. The St. Louis Jefferson, on the other hand, is alone in the center of a domed hall and, although not perfectly symmetrical, he looks out through the main entrance with an upright frontality. While the bronze statue in front of the rusticated Cuyahoga County Courthouse is imperfect and rough, the details and surface of the St. Louis Jefferson are neatly finished and the marble figure thereby matches the smooth stone construction surrounding it.

There are other less tangible, but very basic, reasons why the two statues differ in their interpretation of Jefferson. First, they are meant to portray him at different times in his life when he played two contrasting roles. The Cleveland Jefferson was produced for the courthouse to symbolize the Declaration of Independence as an important document in the evolution of Anglo-American law, and not necessarily as a passionate manifesto of American independence. For this purpose Jefferson is not interpreted as a radical revolutionary but is seen as a sincere, heavily laden, and contemplative individual. It may even have been Bitter's intention to show him as he might have appeared during the long debate in the Continental Congress over his draft of the Declaration. Jefferson was not a good orator; his voice was weak and he lacked the fluency and magnetism on his feet that Patrick Henry, for example, commanded. For this reason he sat silently throughout the entire debate, and, as he himself said, "writhing a little under the acrimonious criticism of some of its parts." He explained away his silence by humbly writing: "As for myself, I thought it a duty to be, on that occasion, a passive auditor of the opinions of others, more impartial judges than I could be, of its merits or demerits."[13] From this point of view Bitter's Cleveland interpretation of Jefferson as the quiet creator of the Declaration of Independence is accurate.

While working on the scale model of the St. Louis Jefferson, Bitter wrote in an undated letter to D. R. Francis that he was chiefly guided by a book published in 1901, *The True Thomas Jefferson* by William Curtis. As it discusses the many roles played by Jefferson and includes a wide variety of reports concerning his personal appearance, ranging from that of a shabby, large-boned farmer to a fastidious, well-bred gentleman, this account of Jefferson may well have been the basic source of Bitter's information for both of his portrait statues.

Regardless of the research material, the changes in attitude, dress, and expression that Bitter introduced in the later work were appropriate for a portrayal of Jefferson the President. In contrast to the earlier image, Bitter now had to portray the administrator who used personal and political influence to push through Congress an act of annexation which he himself had declared unconstitutional. The marble figure enshrined in its classical temple is placed far back in a heavily draped chair. With his head held upright he almost scowls as he stares sternly ahead. This Jefferson does not slump in relaxed contemplation, but with his shoulders thrown back and his hands tightly clenched, he gives the impression of concentrated power. Instead of representing "Citizen Jefferson," the St. Louis statue becomes the formally installed symbol of administrative force.

Bitter was the first artist to attempt a major portrait of Jefferson since the great Virginian died in 1826, and the difficulty of this task resulted both from the diversification in Jefferson's career and the multiple image that was formed of his personality from contemporary descriptions. Bitter stated that he used about twelve paintings of Jefferson, and each one showed a different conception, but together they gave him what he believed to be a "correct idea of his personal appearance."[14] The only general agreement among the life portraits of Jefferson is that the man's face was characterized by low straight brows, heavy lids, thin lips, and a prominent chin.[15] Otherwise, each differs from the next, and the image varies from a cosmopolitan dandy wearing a fresh lace collar and powdered wig, as painted by Mather Brown, to a dingy old man wearing heelless slippers, as depicted by Thomas Sully. Almost a century later Bitter followed neither extreme, but originated an overdue, sculptural treatment of the great public figure, drawing from two separate phases of his life.[16]

The difficulty of making Jefferson into a consistent image as the patriarchal hero is well established by a leading authority on the subject, Merrill Peterson, who writes: "Jefferson was a baffling series of contradictions;

philosopher and politician, aristocrat and democrat, cosmopolitan and American. . . . None of the ordinary categories of the hero-lawgiver, chieftain, prophet—sufficed for Jefferson. As his character was somewhat labyrinthian, so his mind was bewildering in its range and complexity. Later generations comprehended his thought only in fragments, crossing and colliding with each other, until it seemed that the protean figure, if ever he had genuine historical existence, must never be rediscovered."[17]

The St. Louis statue of Jefferson as president is appropriately accompanied by the high relief "Signing of the Louisiana Purchase Treaty" (Fig. 82), which was finally placed near the featured figure on the east wall of the entrance hall. For this location the relief was reduced in size and cast in bronze with a decorative frame and a projecting, stage-like platform supported by a marble pedestal attached to the wall. The group consists of the American envoys Robert Livingston and James Monroe confronting Marbois, the French Minister of Finance, across a table. Though practically freestanding, these figures are connected pictorially by means of a large, curve coinciding with a studied arrangement of arms. The composition is thus secured as a whole against the anecdotes of books, maps, candelabra, a miniature bust of Napoleon, and the treaty documents that clutter the table. Bitter improved his original design by replacing an overdominant, square-cornered chair with an eighteenth-century example that not only complements the curvilinear composition of the panel as a whole but matches the period costumes. Livingston, who played the key role in negotiating the agreement, is seen sitting on the chair in the foreground, while Marbois is shown signing the treaty and Monroe leans gracefully on the opposite end of the table. To fit the formality of the occasion, the final bronze version, as might be expected, is highly finished throughout. The precisely rendered inscription above the group is a quotation from Livingston's official statement at the time of signing.

This anecdotal composition, celebrating the largest single land acquisition in the growth of the United States, is a slightly revised memento from the St. Louis World's Fair. Otherwise it is questionable if Bitter would have done such a relief at this late date. The bronze "Treaty" panel was installed in the spring of 1913, ten years after it was first cast in plaster. Over this period Bitter moved away from pictorial literalism toward a more generalized and even geometricized, architectural sculpture. This change has been observed in the allegorical reliefs of the two Cleveland

Fig. 82.—"The Signing of the Louisiana Purchase Treaty," model for bronze relief, Missouri Historical Society, Forest Park, St. Louis, Missouri, 1913.

banks and in the archaized figures of the Wisconsin capitol building. Their tendency toward stylized abstraction, aided by ancient classical sources and contemporary European influences, was to be continued in two more public monuments during the last years of Bitter's life. In both, reliefs became quite experimental in technique if not revolutionary in style. The first were developed as part of a portrait monument commemorating a nineteenth-century middle-class moderate who anticipated an age of gradual reform.

XI

The Schurz Monument

DURING THE SAME years that Bitter was engaged in the Jefferson monument for St. Louis, he was occupied with still another architectural, portrait monument for New York City. It too was to feature a heroic-sized statue, and though not a building, this monument also became increasingly utilitarian as its design developed through several stages. The subject of the monument was one for whom Bitter might have felt a great amount of sympathy—the hero of the German-American community, Carl Schurz. When Schurz died late in 1906, a memorial committee was immediately established under the chairmanship of Joseph H. Choate, the prominent New York lawyer. A commemorative program was held at Carnegie Hall, and to the accompaniment of marches from Wagner played by the New York Symphony Orchestra, German choruses sung by the Liederkranz and Arien Societies, and an elegy recited by the fashionable poet Richard Watson Gilder, a fund was started to erect a Schurz monument somewhere in the city. Through private subscription, over $93,000 was eventually raised, and as did the committee for the Sigel monument a few years earlier the Schurz Memorial Committee commissioned Bitter to execute the work.[1]

That Bitter once again had free choice of a site for this monument is revealed in a letter of July 9, 1908, to Mrs. Bitter. In this letter, the earliest available record of his work on the Schurz commission, he states that the front of the new public library had been suggested to him as a suitable location for the monument, and the advantages of this site were so tempting that he was eager to discuss it with Carrere and Hastings, the architects of the building. A rough ground plan which he sketched to accompany his note indicates a place to the left of the library entrance facing Fifth Avenue for a "Schurz," while on the opposite side of the entrance a spot was to be reserved for "some other monument K. B. will do in the future." It is apparent that at this time he conceived of the Schurz monument merely as a statue on a pedestal which could easily be placed in front of almost any existing wall.

One year later, however, this early conception had changed completely. At approximately the same time that he started to think about the Jefferson monument in St. Louis, this New York monument also began to take form as an architectural, as well as a sculptural, design. By June, 1909, Bitter had decided on a site overlooking Morningside Park from Morningside Drive at 116th Street. On the day following his departure for Austria, where he finally returned to receive an amnesty, his preliminary plans for this location in uptown New York were publicized in the *New York Herald* (June 6, p. 9). According to this report the Schurz Memorial Committee had approved Bitter's design for a "sitting figure of Mr. Schurz on a pedestal" that was to be placed in "surroundings" which "have all been planned by the sculptor." The article is illustrated by a large photograph showing Bitter's model of a seated figure on a round pedestal in front of a very plain and low semicircular wall.

By summer of the next year this second plan had also been abandoned, and the monument as it now stands started to evolve. Throughout the middle months of 1910, Bitter and his family were once again in Austria. While there he borrowed a studio in Vienna to start not a seated Schurz but a full-length standing figure, probably intended for the final version of the architectural setting above Morningside Park.[2] Returning to New York in September, he continued to concentrate on the monument, and on March 11, 1911, he wrote to Kestranek that since returning he had altered the statue considerably by modeling a new head and new hands. He furthermore said that he had spent even more time with the reliefs than with the statue, and after many experiments had decided to design them for granite rather than following earlier intentions of using marble. This clearly indicates that the permanent form of the Schurz monument, which is constructed of granite and includes three reliefs of the same material, was well under way in 1911. Finally, at the beginning of 1913, Bitter re-

Fig. 83.—Carl Schurz monument, Morningside Drive and 116th Street, New York City, 1909–1913.

Fig. 84.—Carl Schurz monument, Morningside Drive and 116th Street, New York City, 1909–1913.

ported that he was pleased with the progress being made on the granite reliefs and believed the project would soon be finished.[3] It was in fact completed by the end of April, and on May 10, ten days after the dedication of the Jefferson monument in St. Louis, the Carl Schurz monument was unveiled and presented to the City of New York.[4]

As completed, the Schurz monument (Fig. 83) occupies a circular platform fifty feet in diameter built out from Morningside Heights over the park below. The supporting walls of the platform and the broad stairway rising up to meet it from the south (Fig. 84) are constructed of large rough-faced blocks of stone. The smooth gray granite walls of the monument itself curve outward from the elevated plinth of the portrait statue. They are stopped halfway around the platform by rectangular sections that serve as frames for two large reliefs. These, in turn, create a frontal plane in line with the supporting wall of the stairway. The function of the wide, free area in front as a stair landing is complemented by the exedra which provides a bench for rest. This simple utility is unhampered by over-ornamentation and the clean, unbroken lines of the monument suggest quiet repose.

According to *The New York Times* (May 11, 1913), the architect Henry Bacon "was associated with Bitter in the general design," of the Schurz monument, but no record has been found that indicates how much he had to do with the plans. Bacon, designer of the Lincoln Memorial in Washington, favored Greek forms above any others. The only thing about the Schurz monument directly related to ancient Greece is the style of Bitter's reliefs. It is likely that Bacon engineered the huge foundation for the monument. He was probably also responsible for the stairway. The monument itself, however, especially its semicircular ground plan and the rectangular front sections, remains so similar to the preliminary model which Bitter made in 1909 that it seems altogether appropriate to give him credit for its basic design. He wisely moved his portrait statue from a freestanding pedestal and placed it on top of a plinth incorporated into the exedra. In doing this he may have been thinking of Saint-Gaudens' Farragut monument, which he immediately admired upon his first arrival in America.

But the simplicity of the Schurz monument and the subtle curves of the wall and bench as they meet the buttress-like frame of the statue might have been suggested by the contemporary style of architecture advanced by the students of Otto Wagner in Austria. During his trip home to Austria in 1909, Bitter visited the Vienna Secession,[5] and when he returned for the entire summer of 1910, he had ample opportunity to become acquainted with the monuments that were being designed there by the young architects and sculptors. For example, he must have seen the Strauss and Lanner monument designed by the architect Robert Orley for the Rathaus Park. Anticipating any new knowledge he might have acquired during his return to Austria, he had already demonstrated a familiarity with recent trends in European design. In fact, after his unsuccessful Beaux-Arts proposal for the Lafayette monument in 1899, the architectural settings for his sculpture, when under his control, tended to become clear-cut and direct.

The portrait statue of Schurz (Fig. 85) is plainly posed, draped, and framed to correspond with its architectural support as well as with the supplementary relief panels. From the waist down the figure itself is in high relief, and the bronze base and panel to which it is attached are only slightly trimmed with the ancient bead and reel that Bitter used so much as a decorative device. To avoid depicting an ordinary suit of clothes in full, he draped the nine-foot figure in a long military greatcoat with cape, which actually was one of Schurz's favorite garbs.[6] As was the practice of Bitter in posing his portrait statues, the figure of Schurz is slightly asymmetrical in stance and when viewed from the left side of the monument seems to push out forcefully from its support. In contrast, as the observer moves to the right side, the forward foot of the figure and the aggressive thrust of the hat-side arm and shoulder lose their prominence. The man now seems to stand at rest. Thus a duality of force and restraint corresponds with the division of the allegorical relief panel underneath the statue into a masculine and a feminine side. Also, the linear simplicity of the long folds in the heavy drapery and the smooth, only subtly textured, undulations of the bronze are consistent with the surface and curves of the granite benches that lead up to it from either side.

Serving as an apex of the entire scheme, the head of Schurz is a carefully detailed portrait of a cantankerous old man who had spent all but the last few months of his mature years as an independent critic of the government. When Schurz died Bitter was called upon to make a death mask, and it was this immediate contact,[7] as well as late photographs and his personal recollections of the German-American leader, that enabled him to achieve such an accurate likeness. When he was commissioned to do the

Fig. 85.—Portrait statue, bronze, Carl Schurz monument, Morningside Drive and 116th Street, New York City, 1911–1913.

Fig. 86.—Portrait bust of Carl Schurz, clay, 1911. Destroyed.

monument the first thing he completed was a bust of Schurz (Fig. 86),[8] and the Mephistophelean appearance he gave to the aged head was retained in that of the bronze statue. A broad, high forehead arches back from the jagged, frowning brows, and the full mane of hair comes to a conspicuous cluster at the back. As a counterthrust, the pointed nose curves out from beneath protruding brows that practically conceal the narrow, well-shaded eyes. Finally, the lower half of the face is completely covered with a full, coarse beard, and the fall of the moustache amplifies the down-turned mouth that matches the expression of the eyes and brows.

In his statement concerning the St. Louis Jefferson, Bitter maintained that the silhouette of a black bronze figure seen against the sky was not "reverence inspiring." His choice of exactly this position for Schurz was apparently considered appropriate for the man's career and personality. Unlike Jefferson, Schurz did not present a complex image revered from many points of view. Quite the contrary; throughout his life he was a militant, egocentric agitator for administrative reform who seemed to thrive on controversy, and thus provoked either an extreme dislike or a loyal admiration. Although very young when he established his lifelong reputation as a daring revolutionary in 1848, he never attained lasting fame in any one profession. As soldier, statesman, politician, newspaper editor, and businessman he was only partially successful. However, he was a master of oratory, and was at his best when he could lend his voice dogmatically to such pet causes as civil service reform, which became a near-monomania with him. At home on the speaker's platform in life, Schurz was properly posed high on a pedestal when perpetuated in bronze, and at his feet a theatrical setting was spread to welcome an audience. He seems to be pausing between verbal attacks and, while waiting, scowls with an air of self-assurance in the direction of the country that adopted him.

As noted earlier the Schurz monument was designed as a basic semicircular exedra with a paneled pedestal interrupting the bench as an altar-like support for the portrait of Schurz. Also, a horizontal rectangular partition was placed at either end of the exedra to flank the steps leading up to the half-enclosed platform. The two end partitions as well as the front of the pedestal provided convenient areas for ornamentation, and Bitter took advantage of all three to display an unusual kind of low relief.[9]

Even though it bears the inscription CARL SCHURZ, A DEFENDER OF LIBERTY AND A FRIEND OF HUMAN RIGHTS, the central panel underneath the portrait statue is the least literal in treatment (Fig. 87). On the left side of an unadorned altar, a partially draped, muscular youth balances a dagger on its point in the role of Defender. On the other side, a female figure holds out her hands as a Friend. This division of the pedestal relief into a masculine and feminine side is transferred to the ends of the exedra where the inscription is even more explicitly illustrated. The right relief contains a female figure of Liberty leading the people with a graceful eagle in flight (Fig. 88), a reference to Schurz's lifelong dedication to the promotion of civil liberties. In contrast, the left relief panel is the more forceful or masculine side, with a warrior breaking the shackles of slavery while three Negroes look on (Fig. 89). An allegorical female figure is included, however, grasping the arm of an American Indian as if to urge him to join the Negroes in participating more actively in the development of modern civilization. The dominant theme of this two-part panel repre-

Fig. 87.—Carl Schurz monument, central relief panel, gray granite, Morningside Drive and 116th Street, New York City, 1910–1913.

Fig. 88.—Carl Schurz monument, right relief panel, gray granite, Morningside Drive and 116th Street, New York City, 1910–1913.

Fig. 89.—Carl Schurz monument, left relief panel, gray granite, Morningside Drive and 116th Street, New York City, 1910–1913.

Fig. 90.—Carl Schurz monument, clay sketch for left relief panel, Morningside Drive and 116th Street, New York City, 1910.

sents the role Schurz played in the Civil War, first as an abolitionist and then as a general in the Union Army. The Indian is included as a reminder of his term as Secretary of the Interior under President Hayes. While holding that office he worked to civilize the Indians by putting them on small reservations where they were supposed to become sedate farmers, and by providing them with Carlisle Institute, an industrial school in Pennsylvania.

As first planned, the Schurz monument relief panels were to be marble, and Bitter's early clay sketches were hardly the compositions he eventually produced for tough gray granite. For example, the left panel, devoted to emancipation (Fig. 90), was initially a compact crowd of Negroes in contemporary work clothes joined by an Indian to witness a symbolic ancient Greek soldier break a whip. In the form of a rapid sketch the figures were naturally very rough textured. But even allowing for this, there was little indication of the precisely cut, linear technique that the final version of the panel would assume. The only obvious similarity in the composition of the two was Bitter's retention of certain poses, for example the seated female figure, plus the gestures of encouragement and confidence that he originated in the sketch.

The pronounced change in treatment from the first sketches to the final version of the reliefs occurred after Bitter returned from Europe in the autumn of 1910. He later wrote that throughout the following winter months most of his time was spent with them, making "experiment after experiment in order to find a worthy solution."[10] However, much of the research for this experimentation had already been done during his visit to Greece in May, 1910. To this he himself testified from the National Museum at Athens when he wrote Mrs. Bitter, on May 16, that he saw "some magnificent reliefs of which I took special notice in relation to the Schurz Monument." The archaic relief figure on the Stele of Aristion was one work in the National Museum that apparently received special attention. Evidence of this is seen in the pose Bitter gave to the male Negro figure in the left panel and to the "Defender" of the pedestal panel. The legs of both are separated by a distance commensurate to that used for Aristion, and their feet are also placed in profile with the toes of each outside foot overlapping the heel of the inside one. The exaggerated buttocks and the way in which the slightly bent arm of the Negro falls to his thigh are still other characteristics that Bitter's two male figures share with the late sixth-century Greek figure.

While Bitter's low-relief figures project high enough from the blank surface of their panels to cause a deep dark shadow to run along one edge and a highlight along another, the details within these contrasting contours are inconspicuous. The drapery folds of all the figures are either inscribed as single parallel lines or are slightly raised as narrow relief bands with a tendency to widen. The latter are somewhat more precisely rendered than is usually the case in Greek archaic sculpture. But both the intaglio and the relief techniques were inherited from ancient predecessors who arranged curving folds in patterns less descriptive than decorative. To indicate the muscles of his figures Bitter employed a subtle shallow furrow which he could have seen in a number of archaic relief figures. Once again, however, these tend to be more pronounced than the ancient examples and occasionally they are drawn with single incised lines identical to those he used elsewhere for drapery.

To approximate the appearance of an archaic relief, he scattered his figures across the two end panels, and with the exception of the graceful, very unarchaic eagle, nothing else was carved into the granite. Therefore, any illusion of depth or solidity necessarily results from the treatment of the figures themselves. Legs, arms, and shoulders are related to their respective opposites as parts of a form existing in space. However, profile positions are consistently favored, causing the action to take place in movements back and forth across a single plane, and the two leading figures in each panel twist around rapidly with an abrupt, momentary manner. When a head turns, the rest of the figure, except the feet, follows accordingly. In contrast to most Egyptian or Mesopotamian reliefs, no figure by Bitter could be a physically impossible combination of front and side view. In this respect his Schurz monument reliefs are once again similar to late Greek archaic sculpture, and only the two female Negro figures include details that give them an Egyptian appearance. These are the facial features, the skin-tight skirt of the standing figure, and more than anything else the headdress of the seated figure which evolved from a bandanna suggested in the original sketch. Otherwise, Bitter's figures, while both flat-surfaced and sharply patterned, project from the panel more than the typical Egyptian or Mesopotamian relief. They also lack the extreme anatomical exaggerations and the rich, brocade-like ornamentation that are characteristic of the latter.

Regardless of what reference Bitter made to ancient historical prototypes in designing his relief figures, he continued to depend upon nature and his imagination as well. If not completely nude, most of these figures are draped in clinging "wet linen," and the emphasis he placed on accuracy of structure is clearly evident. At the same time, much of the stylization is not at all imitated from the past, but is worked out to express the particular theme of the figure involved. For example, the outside contour of the Defender in the pedestal relief (Fig. 87) reflects the reduction of a muscular physique to general forms and its angular succession of small curves clearly suggests the masculine in contrast to the soft feminine contour on the opposite side of the panel. The hair of the male figures in the end panels corresponds in its stylization to the three races represented. Therefore, the Negro, the American Indian, and the Caucasian have their hair cut in patterns peculiar to each. The feminine headdress also differs from one figure to the next, and only in the case of the female figure on the

Fig. 91.—Pencil drawing by Karl Bitter, *ca.* 1912. Owned by Mr. Karl Gruppe, New York City.

pedestal panel and the two figures wearing circlets, does it necessarily resemble that of Greek archaic sculpture. None of the faces have archaistic features, and together with the Indian and the Negroes the figures following Liberty are not idealized in pose or profile, unless a finely featured face is to be considered a contemporary ideal type.

A pencil line drawing that Bitter did of a female head in profile (Fig. 91) could very well have been a preliminary sketch for the Schurz monument relief panels. The face is small in proportion to the head as a whole, and the hair is swept back ending in a chignon. The nose projects from beneath a low, angular brow, comes to a sharp point, and is squared off with a diagonal line that then meanders its way to the slightly parted lips of a small mouth. The chin is prominent and also somewhat pointed, while the jaw in general is strong. Such a profile represents a type of female face that became very fashionable toward the end of the nineteenth century. Its place in American sculpture was secured by Saint-Gaudens in the development of a Victory figure for his equestrian monument to General Sherman.

Bitter used line drawings as the first step in carrying out his compositions for the Schurz monument. Once his figures were completely designed, he drew them in full scale on tracing paper and had them rubbed with carbon on the reverse side. The lines were then transferred onto sheets of plasteline from which he carved the figures as if he were working in stone. These full-scale models were cast in plaster and used as guides for the permanent granite versions which were pointed and carved in the Bronx workshop of the Piccirilli brothers.[11]

The final design of the reliefs had begun during the same winter Bitter executed the four groups on the Wisconsin capitol building. Following the lead of those huge, fairly freestanding figures, the comparatively small figures of the Schurz monument assumed their basic characteristics. That is, Greek archaic techniques and motives were applied to accurately constructed figures and combined with Bitter's own stylization. An American Indian, whose very presence increases the distance of the work from early fifth-century Greece, has no archaistic features. But he is concisely designed, with such details as there are in his brief costume incised in single lines. The eagle is probably the most original detail of the whole project, and it flies by as an inconspicuous impression, hardly more discernible than the veins running through the granite. On the other hand, Bitter's inventiveness is clearly demonstrated in the illusion of solidity he achieved in spite of projecting, flat-surfaced figures in sharp, perpendicular relief. An over-all preciseness of pattern harmonizes with the severe lines of the exedra to such a degree that the panels do not distract from the apex of the architectural composition, the portrait statue.

XII

The Lowry Monument

BITTER'S insistence that a portrait monument was to be architecturally accommodating to the public, as well as a sculptural tribute to an individual, was never more tenaciously demonstrated than during a three-year struggle to carry out his last commission of this kind. Late in the summer of 1911, when the Schurz monument was well on its way to final form, he was approached by a private committee to design a portrait monument for a large midwestern city. In contrast to most of his previous public portraits the subject for this monument was only of local importance. It was Thomas Lowry, a businessman whose major accomplishment was the establishment of a street-railway company between the twin cities of St. Paul and Minneapolis. After his death a group of friends joined together and petitioned the Minneapolis Board of Park Commissioners for permission to erect a monument in his memory.[1]

A site for the monument had been designated by late August when Bitter described the new commission in a letter to Kestranek (Aug. 24, 1911). An oblique-angled triangle, approximately two hundred feet long by seventy-five feet at its base, formed at the intersection of two major avenues, Lyndale and Hennepin, was placed at Bitter's disposal by the Park Board. At this early date Bitter had not yet determined exactly what the monument should be, but he wrote that he wanted to produce something different from the ordinary exedra, and he urged Kestranek to come to America to collaborate with him on the architecture.

Within two weeks Kestranek agreed to come, and Bitter responded by describing his proposal for the Lowry monument in greater detail.[2] From his observations there were two unavoidable limitations about the site. First, it was necessary for the monument to face north; and second, an unpleasant apartment building stood at the south end of the triangle. "The 'Virginia Flats' is an abominable, red brick building and must be concealed by planting trees." Between the Virginia Flats and the proposed monument a sidewalk connecting the two avenues would have to remain, even if it became necessary to move it farther north to allow space for a screen of trees. Bitter had also encountered certain difficulties with his patrons, Mrs. Lowry and Judge M. B. Koon, the chairman of the monument committee. They had attempted to "meddle" in the project by making some suggestions of their own about what the monument should look like. He vetoed whatever they had recommended immediately and was grateful when "they dropped the insane idea of 'beautiful columns.' " Undaunted by these initial problems Bitter had constructed a model of the proposed monument which, according to his brief description, included a portrait statue in front of a freestanding screen decorated with allegorical figures in relief.

In explaining a photograph that he sent to Kestranek of the rough clay model, Bitter expressed his attitude toward the subject of the portrait, hinted at the personality he thought his statue should represent, and revealed what part of the monument he considered most significant. "The chief concern of the monument is Mr. Thomas Lowry, a good-natured gentleman in a morning coat with an overcoat over his arm and a cylinder hat in his hand. He stands by a busy Minneapolis corner and greets the passers-by. No singular deeds by him are recorded; the man had merely grown up with this swiftly flourishing city in such a manner that everyone wanted his monument. Thus I am putting him on a busy corner. In the background two children are visible which indeed are still very vague and crude. However, they are intended to provide a certain ornament for the place and besides I would like to do something more creative than just Mr. Lowry."[3] Although Bitter assured Kestranek that he need not be influenced by these preliminary considerations, it is obvious that he had settled on a fairly clear idea of how the monument was to be designed. He concluded by saying, "The monument should embellish the city and I would like to make something beautiful. It does not have to be too conservative; however, it also need not be the very latest in reform architecture."

Through the winter and spring of 1911/1912 Bitter and his friend worked on the design for the Lowry monument, including the plans for a miniature park that would lead up to it from the northern tip of the triangular site. In early June Kestranek returned to Vienna and Bitter placed a scale model of their entire scheme on display in Minneapolis. This was the first public appearance of the Lowry monument project, and the *Minneapolis Journal* of June 9, 1912, publicized the occasion with a description of the work in a lengthy illustrated article. Well-photographed by the newspaper, the model displayed the monument on an elevated platform reached by five stone steps extending from one side of the triangle to the other. The four corners of this platform were to be punctuated with ornamental lamp posts. The remainder of the site down to its northern point was to be divided into walks and flower beds. Since the triangle was on the side of a hill and fell away to the east, it was also to be terraced and retained with a stone wall parallel to Lyndale Avenue.

Although featuring a nine-foot bronze statue, the monument itself was to be largely architectural. Divided into three parts, it was accented by a vertical panel in the center with a slightly curved crown to frame the figure. Two somewhat shorter flanking panels, each with a modest allegorical figure in relief, were to bear commemorative inscriptions. Along the top a pronounced border of geometric swags would end in protruding scrolls. At the base, stone beds for plants were to be constructed on either side of the pedestal. According to the newspaper, the committee in charge of the Lowry monument planned to have everything completed in one year. It was to be paid for by contributions from Lowry's friends. In addition, even though there would be no solicitation, the people of Minneapolis would have an "opportunity to subscribe to the fund."[4]

As optimistic as the newspaper seemed to be, the $60,000 that was initially promised Bitter to cover the total cost of the project was not raised by the friends of Lowry or their committee. In fact, a thinly veiled public plea was finally published in a futile attempt to fill the deficit.[5] Bitter, of course, was fully aware of the difficulty and reported to Kestranek that while the model was received with great enthusiasm, the matters of money and contract were not being resolved so smoothly.[6] He was forced to lower his estimate by four thousand dollars, and still the affair was not settled.

Even though such obstacles hindered the project from beginning to end, Bitter never seemed to lose patience. He persistently held out for the completion of both the monument and its triangular park as he and Kestranek had designed them. At the end of June, 1912, he was almost forced to look for another site when the owner of the Virginia Flats complained to the Park Board about the monument, maintaining that a large wall was to be placed in front of his building.[7] During the next month, in spite of the complications, Bitter received his contract from the committee. While it was not as liberal as hoped for, he was satisfied, and wrote that "the monument is important enough from an artistic point of view to put other considerations into a secondary place."[8] By this time the committee had agreed to the use of Bethel granite, as initially recommended by Bitter, and a subcontractor was engaged to begin construction.

Sufficient funds to carry out the small park, however, were still lacking when, to make matters worse, the committee chairman, Judge Koon, died. In desperation Bitter turned to Thomas Lowry's brother-in-law and business partner, Calvin Goodrich, requesting him to take over the responsibility of filling the deficit in order that the work on the monument could be continued and its landscaped setting begun.[9] Apparently nothing came of this request, since letters from Bitter to Kestranek continue to report a failure of funds throughout 1913. Finally, after an unpleasant argument with an indifferent committee, Bitter wrote Kestranek on September 8 that the park plans would have to be reduced to their simplest possible form. New plans were actually prepared late in the summer of 1913, and in August the Park Board was informed that the Lowry monument triangle would not include all of the granite that was initially called for. Most of the stone work would be eliminated and in its place the modified plans substituted "lawns, walks, and plantations."[10] Bitter tried to pacify Kestranek by assuring him that the reduction of their design was not really so bad and, since there was obviously no other solution, they would merely have to "swallow and digest the fragments."[11]

Exactly what, if indeed utimately anything, was eliminated from the original design for the small park in front of the monument is now impossible to tell. In December, 1913, Bitter confessed that he had practically given up all hope for saving the project; and at one point he had even told the committee to abandon the design and approach another architect if they thought it could be done more economically.[12] Soon after this climax was reached the crisis suddenly broke when Horace, the only son of Thomas Lowry, visited Bitter's studio. As Bitter explained to Kestranek, a change in their fortune then took place. "The son of Lowry, who was especially against the large costs, is of a completely different opinion since he saw the full-scale model of the monument. Likewise are the two sons-in-law. All of them are now *Feuer und Flamme* for the whole affair which was not the case several months ago. It may be that these members of the family fear a curtailment of their inheritance."[13] With renewed confidence Bitter was now certain that the park would include much of the granite work meant to harmonize with the monument, and that this would be paid for by the Lowry family itself. This prediction proved correct, and from then on the work progressed free of major barriers. By the end of 1914 the monument, while uncarved, was erected. The park was actually supplemented with a semicircular granite bench that Bitter introduced at the apex of the triangle, plus a variety of borders in the same material around the flower beds (Fig. 92). The four ornamental lamp posts were among the finishing touches.[14]

During the many months of struggle and negotiation to keep the Lowry monument and its park plans intact as a single composition, Bitter was unable to work on the sculpture. In June, 1913, nearly a year after signing a contract, he finally began to prepare models for the portrait statue, followed by the two allegorical figures (Fig. 93). Instead of remaining surface reliefs, as originally planned, the latter, which Bitter insisted on including for their decorative as well as their symbolic function, were to turn out uniquely in the round. As for the figure of Lowry, Bitter had started to acquaint himself with his subject before he and Kestranek went to work on the scale model of the monument.

According to the *Minneapolis Journal* (June 9, 1912), his research was pursued in a very methodical manner. "He came to Minneapolis, obtained every picture of Mr. Lowry that was available, studied the daily habits of the man, his daily life, talked with men who had been his intimate friends, and went away. But he came back to go all over the ground again." Bitter's meticulous attempt to produce an accurate portrait was benefited in the summer of 1913 when he found a man who could wear Lowry's clothes and was willing to pose in them until the clay model was completed. The live model, he wrote, was over six feet tall, had broad shoulders and a "Dickbauch" that could not have approximated Lowry's measurements more perfectly. Furthermore, he was a wholesale grocer from Schleswig-Holstein which was all to the good since Bitter had agreed with

Fig. 92.—Thomas Lowry monument, granite, Lyndale and Hennepin avenues, Minneapolis, Minnesota, 1911–1915. Courtesy of the Minneapolis Park Board. To make way for a new intersection the bronze portrait and its granite screen will soon be removed from the doomed triangle and will be relocated in a park at Twenty-fourth Street and Hennepin Avenue.

Fig. 93.—Thomas Lowry monument, clay sketch, Lyndale and Hennepin avenues, Minneapolis, Minnesota, 1911–1915.

Mrs. Bitter beforehand that Lowry looked like a "*plattdeutsch* grocer."[15] To model an exact likeness of his subject's head, Bitter depended upon the aid of Mrs. Lowry, who came to his studio in New York to advise him while he worked.[16] The bronze statue was at the foundry in March, 1914, but it was not installed until the allegorical figures were carved to completion on the site. Then the monument was not dedicated until August 19, 1915, a few months after the death of its sculptor.[17]

While very much concerned that the Lowry monument, with its architectural landscape setting and allegorical figures, should "embellish the city,"[18] Bitter had been, above all else, commissioned to produce a portrait statue of Thomas Lowry. In contrast to any of his previous portrait subjects, Lowry was not famous, and in spite of his financial success as the owner of the local traction company, his career was apparently rather pedestrian. As Bitter pointed out, no singular deeds by him are recorded and the demand for his public monument, if indeed very widespread at all, resulted simply from the association of his business with the growth of a city.[19] In appearance, Bitter's Lowry, unlike his Pepper, Tappan, or Schurz, is not poised in a duality of restrained movement and restless calm. "Tom" Lowry shows no tension in his flat-footed stance, and the drowsy expression of his eyes is in complete accord with the relaxed fall of one arm and the deliberate gesture of the other in holding out a hat. To harmonize with the casual pose and as a means of enlivening the drab surface of commonplace, contemporary clothes, Bitter allowed his last portrait statue to remain "clay-modeled" in bronze. In short, a rather colorless subject was treated to some textural color.

The chief problem that plagued not only Bitter but many of his colleagues in fulfilling portrait commissions of modern men was recognized in a tactful understatement by the *Minneapolis Journal* (June 9, 1912). "When Mr. Bitter undertook the work he faced the hard problem encountered by sculptors who have made statues of Lincoln, of handling the tall, spare figure of a man in trousers and frock coat, presenting no opportunity for the heroics. Some of the severest criticism of the world of art has been directed toward such figures now existent and Mr. Bitter approached the work with a realization that he had taken a difficult task."

The inherent difficulties of portraiture do not prevent people from commissioning it, and Bitter's career in America happened to coincide with a period when the demand for public portrait monuments increased out of a growing desire to commemorate national heroes and local leaders. In fact, by the time Bitter came to this country, a thriving tradition of portrait sculpture had already been firmly established. Such well-known sculptors as John Quincy Adams Ward and Augustus Saint-Gaudens were turning out realistically rendered figures to sit, stand, and ride as bronze or marble sculpture on public places. Within this tradition certain conventions were maintained as a matter of course. The most obvious of these was the faithful depiction of contemporary suits and uniforms, a practice inherited from the late nineteenth-century academies of Europe and applied to American subjects. The classical frame used on high relief portrait panels, and the so-called exedra, used as an architectural setting for a statue in the round, were introduced and formularized by Saint-Gaudens in collaboration with Stanford White during the 1880's.

The tradition and its stylistic conventions were carried on by Bitter, who, in accepting commissions for portrait monuments, was, as he said, thrown into competition with the disciples of Saint-Gaudens.[20] Throughout the twenty years that he produced portraits he was consistently diligent in his attempt to achieve an accurate account of each personality. If a subject were no longer alive for direct observation, he would research thoroughly to find photographs, paintings, biographical accounts, or word-of-mouth descriptions in order to portray his man faithfully. In no way would he have intentionally distorted or diminished beyond recognition any essential feature of a portrait subject. He also complied with the familiar process of working out a full-scale model in clay to be cast in plaster. This finished version was then usually recast in bronze, although occasionally pointed up and carved in marble.

As traditional as Bitter was in producing portraits, he did nevertheless introduce a variation of surface treatment among his permanent figures. While one might be carried to a precisely detailed exactness, the next might be left in the rough, suggesting an almost Rodinesque quality in its texture of deftly modeled clay. This contrast in finish from one portrait to another seems to have been determined, along with a particular pose, by the general character of the person involved. When a down-to-earth informality was suggested in the life of a man, a corresponding appeal for a direct tactile response was made by allowing the natural pliable quality of the original earthen material to remain in the bronze cast.

A much more crucial concern in the designing of Bitter's portrait monuments was the interest he revealed for composing a figure in harmonious relationship with its architectural setting. Primarily an architectural sculptor, he frankly confessed that portraiture alone, especially portraits of contemporary subjects, offered only secondary satisfaction to him. For that reason when the opportunity arose he applied himself enthusiastically to the architecture as well as to the sculpture of a monument. As the evidence plainly proves, it was Bitter himself who sketched the initial designs of his major independent monuments, and while he did not invent any revolutionary architectural forms, he at least became less dependent on academic antecedents. The exedra for the Schurz monument was thus denied the classical columns and rusticated pillars used in the model for a Lafayette monument. Consequently it became a simple and yet dramatic setting for the featured figure. Bitter then did away with the exedra altogether, and his Lowry monument became part of a small park plan that was even more utilitarian than the monument to Schurz. In addition to the supplementary, allegorical sculpture, which in the end was literally assimilated into the fabric of the monument itself, the immediate architectural setting of Bitter's portrait figure became an increasingly practical embellishment of the city.

An opportunity for original architectural sculpture was provided by the allegorical ornamentation of the Lowry monument. From the time Bitter first started on this project in the autumn of 1911 he insisted on providing "something more creative than just Mr. Lowry."[21] But it was not until the spring of 1913, when he finally was able to complete a full-scale model of the monument (Fig. 93), that he came up with a solution for the two allegorical figures that completely satisfied him.[22] The background screen of three sections was to be constructed in white Bethel granite (Fig. 94) with a total width of approximately twenty-five feet. Each wing was to be built to a height of about twelve feet with stones roughly two feet thick. Initially Bitter intended to carve his allegorical figures in relief, but by the time he finished the model of the monument this conventional technique was abandoned for a unique architectural design.

Instead of restricting the figures to only one surface, Bitter decided to pierce the screen by cutting through from both sides (Fig. 95). In this way each figure remained an integral part of the stone, attached inside, even though realized almost entirely in the round. Since the monument was erected in the middle of an elevated platform the avoidance of a negative

Fig. 94.—Thomas Lowry monument, Lyndale and Hennepin avenues, Minneapolis, Minnesota, 1911–1915.

Fig. 95.—Thomas Lowry monument, rear view, Lyndale and Hennepin avenues, Minneapolis, Minnesota, 1911–1915.

Fig. 96. Thomas Lowry monument, left relief panel, granite, Lyndale and Hennepin avenues, Minneapolis, Minnesota, 1913–1915. Photo by Bob Perrizo.

Fig. 97.—Thomas Lowry monument, right relief panel, granite, Lyndale and Hennepin avenues, Minneapolis, Minnesota, 1913–1915. Photo by Bob Perrizo.

Fig. 98.—Thomas Lowry monument, left relief panel, model for granite figure in Minneapolis, Minnesota, 1913–1915.

side was desirable. Bitter's unusual open-air reliefs resourcefully solve this problem and provide a figural composition from all major views. Another good reason for piercing the screen was to expose the allegorical figures to a southern light necessarily denied the portrait statue.

As in the case of the Schurz monument relief panels, the allegorical figures for the Lowry monument are meant to represent the career of the honored man. Since Lowry's sole contribution to his community was the development of a street railway company, municipal growth became the object of Bitter's symbolism. A male figure in the east panel is seen tying up young vines, while the west panel contains a seated female figure busily harvesting grapes. Bitter had already used a similar allegory for a small bronze relief panel on the pedestal of his first portrait monument, the monument to Dr. William Pepper. However, the architectural sculpture on this final portrait monument is far removed in technique and style from that in the early period of his career.

Among the last works by Bitter the Lowry monument reliefs bear the

Fig. 99.—Thomas Lowry monument, right relief panel, model for granite figure in Minneapolis, Minnesota, 1913–1915.

closest resemblance to the short-lived pairs of figures executed for the façade of the First National Bank in Cleveland. While in no way directly derived from Greek archaic sculpture, the Minneapolis figures are highly stylized (Figs. 96 and 97) in a contemporary Secessionist manner that is even more comparable to the sculpture of Franz Metzner in the Haus Rheingold. A touch of *Jugendstil* ornamentation is also apparent in the foliage that accompanies them, forming a decorative pattern that complements the swag-and-tie motive along the top of the monument. From the four bottom corners of each open container, a flat stem rises out of a plain border that marks a rectangle measuring three and one-half by two feet. In the Planting relief it grows upward as a vine of evenly overlapped leaves, which gradually turn into an abstract, saw-tooth pattern as they reach the top of the arch. The same transformation occurs in the Vintage relief, except that bunches of grapes hang down from the top in perfect symmetry.

Each figure sits hunched over with one leg tucked underneath the other while industrious hands are raised to the top of the arch. The heads, connected to the uncarved stone above, are held upright, with facial expressions of stern sincerity (Figs. 98 and 99). The hair of both falls from beneath the arbor in thick, flat, looping strands, and the body of each figure is almost as stylized. Muscles and creases are incised as pronounced lines into the granite. Bottoms of feet are sketched in abruptly and the hand holding a basket of grapes in the Vintage relief remains a flat, linear, leaf-like shape. A similar treatment, possibly derived from Metzner, was applied to the wisps of drapery, with flat-surfaced folds helping to draw each figure into a compact composition.

These unusual open-air reliefs are the last examples of applied architectural sculpture that Bitter was able to complete. Although modest in size, they are a fitting climax, both in theme and in style, to a career which pursued the integration of sculpture with architecture and, conversely, promoted the architectural relationship of a setting to its sculpture.

XIII

Municipal Affairs And the City Beautiful

IN THE COURSE OF his career Bitter gained a reputation for his interest in public art and in the promotion and protection of sculpture in America.[1] A chapter on Bitter's public services and public commissions formed part of the brief commemorative biography written by his brother-in-law, the historian Ferdinand Schevill.[2] In a lengthy review of that book, the New York *Evening Post* offered a final statement of praise for Bitter's role as a public servant. "Art for art's sake he considered an abomination, if the slogan meant the divorcing of the artist's work from the needs of the community. For Bitter the sculptor was first and formost the citizen and the idealist convinced that his art had a mission to serve. He held that it was not only the handmaid but the inspiration of civilization, and in his biographer's words, that while its 'immediate concern was to enhance man's environment by adding beauty to utility,' its final justification lay in social service."[3]

As an architectural sculptor, Bitter quite naturally preferred what he termed "open-air" sculpture located upon or within an architectural setting, as opposed to the isolated exhibition piece which was merely placed on display in a drawing room or museum gallery. However, there is no convincing evidence that he had a strong sense of social service or any intention of contributing to the public needs of a community when he embarked upon his career in America. With the exception of the Administration Building at the Columbian Exposition and the Broad Street Station in Philadelphia, his first major works were for the exclusive gratification of

America's wealthiest families. Lucrative commissions to decorate their town houses and country mansions provided him with the opportunity to achieve material success, leading, for example, to the construction of his own home above the Hudson. With its completion in the spring of 1896 he abandoned the *Wirtshausleben* of an uprooted immigrant and wrote that he found security not only in the ownership of a house but also in his newly acquired citizenship.[4]

While the next two years were probably the most unproductive of his career, they did lead to the first recorded statement now available that Bitter, besides having acquired a secure sense of belonging in his adopted land, had developed an interest in lending his talents to the community as a whole. This statement appears in the form of an extensive article that he wrote for the March, 1898, issue of *Municipal Affairs,* a short-lived New York quarterly devoted to civic reform. Anticipating the muckrakers, who were to be inspired by Lincoln Steffens' "Shame of the Cities" series for *McClure's Magazine* in 1903, an organized municipal reform agitation arose during the nineties. Improvements in physical, social, and moral conditions were demanded by various groups, and *Municipal Affairs* observed in its first issue in 1897 that the "Civic Renaissance," or widespread revival of interest in municipal affairs, had to be educational in nature. One of its leading contributors, the editor of the *Nation,* E. L. Godkin, urged American intellectuals to take a greater interest in community problems. Jane Addams and the militant liberal, R. R. Bowker, also contributed many articles to the quarterly. Each issue contained a "debate" on some problem of the city, and Bitter's article, entitled simply "Municipal Sculpture,"[5] was one of several devoted to the subject of municipal art.

With an eye cast mainly on New York, the American city with which he was best acquainted, Bitter observes that the engineer and architect are apparently appreciated by the public while the sculptor remains neglected and has cause to lament the absence of municipal sculpture. Even though it had been of great importance in the ancient and Renaissance worlds, such sculpture in America had thus far only been accorded the opportunity of a "foster child of accident." This he cannot understand, because sculpture, in his opinion, is more readily comprehended by the masses than is architecture. Furthermore, as an outdoor art, it should appeal to everyone as a "permanent public possession." The lack of municipal sculpture in America must result from a popular misconception of what constitutes the art of sculpture in general. "To the minds of many it is of little or no usefulness, but rather a very expensive luxury. It has long been conceived as an art producing statuettes or busts intended to ornament the parlors and drawing rooms of the wealthy, there to be covered with white muslin during the summer months. If the piece happened to be of a larger size it was considered a fitting object to donate to a museum. In this manner the figures of little boys with upturned trousers, and fishing rods in hand, or a boy and girl under an umbrella or asleep became the typical sculptural ornament of the homes of many who fondly believed these possessions to be works of art. While such crude notions about the artistic scope of sculpture were but the product of popular ignorance, it is not surprising that this art under such auspices gained but a scant foothold in the community" (pp. 74–75).

Bitter also blames the portrait statues in America's parks and squares for giving the public an erroneous conception of sculpture. These figures, he points out, were attired in ungainly garments and planted on pedestals inscribed with the names of those instrumental in their erection. As likenesses they failed to "supplement the imagination concerning their possible characters or achievements" (p. 75). Perhaps more damaging to sculpture than anything else, however, were the soldiers and sailors monuments that were distributed throughout America following the Civil War. From town to town uniformed figures in granite or bronze stand on top of columns and even with slight variations of posture are "apt to be the same man with the same meaningless features." Bitter condemns this trade in monuments as "speculation on the patriotic feelings of the people," alluding to a certain bronze foundry in Europe that stocked different sets of buttons and accoutrements to suit any given regiment required. "With few exceptions such are the average surroundings in which the masses of our people have received their ideas of sculpture" (p. 76).

Having dismissed public sculpture in America as mainly a bad influence, Bitter briefly surveys its successful use in the past. Egypt, for example, left a record of its grandeur in sculpture, while the people of Athens were surrounded by a magnificent outward demonstration of their city's greatness. "They could find the beauty that we seek in our houses distributed throughout the entire city, and thus they grew to consider the city itself as their real home and to be more concerned in it than in their own, at best, but casual dwelling place" (p. 77). Roman sculpture was also largely public, but its standard was lower, with more emphasis placed upon the glorification of a militant state. The sculpture of the Middle Ages was an integral part of the civic and spiritual life of the people; and, finally, the aristocracy of the Renaissance, in addition to the church, erected monuments as an expression of their ideals, or to call forth the pride and power of individuals. While admitting that it would be unfair to compare New York City, which grew so rapidly, with the European cities that developed gradually through the centuries, Bitter accuses the comparatively youthful city of doing very little to advance public art. This could easily be demonstrated by a quick journey through its streets, and the remainder of Bitter's article provides just such a tour.

Starting at Battery Park, he travels uptown, pointing out the need to improve the appearance of major intersections, squares, and parks with the proper integration of sculpture, architecture, and landscaping. Even Bartholdi's Statue of Liberty fails to escape his criticism. Either it should have been three times larger or it should have been placed "in a more advantageous position where even so external a merit as its mere size could be sufficiently realized and appreciated" (p. 79). From that point on Bitter either criticizes the lack of any attempt to make the city an attractive place in which to live or condemns the haphazard use of isolated monuments as being inadequate. At the bottom of his survey lies the question, "How can the effect be ornamental unless the monument be adapted to the place and the place to the monument?" (p. 80). For example, such old, historical monuments as Trinity Church should, naturally, be preserved. But, in spite of the fact that religious interests no longer preclude commercial pursuits and skyscrapers tower above churches, the business buildings surrounding Trinity Church should somehow harmonize with it. They might at least be uniform in color and of an even height.

Many difficulties stand in the way of beautifying City Hall Square. Worst of all, the "exceedingly ugly" brownstone Municipal Court built by the Tweed Ring "mutilates the place." Also, a large, uncomely fountain stands out badly against the delicately proportioned City Hall. All adornments of the park and square should be proportioned to this central building and carefully related to the two natural axes, Murray and Warren streets. With this rule established, the square might be sufficiently emphasized with a fountain designed to represent the recent consolidation of the boroughs of New York into a single city. For the Broadway side of the park, Bitter suggests that a number of portrait statues could be located among the trees and shrubs to accompany MacMonnies' figure of Nathan Hale. But he hopes that a "systematic and general scheme, with a definite purpose in view" (pp. 83–84) would be adopted in placing such works. His final suggestion for the sculptural decoration of the square is a row of busts portraying prominent New Yorkers to face City Hall as an approximation of the Pincio in Rome.

As Bitter continues uptown, he discovers few things to praise and much with which to find fault. Saint-Gaudens' portrait monument of Peter Cooper is an example of the way a city should commemorate its great men. On the other hand, he feels that it too suffers from unfavorable surroundings. An elevated railroad runs too close by, and the little triangle upon which the monument stands is marred by a cast-iron drinking fountain, listed by Bitter as a "toilet facility." Even lanterns, benches, hydrants, and the like should be designed and placed to meet the demands of a monument commanding the immediate area. A lack of such "architectural principles" characterizes Union Square, which, according to Bitter, gives the impression of a large empty lot with pathways winding through monotonous gardens. It is in need of a symmetrical plan with a prominent object proportioned to the size of the place as a central focal point. Two ornamental fountains, one of which had been boxed up for years; a "discouraging" monument of Lincoln;[6] a statue of Lafayette; and Henry Kirke Browne's equestrian Washington are scattered over the square; and "not one has any apparent reference or connection with any of the others, or to the place" (p. 87). As Paris glorified the Republic with such tremendous monuments as the Trocadero, New York, in Bitter's opinion, might take advantage of Union Square as the site for a fountain commemorating the American Revolution.

Not only squares but corners attract Bitter's attention, and to him the one at Broadway and Fifth Avenue demands artistic treatment more than any other. From a purely practical point of view, the money spent for a prominent feature at this point would add at least the same amount to the real estate value of the building to which it would be attached. Municipalities as well as private corporations had beautified important street corners in Europe, and if such a work as the Fountain of Saint Michel in Paris could be erected here it would have obvious "advertising qualities." With regard to public buildings, he approves of the new Appellate Court on

Madison Square mainly because its sculpture will certainly benefit the underprivileged, a rationalization for splendor often expressed by reform-minded members of the artistic community. "To the majority of our population who have rarely anything to cast their eyes upon but the fronts of factory buildings and tenement vistas, to visit such a building will be an event . . . . Such buildings should be made to be an educational factor for the lower population which lacks opportunities and means to surround itself with the beautiful to which it is entitled and which the community owes it" (pp. 89–90).

A museum, in Bitter's opinion, is primarily a storehouse where art is removed from the public at large. He advises benevolent citizens to donate money for sculpture in Central Park instead. No park, however, is suitable for portrait statues, and those of poets in the Mall should be replaced by appropriate allegorical subjects and animal groups which would be of more valuable influence on the children who play there. While the plans employed for Riverside Drive and Morningside Heights are grand and imposing, high-cost improvements have not included sculptural adornment. This is disturbing, since a wealth of suggestions for the sculptor are provided by openings of cross streets into the Drive, as well as in the esplanades and recesses of Cathedral Heights.

Of the many places in New York City that Bitter chooses to discuss, the Plaza at Fifth Avenue and Fifty-ninth Street, the open area at the southeast corner of Central Park, demands special attention. It had been suggested that a soldiers and sailors monument be placed on this centrally located site still outside the stream and turmoil of business activity. This suggestion is diplomatically, but definitely, rejected by Bitter. He feels that whatever is ultimately done here must suitably ornament the entire square in relation to the park entrance. "At the outset the idea of a column, or anything rising to a great height must be adandoned as inapplicable to a place that in no sense controls a vista. The natural roadways and crossings will in a great measure determine the general plan upon which carefully studied effects must be based" (p. 92). He recommends a systematic arrangement of individual figures or groups, connected by balustrades or arcades, which in turn would be surmounted by decorative lanterns, vases, or supplementary sculpture. Each should be located to accentuate the necessary thoroughfares and passageways. The resulting corners might be adorned with small fountains surrounded by flower beds. But any ornamentation was to serve as an "appropriate but subdued setting" for one or two monumental centerpieces of imposing sculpture. Such a theme, he maintains, "would not only embrace the entire Plaza, but would also lead up to and culminate in the park entrance" (p. 93).

Bitter closes his article with a plea for long-term plans to be drawn up as a guide for the rejuvenation of the city. Instead of a central circle from which streets radiate as they do in Paris and Washington, New York has the aesthetic disadvantage of a rectangular grid system. However, it does have squares, and it remains the task of civic sculpture to cultivate their local character. At the same time, it is particularly imperative that a "definite program or system" be devised to which the large squares would conform for the sake of harmonious artistic development. The existing conditions provide a poor basis upon which to build, and must be reformed. "Momentary needs have dictated the present plan and we accordingly find statues, fountains for man and beast, toilet facilities, and other huts, hydrants, and lampposts planted about in a most empirical manner without the slightest consideration or reference to each other, like dice cast from a dice box . . . . To produce monumental effects, it will be necessary for the landscape gardener, the architect, and the sculptor to go hand in hand to develop, decide upon, and lay down the required measures to which every change and every innovation shall conform" (p. 95).

Since the city is in the process of being rebuilt, the importance of taking immediate action must not be underestimated. Bitter appeals to the wealthy to contribute at least toward replacing the numerous cast-iron drinking fountains with fountains that have some artistic merit. For such extensive projects as modifying the Plaza "until it shall compare favorably with places like the Place de la Concorde in Paris," the city must bear the expense. Whatever the source, a large expenditure will be required before New York can be made architecturally, as well as sculpturally, worthy of its reputation as the wealthiest city in the world. "Before all we must arouse the required civic pride and foster unanimity of purpose where the common interest is set above private or individual interests" (p. 97).

Bitter was far from being alone in criticizing the appearance of New York City, or in recommending a carefully planned scheme of artistic reform. The American city in general was falling under the scrutiny of the reforming eye, and municipal art was considered important for a variety of reasons. One proposal of peculiar practicality was offered by Brooks

Adams in an article he wrote for *Municipal Affairs*.[7] The United States had entered into a struggle for supremacy with Europe, and Adams believed that art should play an important role in the competition. By this he meant that an American city should include a practical public or "commercial" art to attract foreign tourists. By the same token it would keep its own country's citizens from touring abroad, where they spent their money in such cities as Paris, probably profiting France as much as iron and steel did the United States. To be completely "self-sufficing" by avoiding this "waste" was Adams' goal, and to serve this purpose a form of architecture should be developed in the same spirit that produced the Greek temple. The ancient Greeks were to be admired as men of business whose genius was found in finance and colonization. Being commercial and materialistic, they developed a materialistic form of expression in their temples, which were not mysterious shrines but parts of a logical scheme of civic decoration. To Adams the Greek temples were the "most refined, most effective and the cheapest form of advertising ever devised and they still pay off by attracting American tourists and their money."[8] America could profit from the example of the Greeks, who also made Alexandria a great attraction by applying business methods to their art. New York, Adams maintained, had the duty of leading the way by becoming an artistic as well as a financial capital. In this enterprise the city would succeed "if she would devote to it a tithe of the genius which she lavishes on railway administration or on the stock exchange."[9]

That the American city could ever reverse the flow of tourists across the Atlantic is highly doubtful, and more than likely Brooks Adams himself did not really believe it possible. However, an optimistic attempt to rid America of urban ugliness was under way by the turn of the century. In the same year that Adams wrote his article, Senator James McMillan of Michigan formed a commission to revive the L'Enfant plan for Washington, D.C. Daniel H. Burnham, Charles F. McKim, Augustus Saint-Gaudens, and Frederick Law Olmsted were appointed to study the original scheme of the 1790's, and restoration of the central portion of the city was soon begun. Alexander Cassatt, brother of Mary Cassatt and president of the Pennsylvania Railroad, agreed to remove his company's station from the Mall, and Burnham designed the present Union Station for a location north of Capitol Hill.[10]

In 1906, Burnham, the leading architect-planner of the period, began work on his comprehensive plan for Chicago. This effort at least resulted in the improvement of the lake front and the widening of Michigan Avenue. Similar projects were introduced in other major cities where park systems were expanded and civic centers planned. In St. Louis, for instance, Forest Park was developed around Cass Gilbert's Art Museum, the only permanent building of the 1904 World's Fair. In fact, the international exposition played a key role in the City Beautiful movement, as this phase of municipal development was called. Above all, the Court of Honor at the Chicago Columbian Exposition provided a prototype for such civic centers as those in Cleveland and San Francisco, where colonnaded buildings with uniform cornice lines were constructed around open malls.

As director of sculpture for three major expositions, Bitter participated in the City Beautiful movement by devising for its proving grounds large formal schemes of ornamentation. Besides this rather indirect contribution he also added several permanent improvements to the American city in the form of architecturally conceived public portrait monuments. The largest of these was made possible by the St. Louis World's Fair, and because of his connection with the Exposition Bitter was subsequently given the opportunity to collaborate with an architect and a landscape architect in designing the Jefferson Memorial Building as a prominent feature of the Forest Park development. Following its completion he devoted a great amount of time and effort to the fulfillment of his own plans for the Lowry monument, which upon his insistence included a small triangular park as a utilitarian embellishment of Minneapolis.

In connection with his early concern for the beautification of New York City, Bitter was fortunate enough to be able to utilize two of the locations that he had designated in his *Municipal Affairs* article as appropriate for municipal sculpture. Above the stairway descending from the end of West 106th Street to Riverside Drive he placed his equestrian statue of General Sigel, and as a site for his monument to Carl Schurz, a platform was extended dramatically from the eastern slope of Cathedral Heights out over Morningside Park. It was the Plaza on Fifth Avenue, however, that received Bitter's most dedicated attention for many years. He approached this long-term project as a conservative architectural sculptor progressively committed to the necessity of artistic public planning.

XIV

The Plaza

THE PLAZA on Fifth Avenue became Bitter's personal City Beautiful project, one in which he concentrated a strenuous effort to reform the appearance of New York City. As discussed in the previous chapter, his special interest in this site was first expressed as part of a general survey of the city that he prepared for *Municipal Affairs* in the spring of 1898. On December 19 of the following year the National Sculpture Society held a symposium with the intention of solving the problem of the Plaza embellishment, but the program was finally expanded to cover all of Manhattan. Subjects that Bitter had previously touched upon in his analysis, such as Battery Park and Madison Square, were assigned to the participants, each of whom was to suggest how his given place might be redesigned. Bitter was asked to discuss the featured topic, the Plaza. Once again *Municipal Affairs* served as an outlet for this professional concern toward public art when the symposium speeches were published as an article entitled "From Battery to Harlem: Suggestions of the National Sculpture Society."[1]

In contrast to the other eight speakers at the symposium, Bitter does not promote a pet structure for his special square. He merely maintains that the Plaza must be treated as a single well-integrated composition.[2] At the beginning of his speech he states that his friend and patron, the late Richard Morris Hunt, had also been very much interested in this space on Fifth Avenue. This is demonstrated by a view with proposed monuments that the architect had drawn some forty years before. As indicated by Hunt's drawing, the Plaza was traditionally considered to be the square between Fifty-eighth and Fifty-ninth streets, while the adjacent block of the same size between Fifty-ninth and Sixtieth streets was called the Circle. That the two were still looked upon as being separate and distinct had lead to the recent proposal to erect a soldiers and sailors monument in the form of a high column on the Circle accompanied by an equestrian statue on the Plaza. According to Bitter, "both propositions were entirely independent of each other; and the effect of one upon the other was not for a moment considered."[3] This he finds very disturbing. Together the two equal squares should be called the Plaza and always be treated as a whole.

From Bitter's point of view a symmetrical ground plan was basic to the proper planning of the two-part Plaza. If, for example, a circular base or basin were to be constructed near Sixtieth Street it should be duplicated on an axis parallel with Fifth Avenue at the opposite end, near Fifty-eighth Street. However, as may be seen in the carefully executed perspective drawing and ground plan which Bitter made to illustrate his remarks (Fig. 100), he would not have been satisfied with two widely separated circles or ovals alone. Instead, he visualized a pair of relatively large islands with the same shape as those on the Place de la Concorde minus the central obelisk. Such expanded areas would not only minimize the passageways for horse and carriage, but by the same token would leave uniform lanes around the Plaza through which pleasure traffic could move in a more orderly fashion. Furthermore, the existing distance from one sidewalk to another was too great for the safety of the pedestrian, who needed adequate "isles of refuge" in order to cross the Plaza casually on his way to Central Park.

To accommodate the stroller, Bitter included a sidewalk around each island as well as a broad central promenade. Flanking balustrades were to be punctuated with pedestals of sculpture and stone benches. To make up for Fifty-ninth Street and its trolley cars the matching islands would face one another without permanent obstructions on either side in order to enhance the impression of one uninterrupted composition. Finally, Bitter indicated cascading baroque fountains at both ends, with nude figures and aquatic animals, as the predominant features of his projected scheme. But, as he assures his readers, "there is no reason why two equestrian statues could not be substituted, as could any other monumental features, so long as they are either symmetrical or in some distinct and clearly visible relation to the square as a whole."[4]

Along with his plan for the Plaza as a single, well-integrated square, Bitter proposed a way in which it might also serve as an introduction to Central Park. A double row of trees, starting at the Plaza, ran along the west side of upper Fifth Avenue. Although they were separated from the park by a rough wall "of the brownstone period," the trees were under the jurisdiction of the Park Board and could be incorporated into a boulevard for pleasure driving, riding, and walking. Bitter regretted that New York lacked such a *corso* and urged that the old stone wall be removed as the first step in constructing one. Once that was accomplished another double row of trees (Fig. 100) might be planted to shade the alternate thoroughfares and sidewalks, an arrangement that Bitter believed would benefit both Fifth Avenue and Central Park as two parts of a single scheme. What is more, the new boulevard would fall in line with the principal axes of the Plaza and thereby create a long narrow vista from Fifty-eighth Street northward.[5]

While Bitter's proposals for the Plaza were to remain suspended throughout the first decade of the new century, he did succeed in saving this open area from being mutilated by a soldiers and sailors monument, or by any other "affair of incongruous scale and shape."[6] On Decoration Day, 1903, the Plaza became a parade ground for the ceremonies occasioned by the unveiling of Saint-Gaudens' long-awaited Sherman monument. However, the mounted general and his comely companion were not permitted to invade the square, having been placed to the north, on the edge of the park.[7] In the spring of 1912 Bitter maintained his role as protector of the Plaza when the question of its development was suddenly revived. This was brought about by the death of Joseph Pulitzer who bequeathed $50,000 "for the erection of a fountain at some suitable place in Central Park, preferably at or near the Plaza entrance at 59th Street, to be as far as possible like those in the Place de la Concorde, Paris, France."[8]

In March, 1912, Pulitzer's son, Ralph, and his attorney, George L. Rives, acting as executors of the estate, obtained the permission of Park Commissioner Charles B. Stover to erect the fountain on the southern half of the Plaza. With this so easily accomplished there was no apparent reason why arrangments for its design and erection should not be made as soon as possible. Therefore, Rives immediately informed the National Sculpture Society.[9] Hermon MacNeil, its then president, appointed a committee consisting of Daniel Chester French, Herbert Adams, and J. Scott Hartley to advise the executors and to provide a tentative program for a limited competition.[10] In the middle of May a special meeting of the sculptors was held at which it was decided that ten names would be elected by means of a plurality vote. Balloting was to be done by mail, and the five sculptors receiving the highest number of votes would compete for the Pulitzer commission.[11] Two weeks later the ballots were counted. Bitter received more votes than anyone else, followed by Calder, MacNeil, Adams, and Adolf Weinman, who were all eligible to submit a design.

Any plan proposed for municipal property had to be approved by the Art Commission of New York City. Since Bitter had just been appointed by the mayor to serve as a member of that commission (as of January 1, 1912), he was in an excellent position to carry on his watch over the Plaza. In early June, Ralph Pulitzer finally informed the Art Commission of his father's bequest and asked that the Plaza be endorsed as the best possible site for the fountain.[12] As chairman of a subcommittee created to investigate this request, Bitter, in spite of his participation in the competition, rejected the Pulitzer proposal. His reasons for doing so were explained in a letter to Herbert Adams, the newly elected president of the National Sculpture Society. On the day of his writing Bitter had met Park Commissioner Stover at the Plaza and succeeded in persuading him that nothing should be undertaken that would not "comprehend the entire area." A comprehensive plan, he felt, could not be fulfilled with the amount of money provided in the will. "With $50,000 we can only succeed in ruining the place and the hope of its future and proper development." Bitter also explained to Adams that he and the other two members of his subcommittee had investigated the possibility of using the southern end of the Central Park Mall for a fountain site, but concluded that this too would exceed the funds on hand.[13]

As a counterproposal, Bitter suggested that a fountain, comprising a low basin flanked by two groups of recumbent figures supporting water spouts, could be erected on the southeast corner of Central Park in place of the unattractive park wall still standing there. Also, a disreputable cast-iron shelter, a drinking fountain, and several rubbish cans close by should be removed to allow a clear view of the small pond below, which he con-

Fig. 100.—Plan and perspective drawing by Karl Bitter for the Plaza, Fifth Avenue and Fifty-ninth Street, 1899. Owned by Prof. John Bitter, Coral Gables, Florida.

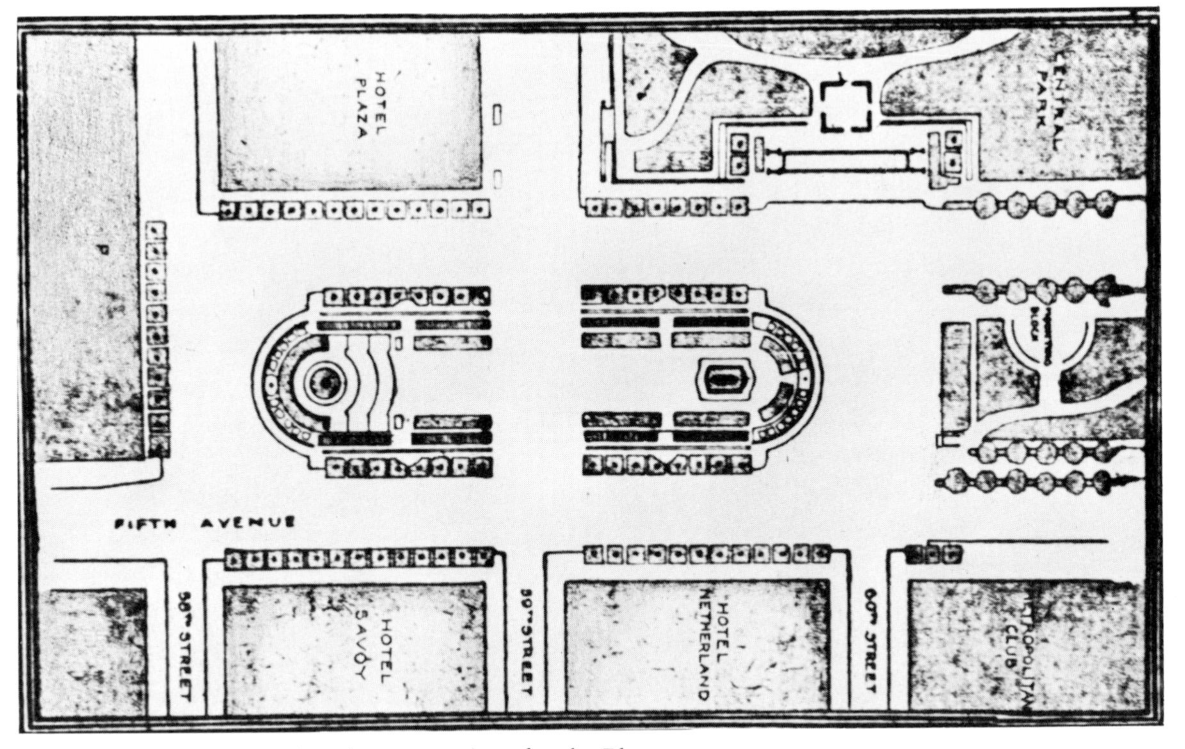

Fig. 101.—Plan by Thomas Hastings for the Plaza, 1913.

sidered "one of the sweetest landscape effects in the entire park." Provided Adams, French, and Hartley agreed to his suggestion, Bitter intended to recommend the corner location as the most promising site "on" the Plaza for a Pulitzer Fountain.[14]

In his reply Adams agreed with Bitter's perennial demand for a treatment of the Plaza as a whole. At the same time he was not certain that a fountain on the corner of the park was the best way to "frame" the landscape. He further warned that the executors of the Pulitzer estate might not feel that Bitter's suggestion complied with the will, especially with the stipulation that the fountain was to resemble those on the Place de la Concorde.[15]

Before placing his counterproposal in the hands of the executors Bitter attended a special meeting of the Art Commission on July 2 and reported the findings of his subcommittee.[16] Three weeks later a letter of explanation was sent to Ralph Pulitzer underlining Bitter's contention that it was basically the sum of money that prevented the construction of the fountain proposed in the will for the southern half of the Plaza. The letter also advised that even though the official duties of the Art Commission were confined to action upon a particular design submitted for a specific location, Bitter and his subcommittee would nevertheless be glad to suggest an alternative location near the Plaza entrance where an appropriate fountain might be placed.[17] Pulitzer was understandably disappointed with the decision but ignored its financial basis when he wrote that the subcommittee had rejected his father's fountain because it "would not be adequate for the site of the Plaza."[18] As for another location nearby, an informal discussion with Bitter and his subcommittee concerning the matter was out of the question until his fellow executor, Rives, returned to New York from a summer abroad.

The negotiations between Pulitzer and Bitter via the Art Commission finally came to a climax on October 10, 1912, when the subcommittee for the Pulitzer Fountain met the executors of the will in front of the Plaza Hotel, at the controversial site itself. Throughout the morning they went over the ground, and as disclosed in a long letter written by Pulitzer to Park Commissioner Stover, the face-to-face encounter resulted in a workable agreement, but only after Bitter had convinced Pulitzer that his way of approaching the Plaza was the reasonable one.[19] Therefore, the basic assumption of the agreed-upon scheme was that no fountain could be approved if it were placed anywhere on the Plaza or its immediate vicinity without consideration for the entire area. Moreover, if the location and design of the fountain were to be viewed properly as an architectural problem, a competition of architects would have to precede the one already arranged for among the sculptors.

All those attending the meeting at the Plaza consented to the idea of inviting five architectural firms to submit plans for the reconstruction and embellishment of the site as well as to present a design for a fountain. Obviously under the influence of Bitter, Pulitzer maintained that these plans "would involve, in the first place, the laying out of the Plaza in such a manner as is worthy of the principal entrance to Central Park and would provide as one feature of the general plan the erection of a fountain at the expense of Mr. Pulitzer's estate."[20] Pulitzer also hoped that the project would commend itself so strongly to the public authorities and to public opinion in general that the other features required in developing a good architectural treatment of the whole Plaza would be paid for by the City, just as Bitter had suggested many years before.

Sometime in the middle of November the Art Commission approved the plan of procedure outlined in Pulitzer's letter to the Park Commissioner. One month later the five architectural firms taking part in the competition, as well as the jury, were announced by the press.[21] On January 21, 1913, the five designs were placed on exhibition in the new public library, and its architect, Thomas Hastings of Carrere and Hastings, was named the winner.[22] Although comprising only one fountain, the Plaza design by Hastings (Fig. 101) bore such a remarkable resemblance to the design proposed by Bitter in 1899 that it must have been directly determined by it. The ground plan consisted of the same twin islands that Bitter had adopted as an introduction to Central Park and to his projected *corso*. Separated by Fifty-ninth Street, they remained aligned on an axis exactly halfway between the east sidewalk of Fifth Avenue and that serving the Plaza Hotel. A walk was to circle the outer ends of each island, and two parallel balustrades, "suggestive of those on the Place de la Concorde,"[23] were to flank a pair of narrow garden plots with a broad stroll-way down the middle.

Bitter's original proposal of matching fountains was not necessarily compromised when it was decided that Saint-Gaudens' Sherman would serve as the focal point of the north end. It should be recalled that he had suggested equestrian monuments as alternatives to his fountains. In order that it might assume its new architectural role, the popular equestrian monument had to be moved sixteen feet to the west, which made the distance from its pedestal to the Pulitzer Fountain one hundred and eighty feet.[24] Bitter's desire to have a pleasure boulevard or *corso* between Fifth Avenue and Central Park was apparently considered impractical for the new automobile age already well under way. However, Hastings did propose to reconstruct the upper edge of the Plaza area as an entrance to the park. Two large rostral columns were to be placed on the corners of the tree lawn between the avenue and the parkway in line with the balustrades of the Plaza islands. Also, a long-term plan called for the erection of a shelter just inside the park, opposite Sixtieth Street, to replace the wall and the small cast-iron shelter which Bitter disliked so much.[25]

As the Plaza now exists the Bitter-Hastings design has undergone certain changes. The most noticeable of these are the replacement of hedges

Fig. 102.—Pulitzer Fountain, Plaza, Fifth Avenue and Fifty-ninth Street, New York City, 1913–1916.

Fig. 103.—Pulitzer Fountain, Plaza, Fifth Avenue and Fifty-ninth Street, New York City, 1913–1916.

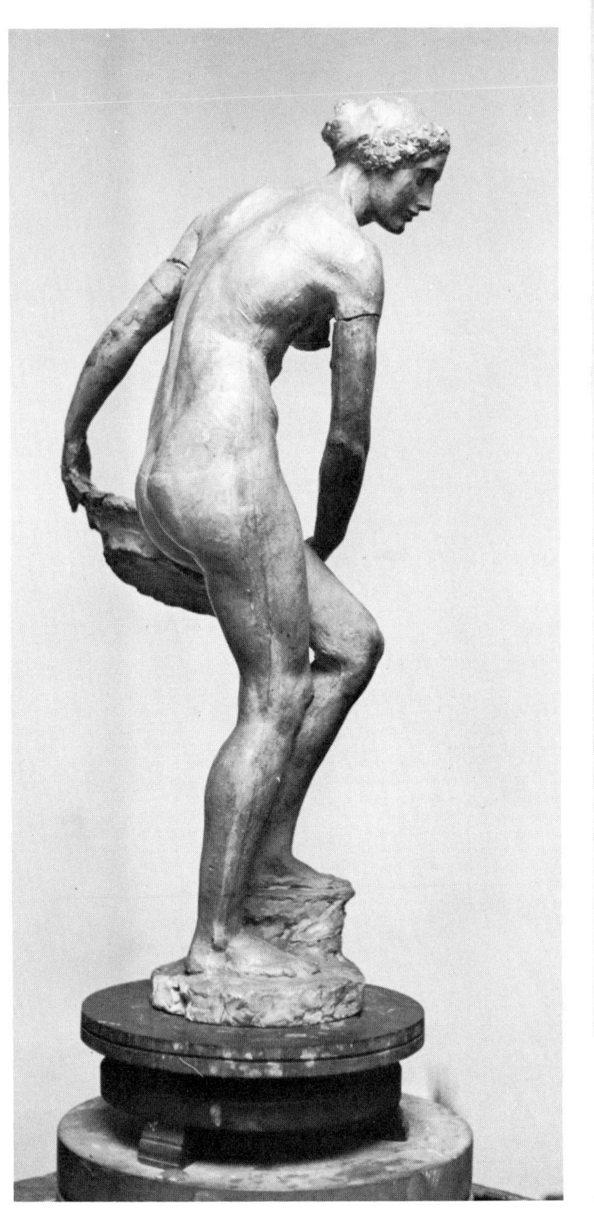

Figs. 104 & 105.—Pulitzer Fountain figure, "Abundance," original scale model in plaster, 1914–1915. Owned by Mr. Karl Gruppe, New York City.

instead of the balustrades that ran intermittently around the two islands, and the elimination of the paired rostral columns that were erected at both ends of the oblong square.[26] The fountain itself, however, remains unaltered (Fig. 102). Made of limestone, it is approximately sixty-five feet in width at ground level and comprises a succession of six late Renaissance basins ornamented with a pair of flanking ramshead horns of plenty.[27] The upper basin is sixteen feet in diameter and the figure on top is about thirty feet from the ground (Fig. 103).[28]

Out of due respect for his vigilance over the Plaza, and as a fitting reward for his determination of its plan, it was only appropriate that Bitter should be chosen to provide the figure for the Pulitzer Fountain. Hastings' design specified a nude female figure, and Bitter started to work on a scale model in the fall of 1914.[29] At the beginning of spring he cast a plaster figure two feet in height (Figs. 104 and 105). It was left behind in his Weehawken studio when he was struck down and mortally injured by an automobile while leaving the Metropolitan Opera on the evening of April 9, 1915. Following Bitter's untimely death, Karl Gruppe, who had been his student and assistant for more than three years, carried on with the project by enlarging the plaster model to full scale. This reproduction was in turn worked upon briefly by Isidore Konti before it was cast in bronze and installed on top of the fountain in time for dedication in May, 1916.[30] Except for the more precise modeling of the hair, and the definition of fruit and drapery in the basket symbolizing Abundance, the bronze figure on top of the Pulitzer Fountain accurately represents its original conception by Bitter.

He chose a pose that had been repeated with slight variation for many nude allegorical figures down through the baroque era. An appropriate comparison for Bitter's Abundance is the figure of Florence on top of Niccolo Tribolo's Fountain of the Labyrinth at the Villa della Petraia.[31] Above a type of high basin that established a precedent for Italian fountains, the mid-sixteenth century figure turns in a motion of wringing water from her long hair. The arms of Abundance, holding the overladen basket, assume approximately the same relationship to the figure as do those of the Tribolo figure. They swing elliptically in opposition to the force of the bent leg and they counter the forward thrust of the head, which was no doubt purposely limited in size.

The scale model of Abundance, the last work touched by Bitter, may be

Fig. 106.—"Stretching Model," Miss Anderson, bronze, 1897. Owned by Dr. Francis Bitter, Centerville, Massachusetts.

Fig. 107.—Diana, bronze, 1909. Owned by Mrs. Walter Abel, New York City.

better appreciated as a final statement when viewed alongside two of his earlier nude figurines. Together the three modest works, produced at widely separated intervals, represent a concise review of Bitter's stylistic development.[32] The first is a clay sketch of a seated figure dated 1897 and cast in bronze (Fig. 106). Less than ten inches high, it is a spontaneous impression of his youthful model, a certain Miss Anderson, stretching her arms and legs at the moment of breaking a long pose.[33] The sensuous little nude was modeled into energetic existence on top of a roughly defined chair form and, whether intentional or not, represents the closest approximation of Rodin that Bitter ever produced in permanent material. That he would not have continued in this vein at the expense of a classicistic direction is demonstrated in another small bronze of 1909 (Fig. 107).[34] Only sixteen inches tall, it depicts the goddess Diana, and while it has a Houdinesque surface, its haughty pose corresponds to the austere monumentality of Bitter's mature style of architectural sculpture.

The slightly larger, scale model for the Pulitzer Fountain includes characteristics of its two predecessors in that it combines an energetic, baroque pose with classical details. Its head, though small in relation to the elongated body, bears a stylization of hair and facial features that reflects Bitter's part in reviving and revising archaistic motives for a contemporary public sculpture.[35] The figure in full sums up his stylistic development and from its imposing position looks out across the Plaza, a final memorial to Bitter's efforts as an architectural sculptor with aspirations for the City Beautiful.

XV

A Stewardship Of Sculpture

THE INTEREST that Bitter developed in producing sculpture as a public art for the American city was closely related to the administrative role he played in promoting and protecting the position of the sculptor in a newly urbanized culture. Only four years after his arrival in the United States he participated in the foundation of the National Sculpture Society, which provided him with the opportunity to help organize the advancement of his profession. As its constitution states, the object of the Society was to spread the knowledge of good sculpture; that is, it intended to foster a taste for "ideal sculpture" in America and to encourage its use in the decoration of public buildings, squares, and parks. In order to achieve this end it was necessary for the sculptors to display their wares, and aside from a periodic international exposition, or such joint efforts as the Dewey Arch, exhibitions provided the only outlet through which they could collectively reach the public. New York, however, contained few halls, let alone proper galleries, that could suitably accommodate the great size and weight of the more ambitious works, and these places were seldom available. Prior to the turn of the century the Society held no independent exhibitions, and while the New York Architectural League included modest examples of sculpture in three of its annual exhibitions, it refused to invite the sculptors as an organization.[1]

After a costly and disappointing collaboration with the New York Florists Club at Madison Square Garden in 1902, six years were to pass before another exhibition was attempted by the Society. During that time, Bitter, as chairman of a standing committee on current work, investigated the possibilities of exhibiting sculpture, only to find that the other professional art societies refused to rent or share what limited facilities they controlled.[2] An immediate solution was to support the recently established Fine Arts Federation of New York in its effort to bring the many societies together under one large roof. Early in 1905 the construction of a United Fine Arts Building was discussed among the representatives of the Federation with no tangible results. A committee of three from the National Sculpture Society insisted that only the National Academy of Design and the American Fine Arts Society could afford to shoulder the financial burden involved in erecting and maintaining the building. It also felt that a site should either be supplied by the city, subscribed by a group of "public spirited citizens," or suddenly appear as a gift from some wealthy individual. Once constructed the building itself was expected to bring in additional funds from the gate receipts of a "General Annual Exhibition," from the leasing of permanent quarters to the cooperating societies, and from the rental of space to "outside parties."[3] In spite of the rather presumptuous demands of potential participants, the hope of erecting a United Fine Arts Building was kept alive by the painter, Howard Russell Butler. He had previously succeeded in administering the construction of the Fine Arts Building on Fifty-seventh Street which was currently shared by the Architectural League, the Art Students League, and the National Sculpture Society. However, the individual societies could not be united in purpose and the idea finally fell by the wayside.

Throughout 1906 and 1907 Bitter served two consecutive terms as president of the National Sculpture Society, and the search for adequate exhibition space continued under his leadership. Mrs. Harry Payne Whitney offered to finance an exhibition in the autumn of 1907, and three hundred American sculptors were invited to take part.[4] Once again, however, the National Academy of Design and the Architectural League had already leased the cramped gallery space, and since the cost of renting Madison Square Garden had proven to be much too costly, the exhibition of sculpture was canceled.[5] As a consequence, Bitter decided that if the Society were ever to exhibit its work, arrangements would have to be made in some city other than New York. In May, 1907, he sent letters of inquiry to such outlying centers of art as the Art Institute in Chicago, the Albright Gallery in Buffalo, and the Corcoran Gallery in Washington, D.C. In contrast to the Metropolitan Museum, all were agreeable to the exhibition of contemporary American works of art.[6] However, since problems of transportation, convenient dates, and gallery space could not be solved for the time being, Bitter passed by the museums altogether to enter into negotiations with the Municipal Art Society of Baltimore.

After a rapid exchange of letters with William M. Ellicott, a local architect representing the Art Society, it was agreed that the Fifth Maryland Armory would be placed at the disposal of the National Sculpture Society during the month of April, 1908.[7] In handling these arrangements Bitter used clever strategy. He never disclosed that the Sculpture Society had not been able to put on an exhibition for many years and was desperate to do so. Instead, he created the impression that it would be a great privilege for Baltimore to have an exhibition of American sculpture from New York. He even risked a threat to withdraw his "offer" when Ellicott tried to press him for information concerning past exhibitions of the Society.

As chairman of the Baltimore Exhibition committee and foreman of the jury to select the works for display, Bitter continued to lead the Society's experiment of exhibiting out of town. The Baltimore Art Society, which raised an initial fund of approximately five thousand dollars, paid all of the expenses except transportation and installation costs. The number and size of the exhibits were left completely to the discretion of the National Sculpture Society. By the end of February, 1908, about four hundred examples, including equestrian statues, bronzes, marble groups, busts, and reliefs were selected from over one hundred American sculptors. In order that the sculpture should have a proper garden setting the florists of Maryland furnished more than enough plants, flowers, shrubbery, and trees to fill the armory. On the eve of the opening an elaborate subscription banquet was held with the French ambassador as the featured speaker.[8]

Measured in attendance and catalogue sales alone the exhibition was an unprecedented success. Upon its close at the end of April, over sixty thousand persons had been admitted, and it was reported that there were times when the crowds practically exceeded the ability of the ticket sellers to keep up with the lines. The total cash receipts were well over $11,500. This not only paid for the incidental expenses but left a generous surplus.[9]

Bitter's solution to the problem of exhibiting sculpture relieved the National Sculpture Society from the lack of space and sympathy in New

York City. After the triumph in Baltimore contemporary works of American sculpture moved inland with further exhibitions. During the winter of 1909/1910 an exhibition of small bronzes was collected by the National Sculpture Society under the auspices of the Art Society of Pittsburgh. Originating at the newly constructed Carnegie Institute, it was sent on to Buffalo, Chicago, and St. Louis with such good results that a similar collection followed the same circuit three years later with Indianapolis, Baltimore, Philadelphia, and Newark added to the itinerary. In January, 1912, the Toledo Museum inaugurated a new wing with a selected exhibition of American sculpture organized by the National Sculpture Society.[10] Bitter, however, was dissatisfied with the limited number of works displayed in Toledo, and soon after his election to the Society's presidency in 1914 he repeated the performance of his earlier two terms by planning another comprehensive exhibition.

Although several members, including Sherry Fry and Herbert Adams, thought another attempt should be made to hold an exhibition in New York, Bitter was corresponding with Cornelia Sage, Director of the Albright Gallery in Buffalo.[11] In December he addressed a regular meeting of the Society and persuaded those present to adopt his recommendation for a Buffalo exhibition to be held in the spring of 1916. If displayed both indoors and out, the exhibition could include sculpture shipped from the Panama-Pacific Exposition in San Francisco. In any case only the expense of transporting works from New York to Buffalo would be borne by the Society. A final surplus fund was impossible, however, since the Albright Gallery had been built by the city with the stipulation that no admission could be charged. For this reason any deficit was to be met by the municipal government.[12] At the next Society meeting a committee of nine was appointed to take charge of the exhibition and Bitter was named its chairman, ex officio.

Soon after the initial arrangements for the Buffalo exhibition were made, Bitter reported an unusual encounter with Royal Cortissoz which further justified his insistence that the National Sculpture Society should hold independent exhibitions in American cities other than New York. Even though the Architectural League had remained willing to include plaster models of sculpture in its annual exhibition at the Fine Arts Building, the well-known critic attacked this practice in a dinner speech delivered before its members. According to Bitter, who was in the audience,

Cortissoz stated that the sculpture interfered with his pleasure of viewing architectural drawings and plans much in the same way "boiled onions would affect a hungry person who had expected to be served peaches à la Melba."[13] Bitter promptly wrote a letter to Cortissoz in which he reviewed the difficulties experienced by the National Sculpture Society in finding exhibition space. Though inadequate, the Architectural League offered the sculptor his only opportunity of exhibiting in New York, and now even that was endangered by the abrupt and outspoken criticism of an influential member of the art world.[14] Cortissoz was so impressed by Bitter's rejoinder that he had the letter printed in the *New York Tribune* along with a plea for better exhibition facilities. He also promised not to oppose the appearance of sculpture at the Architectural Annual but, on the contrary, to encourage it.[15]

The letter to Cortissoz marks the end of Bitter's persistent effort to place sculpture before the public by means of exhibitions. In May, 1916, the Buffalo Exhibition took place at the Albright Gallery, and in memory of its instigator the galleries and grounds included fourteen examples of Bitter's late public portraits, memorial figures, and architectural sculpture.

The stewardship of sculpture that the National Sculpture Society assumed as its responsibility was carried out in many ways besides exhibitions, and Bitter was repeatedly in command of a cause. In 1906 he was sent as a delegate from the Society to a Washington conference on copyrights which resulted in a more protective law as far as the artist was concerned. From the moment a work was completed it was to be protected against plagiarism. Consequently, during the last month of his life Bitter, as Society president, was able to lead an effective investigation into the illegal reproduction of a small bronze figure by the young Janet Scudder.[16]

Another perennial problem confronting the sculptor was the maintenance of fair and standard methods of competition. Certain members of the Society led by Daniel Chester French were against competitions altogether and recommended the direct selection of a sculptor to design a public monument on the basis of his past performance. Others maintained that a design should be chosen from the wide selection provided by an open competition. A compromise point of view was taken by still others who favored a closed competition in which participation was limited to a fixed number of sculptors. Considering all three methods, Bitter was of the opinion that direct selection was advisable in the case of portraiture, while a design for an ideal subject should be selected by means of a competition.[17] The official position of the Society was to recommend a controlled competition for a public work, and if a committee did not live up to the *Circular of Advice,* distributed with a sample program by the Society to guide those conducting competitions, the project was to be boycotted.

Competition in general was a much discussed topic during this age of reform, and the newly organized sculptors shared in the current concern for protecting an equality of commercial opportunity against monopoly. This problem as it applied to sculpture was brought into focus in early 1909 when a group of thirty-two young members of the Society, including Chester Beach and Solon Borglum, petitioned against "well-known abuses" of fair professional conduct and proposed a new code of ethics to prevent their continuation.[18] The code considered unprofessional such things as intentional underbidding, the use of collaborating "ghosts," and the uninvited entrance of a design into a closed competition. Consisting of eight clauses, it was handed over to a three-man committee, to which Bitter was appointed chairman, and in April a majority report recommended its adoption in slightly revised form.

Bitter, however, did not approve of placing a negative code of ethics in juxtaposition with the Society's constitution and bylaws. In fact, he was against any attempt to define or prescribe in specific terms the conduct of the professional membership and recommended that the matter be covered by the insertion of a general paragraph into the bylaws. This he believed should simply state that any member accused of unprofessional conduct affecting the good name and common interests of the Society would be investigated by a committee of three and suspended if found guilty.[19] Once again Bitter's influence won out when his recommendation was adopted as a new section in the bylaws. The proposed clauses dealing specifically with unprofessional conduct in competitions were added to the already existing code of ethics.[20]

While the National Sculpture Society worked to protect the opportunity of its individual members to compete for public projects, it also helped in promoting the establishment of governmental art commissions. As early as 1897 it actively supported an organization of prominent artists known as the Public Art League in its effort to create a federal art commission by act of Congress. According to a proposed bill, the commission would have consisted of the presidents of the American Institute of Architects, the National Academy of Design, and the National Sculpture Society, together with two laymen. Their approval was to be required for every work of art purchased, erected, or accepted as a gift by the federal government. Sculpture, painting, architecture, and landscape architecture, as well as designs for coins, seals, medals, stamps, currency, and bonds were to be under their jurisdiction. The commission, furthermore, would have been given the power to institute, organize, and direct competitions for any art work produced for government ownership.[21] In 1908 the National Sculpture Society urged the State of New York to introduce a similar art commission. It also was to include a painter, a sculptor, and an architect who would control the design and location of art works belonging to the state.[22] Although both of these efforts to place public art under government regulation failed, the Society was instrumental in the successful establishment of New York's municipal Art Commission in 1898, the same year the city became a metropolis of five boroughs.[23]

The jurisdiction of the Art Commission in New York City was so widely defined that its approval was required for any structure acquired by the city, ranging from the largest bridge or building to the smallest lamp post. However, the consent of the Park Commissioner was also necessary before a monument could be erected in any park, square, or public place in the city. For this reason, whenever a new commissioner took office, the National Sculpture Society informed him that it stood ready to furnish expert advisors in selecting, placing, and caring for the city's monuments.[24] In the spring of 1912 the Sculpture Society took vehement exception to a proposal to appoint a city custodian of art objects. Its members felt that this would be merely a political plum and offered resolutions to increase the power of the Art Commission in order to make it responsible for the maintenance of municipal art works.[25] Bitter, who had just become the sculptor member of the Commission, moved that a copy of these resolutions be sent to all of the art societies.

Three years later an even sharper protest arose from the Society when it was discovered that Saint-Gaudens' Farragut monument was being damaged by repairs undertaken independently by the Park Department. Once again its members resolved to make the Art Commission custodian of the City's major possessions, this time insisting that the City Charter be amended to that effect.[26] Bitter and French were appointed to confer with the Park Commissioner, who, while finally acquiescing to the assistance of the Society in the erection and care of monuments, insisted that they remain under his control. He was promptly reminded that such matters should be under the supervision of the Art Commission and would not be taken up by the sculptors without first seeking its advice.[27]

During the last few days of his life Bitter concentrated on this difficult tangle of administration. By relating it to the question which he first raised in 1898 of renewing and beautifying the public places and thoroughfares of New York City in accordance with a long-term plan, he brought his concern for public art full circle. On March 20, 1915, he called a special council meeting of the National Sculpture Society to report on his conference with the Park Commissioner and to discuss the monument problem in general. He had discovered that it was difficult to oppose the erection of a monument, no matter how small or insignificant, once it had been proposed in a meeting of the Art Commission. As an example, he referred to a mere flagpole on Madison Square which he had opposed, maintaining that the square should remain unaltered until it could be improved as part of a comprehensive plan of the city. While warning against any action that might conflict with the Art Commission, he suggested that a letter be addressed to George W. McAneny, President of the Board of Aldermen, requesting him to adopt a permanent method for dealing with monuments. The method could then be incorporated into the programs of several newly organized committees on city planning.

Bitter had prepared two drafts of a letter to McAneny before calling the special meeting, and one was adopted.[28] In this letter he strongly emphasized the need for a consistent plan to guide the municipal authorities in granting sites and making provisions for public monuments. As it was, whenever a group of citizens or the city itself proposed a memorial, the matter was taken up by the department into whose province that particular proposal happened to fall before it was finally passed upon by the Art Commission. With constant changes in personnel of these bodies from one administration to another, a continuous policy was virtually impossible. Bitter also stated that the current Park Commissioner, Cabot Ward, agreed that the present system was defective.

Together they maintained that the interests of the city were poorly served when, under the pressure of some powerful faction, an important site was granted to any unimportant memorial. Opposing such an occurrence was extremely difficult when no stronger argument could be advanced against it than the opinion of a city department, even if supported by the judgment of the Art Commission. Bitter was certain that an affirmative or negative ruling would be much more convincing and satisfactory if it were given on the basis of a master plan. This could correspond, "in thoroughness and authoritative substance," with the policies on which the architectural planning committees recently established by McAneny were engaged. With respect to this proposal, he wrote: "It would be possible to demonstrate on the basis of such a guiding plan, that this city must reserve certain of its most prominent squares and places for subjects which only the future can bring to ripe maturity. It would also suggest, and quite properly so, what general forms the memorials and fountains should take to give greater harmony and better presentation of public achievements than our city parks and squares and other open spaces now present."[29]

Bitter's career-long attempt to inaugurate a comprehensive plan for the sculptural ornamentation of his city was for the most part a failure. Yet it expressed his constant concern for the aesthetic welfare of the community at large. It remained a principal motivation behind his promotion and protection of sculpture as a public art in America.

XVI

Influences

BITTER'S life as a sculptor in America covered exactly twenty-five years and may for convenience of evaluation be divided into three distinct periods. The early years from 1890 to 1896 were filled with commissions from Richard Morris Hunt and two of his students. During this period of concentrated wealth and patronage Bitter executed an elaborate style of Viennese baroque sculpture that he had learned firsthand as a student in his native Austria. Next came works more modest in scale and scope. Nevertheless, the groups and figures he designed for buildings and monuments throughout this second period, between 1896 and 1906, continued to be essentially baroque in tradition. The architectural sculpture belonged to large decorative schemes carried out in collaboration with fellow members of the National Sculpture Society to meet the specifications of the architects in charge. It was only when he could take over a project, completely free to embellish a building or monument with whatever design of sculpture he wished, that independence of style emerged. The year 1907 marks the beginning of this third period, cut short by sudden death in 1915.

The decoration of the Cuyahoga County Courthouse in 1909 with standing figures in period costume was the only joint effort in which Bitter participated as a sculptor during this final period. That he must have developed a dislike for collaborating with other sculptors is revealed in the terms he demanded before agreeing to become director of sculpture for the Panama-Pacific Exposition in San Francisco. In the autumn of 1912 he drew up his own contract to provide a general scheme of sculpture for the buildings and grounds, just as he had done for the expositions in Buffalo and St. Louis. However, he refused to go to the exposition grounds to supervise the execution of his scheme. Instead he named Alexander Stirling Calder acting chief of the Department of Sculpture to represent him.[1] What is more significant, Bitter declined to contribute any works of sculpture to the embellishment of the Fair, and thereby avoided a collaboration with his colleagues altogether.

Until he had an opportunity to apply sculpture to structures that were largely his own design, the development of his mature style took place within a very conventional context of academic Beaux-Arts architecture. It first appeared in the pediment of the Cleveland Trust Company where, in a uniquely composed high-relief, Bitter fashioned the central figure in an idealized, classicistic form accompanied by a decorative pattern of leaves. From then on, his allegorical architectural figures and their accessories, while always based on a close observation of nature, became increasingly stylized. Newly discovered Greek archaic sculpture provided a variety of models for this purpose, and after his visit to Athens in 1910, he took greater advantage of this source in his freestanding groups on the Wisconsin capitol and in designing the Schurz monument reliefs.

In addition to searching out a period of ancient art as an aid in developing his own style, Bitter was also inspired by certain forms of contemporary architectural sculpture in Europe. He was in constant communication with Austria, and during the summers of 1906, 1909, and 1910 he made trips abroad. The first took him as far as Munich and Leipzig, while the last two, following his pardon as a deserter, were to his native city. In the journal that he kept throughout a month-long visit early in the summer of 1909, Bitter reported an art exhibition in Vienna where he felt "vulgarity and degeneracy" were predominant. He wrote that this was just the thing he wanted to avoid "by taking the road to Greece."[2] However, he also recorded that the exhibition included "some splendid things by Franz Metzner and Hugo Lederer."

Upon leaving Austria, Bitter went to Leipzig where he visited the huge Voelkerschlacht monument by Bruno Schmitz and Metzner. It was still under construction at the time, and he merely commented that it was a very imposing structure.[3] Two days later he was in Berlin and once more saw the work of Schmitz and Metzner when he dined in the Haus Rheingold Restaurant.[4] Mention of Lederer was made again over a year later when Bitter served as a juror in the competition for a Goethe monument to be erected in Lincoln Park, Chicago. While Lederer's design did not win, Bitter expressed his admiration for the Austrian-born sculptor and wrote that "he especially knows how to deal with architectural forms."[5]

Though Bitter's sculpture never approached the imposing proportions attained by that of Metzner and Lederer, its increased monumentality resulted from methods closely related to those developed by his two fellow Austrians. The most basic of these was the generalization of the human figure as an integral member of a structural scheme. It is obvious, however, that Bitter did not carry this process to the point of architectural abstraction reached by either Lederer or Metzner. He did not anthropomorphize functional parts of a structure as Metzner did in carving huge mask-like faces on the pillars of the Voelkerschlacht monument and the Haus Rheingold. He refrained from distorting the proportions of a human figure beyond an ideal norm. Also, Metzner's use of whimsical double images found no place in his compositions. Nevertheless, the last phase of Bitter's career reveals a growing concern for designing sculpture in conjunction with an architectural structure rather than merely applying an energetic figure, or group of figures, to the surface of a wall as an added embellishment. Often working within a setting of conventional architecture, he composed, for example, pediment groups as single cohesive reliefs instead of repeating the classical method of placing separate figures in a row. A comparable technique was used by Metzner in designing the decorative reliefs of figures and foliage for the gables of the Haus Tietz, a department store in Düsseldorf.

Bitter's admiration for the works of Lederer and Metzner reflects his sympathy for experimentation in architectural sculpture. Late in 1909 he wrote, "It is the younger people from whom we expect the extraordinary (*Besondere*), even if the extraordinary dares to change, as is the case with the innovators (*Neueren*) in Europe."[6] Two years earlier, however, he had confessed that while he attempted to maintain an open mind toward all contemporary trends in art, his training tempered his tolerance. In a letter to Kestranek he stated, "You are a modern with all the *Morgenroth* that this expression conceals. . . . I belong to the modern in longing and spirit (if I dare discuss it in general), but not in education and development."[7]

Although Bitter does not specify exactly what he means by "modern," it is safe to assume that he would not have been able to accept the works of such avant-garde sculptors as Gaudier-Brzeska, Archipenko, or Brancusi as being anything but decadent. Their distortions of the human figure sometimes suggest a primitive inspiration, and Bitter called primitive sculpture "Haschish" in contrast to the sculpture of fifth-century Greece and the Italian Renaissance.[8] Furthermore, he believed that a great style of sculpture evolved gradually from generation to generation rather than springing spontaneously from the inventive genius of an individual artist. He argued that the peculiar beauty of Greek sculpture, especially the archaic style, could not be attributed to "pure invention." On the contrary, it resulted from a chance conjunction of certain traditions, techniques, and materials.

"The simplicity of the archaistic forms," he wrote, "is not a product of free will, but of constraint from the material. Also, tradition produces technique, and technique alone renders richer fashioning possible. Thus we see the step-by-step perfection of a motive and new motives add themselves to new themes only timidly. However, as the material is brought under control, motives are able to evolve in a natural manner. As far as I am acquainted with the antique, nothing suddenly appears by itself as a completely perfected form." Bitter warned that he offered no foolproof formula for a beautiful style, but mainly an explanation for the initial growth of classical sculpture. For contrast, even though the sculpture of the Aztecs, Indians, and Japanese also evolved as gradual, continuous traditions, he considered them far removed from "the greatness and purity of the Greeks."[9]

These same ideas and opinions were advanced in a long lecture entitled "Observations on Ancient and Modern Processes Employed in the Production of Monumental Sculpture" which Bitter delivered on February 28, 1914, at the annual exhibition of the Architectural League of New York.[10] In defense of tradition in art he calls attention to the similarities among early Greek figures. These result, especially in architectural sculpture, not from the fact that a figure was carved with the aid of a plaster model but by means of "descriptive instruments," that is, templets or patterns bequeathed from father to son. Standard forms and types were transferred from one generation to the next, and while a style was gradually refined. there was little interest in uniqueness.

Bitter was concerned about the possible failure of contemporary sculptors to retain the traditional methods of the medium, and exhorted the young to respect the technical accomplishments of their classical predecessors, both ancient and Renaissance. As great masters they had for one thing possessed a thorough knowledge of architecture, as well as sculpture, and to them a figure or group became monumental only as it was integrated with a larger structure. Unfortunately this "healthy relation of the arts" diminished in the eighteenth century with the growth of an open art market, the art exhibition, the academy, and the museum. "Different aims began to separate the arts more and more. The architect took up primarily the housing problem; the sculptor, the modeling of saleable statues and statuettes; and the painter, the gold framed canvasses. The sculptor, coming only occasionally into contact with the architect, devoted himself more and more exclusively to modeling things which would not require foundations and structural bases and frames. He was not trained to mingle with the architect; he was a 'Master' no longer, but a 'statuaire;' this distinguished him from his craftsmen brothers, to whom he left the more mechanical and technical things connected with structure."

The architect, according to Bitter, may still know how to design monumental buildings but he is no longer aware of the possibilities of sculpture, except as a "sort of luxurious dressing." Most often the sculptor is called upon to produce a statue in some historical style, "ala Gothic, or Jean Goujon, or Carpeaux, as the case may be." But seldom do the architect and sculptor work together with supplementing ideas, taste, and expression. "We have modern works, the unity of which delight and inspire, but they are not so much the rule as formerly. More often out of such collaboration we get creations which remind us of some famous work of the past, not by its wonderful and masterly conception and execution, but rather by the adoption of certain forms and details with which we are familiar."

Thus, while Bitter disliked the imitation of historical prototypes, he distrusted the ends and means of contemporary, avant-garde art. Consequently he participated in change as a cautious traditionalist dedicated to Europe's classical heritage rather than as a past-defying revolutionist. When he altered the style of his own architectural sculpture after 1906, he did not forsake his ability to represent nature. He simply ceased to exploit the pliable nature of clay for reproduction in soft stone. He thereby abandoned the energetic poses, complex drapery folds, and much of the realistically rendered detail that characterized the baroque compositions of his youth. To replace these for his new work in granite, he combined certain linear motives discovered in Greek archaic sculpture with his own stylization of the human figure and allegorical accessories. In turning to newly unearthed examples of archaic sculpture for techniques to employ in his own sculpture, Bitter helped inaugurate a revival of interest in early classical art that had had no precedent since ancient times. This interest soon became widespread enough to compete with the sustained influence of Rodin. It can be seen, for instance, in the archaicism of the German sculptors Joseph Wackerle, Hermann Haller, and Karl Krikawa.

From America's community of sculptors the young Paul Manship followed Bitter's footsteps on a pilgrimage to Greece in 1912. Returning to Rome, where he was studying at the American Academy, he read a paper entitled "The Decorative Value of Greek Sculpture." Although he did not share Bitter's interest in the evolution of style, he did provide a good, concise description of archaic sculpture. "It is the decorative value of the line that is considered first. Nature is formalized to conform with the artist's idea of beauty. Just as the sculptor in modeling foliated forms to be used in architectural decoration reduced nature to its decorative essence and considered the relationship of lines and masses rather than reality, so in these statues the artist has subordinated everything to his formal composition. The entire statue can be considered as a decorative form upon which all the detail is drawn rather than modeled."[11]

A few months later Manship was back in New York where his application of archaic characteristics was exhibited in a group of small bronze figures. Since this was the same year that Bitter completed the relief panels for the Schurz monument, it is clear that he and Manship were moving in a similar direction simultaneously. However, Bitter had already applied archaistic details to his heroic figures on the Wisconsin capitol building, and even before Manship left for Rome in 1909, Bitter had revealed his knowledge of Greek archaic sculpture in the central figure of the west pediment in Madison. At that time Manship was an assistant to the Vienna-born Isidore Konti who was in continual contact with Bitter, and it is entirely possible that through this association Manship's interest in Greek archaic sculpture was awakened before he left for Italy and Greece.[12]

At any rate, Bitter was apparently the first sculptor in America to apply archaic motives to his work. It was not until approximately ten years later that this practice became associated with the students who followed Manship to the American Academy in Rome. Of these, Sherry Fry, John Gregory, and Carl Jennewein were three of the most prominent, developing a neoclassical style dependent largely on archaic sculpture. Older sculptors of Bitter's generation, led by Adolph Weinman and Alexander Stirling Calder, also found a way to more concise compositions of precisely patterned forms through the archaicism planted in America by Bitter and nurtured by Manship.

Aside from ushering in a classical revival based on Greek archaic sculpture, Bitter's mature architectural sculpture assumed a "secessionist" monumentality that anticipated a major trend in America after World War I. This postwar trend was led by Lee Lawrie, whose sculpture for Bertram Goodhue's Nebraska state capitol was recognized as a direct descendant of Bitter's late work by the classsicist Walter Agard soon after that building was completed. Crediting Bitter with the invention of a technique suitable for such smooth, streamlined surfaces, Agard states that Bitter's Schurz monument reliefs "demonstrated the value of flat-faced, sharply recessed relief in keeping the walls clean and the sculpture consistent with its architectural setting. What he did on a small scale, Lawrie projected for an entire building."[13]

Further comparison may be made between the open-air reliefs on the Lowry Monument and the three panels depicting the Magna Charta, the Declaration of Independence, and the Constitution on the south façade of the Nebraska capitol building. While Lawrie's historical figures are carved from Indiana limestone rather than granite, they resemble Bitter's two allegorical figures in their stylization. Hair, hands, facial features, and drapery folds are abstracted into concise, sometimes angular shapes. Even more revealing, Lawrie adopted Bitter's innovation of piercing the stone to allow light to enter from both sides, silhouetting the enclosed relief figures. Such direct stylistic influence was eventually absorbed into the compromised classicism that is still procreated by the academic carvers and modelers of the National Sculpture Society. But at least for a moment Bitter's experiments with architecturally consonant forms were adopted as a sincere attempt to establish a conservative, modern sculpture.

Epilogue

IN 1916, Alexander Stirling Calder wrote a concise firsthand sketch of his friend Karl Bitter. While it was meant to be commemorative, it is an essentially accurate account of the man's personality, at least as it appeared on the surface to a close associate. A copy of the following tribute is in the correspondence files of the National Sculpture Society. The original was presumably written at the request of Ferdinand Schevill, who had asked that Bitter's friends contribute material for a biography.

"There can be no doubt that Karl Bitter was an extraordinary person. If a word could describe the qualities by which complex character is expressed, I would say that the essence of his character and contribution to Art might be summarized under the word fluency—dominating fluency—lavish, nervous, searching fluency. Through all his activities, in all his works, this insistence on action with grace is expressed again and again, and finally remains with me as the residue of his influence.

"His work covers a wide range in treatment, the earlier periods characterized by qualities more descriptive and pictorial; the later work by larger sculptural unity. Among his many splendid things of brilliant conception most sculptors will probably agree that his statue of Dr. Pepper is one of his finest, if not his *finest* work, and I find the types of the caryatides on the Metropolitan Museum very noble.

"The intimate period of my friendship with him was very brief but vivid. It began in the spring of 1912. I had known him for years before and retain pleasant memories of a few meetings with him during the development of the sculpture for the St. Louis Exposition, of which he had charge, but until 1912 our paths had not converged. He was continually active in many affairs, I am by comparison hermitical. My return from the West, toward the end of 1909, with keen interest in the renewal of work in the East induced a greater expansiveness that paved the way for our riper acquaintance. A few accidental meetings and talks developed a cordiality and frankness between us that was only terminated by his sudden death. I cannot but regard the instant attraction and sympathy that thus sprung up as extraordinary. Circumstances had a part in it, but the important factor was Bitter's fearlessness and generosity. Few sculptors have been so helpful to members of the profession as was he during his crowded career. He lived a full life and helped others to live with many a keen word of genuine interest, of human kindliness, and of weighty encouragement.

"A broad, impressionable artist, able to accept many different types of products, I remember his laughing retort during an argument charging that I was not so broad as he. Quick to recognize merit, brave to voice conviction, generous to assume inconvenience in advancing the interests of his less fortunate confreres. These qualities combined with a certain dispatch, an alert promptness, native quality, trained by years of executive experience stamped Bitter as a power in Art. My recollections of him are nearly all during an active period of work. I knew him always as an intelligent, positive, serious force in action; it was a free buoyant action with little trace of anxiety. Sure of himself, he never pushed his advantage too far. He could compromise when necessary and had the power of making the best of the inevitable without rancour.

"I would call Bitter's a practical genius. The kind that achieves. He consciously or unconsciously followed Polonius's advice, giving 'only proportioned thoughts their acts,' and no man knew his dreams. He had little of the dreamer in his composition that did not find expression, certainly none of a thwarted ambition that might have begot moroseness.

"He was a man of wide information from many surprising sources, scientific and political principally, and could talk interestingly on those subjects. In fact, if a word be needed to describe his qualities further, I would say that he was the true type of the ready man that conversation develops.

I made two transcontinental trips with him and recall many themes and theories touched en-voyage that proved wide reading, ready memory, and power to appropriate and use what he had acquired.

"He always retained a slight foreign accent in English, but of a kind that rather lent distinction to his conversation. His physical bearing was marked by a carriage almost military, but without stiffness.

"I believe that Bitter viewed his art and considered all art from a social-political basis. That is, he considered that the progressive democracy of a people must be expressed in its art.

"Eccentricities in achievement or decadent manifestations found little sympathy with him; timidity distressed him. He admired power but withal had a strong vein of sentiment which at times bordered on weakness. He was as just a man as I have ever known, rarely betraying national bias and although positive in assertion and impatient of ignorance, was open to argument and the conviction of right.

"Professionally his thorough grasp of both technical and executive detail was amazing. He was at once both economical and lavish following a conceived plan of achievement in any large project.

"His correspondence was distinguished by the same qualities as his conversation. Promptness, thoroughness, and tireless humanity filled its pages. He relished a certain formality in the business and pleasures of life and soon tired of laxity or undue levity.

"His friend Dr. Frederick Skiff once remarked to me that 'Bitter was a good judge of men' and he added, 'He is your friend.'

"I cherish the memory of that friendship.

> " 'He was a man, take him for all in all
> I shall not look upon his like again.'

A. Stirling Calder
May 16, 1916"

REFERENCE MATTER

Notes

INTRODUCTION

1 John Sloan, however, refers to Bitter in his diary which he kept from January, 1906, to April, 1913. On June 17, 1906, Sloan made his first trip to the heights of the Hudson at Weehawken to visit Henry Reuterdahl, a painter of naval scenes and seascapes. He recorded: "The popular sculptor, Bitter, has a house that rises sheer from the cliffs." On September 20 and 25, 1909, during the Hudson-Fulton Celebration, Sloan went to Bitter's Weehawken house where Reuterdahl was staying. Robert Henri was also there on the 25th. See Bruce St. John, ed., *John Sloan's New York Scene* (New York, 1965), pp. 42, 335, 336.

2 This portrait is in the possession of Emerson's niece, Mrs. A. W. Penniman, of Saratoga, California. Also in California is a small, marble, low-relief portrait of Josephine Crane Bradley, daughter of the wealthy reformer Charles R. Crane. It belongs to Dr. Harold C. Bradley of Berkeley and represents his wife in profile with head gently bowed.

Other examples of small commemorative works:

a) Memorial relief portrait panel of Ensign Joseph Cabell Breckenridge, *ca.* 1900, location unknown.

b) Allegorical medallion in memory of Dr. Fritz Schwyzer, 1901, location unknown.

c) Memorial relief portrait of Antoinette Seilern, *ca.* 1902, location unknown.

d) Memorial portrait tablet dedicated to Edward M. Brown of the New York Fruit Exchange, 1904, location unknown.

e) Decorative relief panel of six children for the C. Goodyear residence, before 1904, Buffalo, N.Y.

f) Commemorative relief portrait panel of Kirby Spencer, marble, 1906, Minneapolis Public Library.

g) Alexander Cassatt, equestrian portrait relief, 1911, Pennsylvania Railroad, Philadelphia.

h) Pair of allegorical tablets dedicated to John Herron, 1911, John Herron Art Institute, Indianapolis, Indiana.

i) Allegorical medallion commemorating Robert Curtis Ogden, educator, on his seventieth birthday, location unknown.

j) Bust of scientist, Morris Loeb, date and location unknown.

3 Letter from Bitter to Hans Kestranek, Oct. 1, 1905.

4 The Kesseler plaque is installed near the high altar of St. Joseph's Church, West 125th Street.

5 The old Criminal Court Building was torn down and replaced a few years ago, and the Tomb's Angel plaque apparently vanished with it.

6 This poem was enclosed in a letter to Mrs. Bitter.

7 Letter from Bitter to his wife, July 29, 1903.

8 Scrapbook-diary, entry dated April 16, 1899.

9 Letter from Bitter to his wife, Feb. 19, 1912.

10 The quotations are from a letter from Bitter to Hans Kestranek, March 15, 1914.

11 An indication of the support among German intellectuals for the cause of the fatherland is suggested by Henry F. May in his very useful study of this period, *The End of American Innocence* (New York, 1964), p. 362. Among ninety-three intellectuals who published a manifesto defending Germany in October, 1914, was the science-philosopher Ernst Haeckel. He was the author of the materialistic doctrine of Monism, a scientific pantheism, to which Bitter subscribed.

12 Bitter's journal of his first return trip to Austria, from June 5 to July 8, 1909; entry dated June 17, 1909.

13 *Ibid.*, June 27, 1909.

14 The war quickly became a depressing distraction that Bitter protested against in a letter to Daniel Chester French at the beginning of the year. "I am made sick at heart by the pleadings of the warring nations for their cause. The conflict of emotions is too much for me, and I avoid it. I cannot get myself to believe that any possible justification can be found for the blight which has befallen the best on earth. I welcome, with you and many others, the New Year which must bring us nearer to the end of this awful conflict." —Letter from Bitter to Daniel Chester French, Jan. 2, 1915 (Correspondence Files, National Sculpture Society, New York City).

CHAPTER I

1 A copy of Bitter's baptismal certificate is among his personal effects now in the possession of his son, Dr. Francis Bitter, Centerville, Mass.

2 This information appears in an unpublished autobiographical sketch dated June, 1896, which is included in the scrapbook-diary that Bitter kept during the 1890's.

3 *Ibid.*

4 Certificates from the Vorberreitungschule des K. u. K. Oesterreichischen Museums fuer Kunst und Industrie are in the possession of Dr. Francis Bitter.

5 Scrapbook-diary, autobiographical sketch.

6 Scrapbook-diary, March 11, 1897.

7 Bitter's student *Bescheinigung* from Die Kaiserlich-Koenigliche Akademie der Bildenden Kunst is in the possession of Dr. Francis Bitter.

8 Scrapbook-diary, autobiographical sketch.

9 Hans Kestranek, "Karl Bitter," *Kunst und Kunsthandwerk,* XXIII (Vienna, 1920), 77.

10 The *Urlaubschein* issued Sept. 11, 1889, by Infantry Regiment No. 84 is in the possession of Dr. Francis Bitter.

11 Ferdinand Schevill, *Karl Bitter: A Biography* (University of Chicago Press, 1917), p. 10.

12 *Ibid.,* p. 20.

13 For photograph see Andrew Tully, *Era of Elegance* (New York, 1947), p. 77.

14 Russell Sturgis, "A Review of the Work of George B. Post," *The Architectural Record,* Great American Architects Series, No. 4 (June, 1898), pp. 83–86.

15 The subjects of the Gold Room panels are the Birth of Venus, the nymph Deianira abducted by the centaur Nessus, Herakles aiming his bow and arrow at Nessus, and Poseidon with Thetis. For a description of Marble House see the guide pamphlet written by Henry Hope Reed, Jr., in 1965, published through the Preservation Society of Newport County.

16 The Diana relief was destroyed by fire along with the house in the fall of 1898.

17 Sculptural ornamentations for Hunt's Columbian Exposition Administration Building and Frank Furness' Broad Street Station in Philadelphia were the largest projects carried out by Bitter during his first five years in America. These are discussed in Chapters II and III, respectively.

18 Sturgis, in *The Architectural Record,* No. 4, p. 56; illustrated on pp. 61–63.

19 *Biltmore House and Gardens* (Asheville, N.C., 1959), p. 8.

20 Oliver W. Larkin, *Art and Life in America* (New York, 1949), p. 314. In a passing reference to Bitter, Oliver Larkin chooses to condemn him as "a cheerful plagiarist who copied Michelangelo's David for a pair of Vanderbilt andirons . . . ." Of all the figures involved in these comparatively minor, fireplace ornaments, only the figurine of Vulcan could possibly resemble the famous marble statue. However, aside from its proportions being similar to those of the High Renaissance nude, Bitter's Vulcan is not a replica. First of all, it bears down on its left leg instead of its right whose foot is pushed back to form a stride. The right arm is held low at the side to support a long-handled hammer. The left arm is bent, but the position of its hand in grasping the chin of a straight forward face, as well as the even height of the shoulders, is hardly close enough to Michelangelo's composition to war-

rant the accusation of plagiarism. If Bitter did use a Renaissance figure as a model, he might very well have looked at Nicola Pisano's proto-Renaissance figure of Fortitudo on the pulpit in the Baptistery of Pisa. It is much more similar in pose to his Vulcan figurine than Michelangelo's David, and was itself obviously based on an ancient prototype.

21 Scrapbook-diary, Jan. 25, 1898: "Ich, der Lump, nun Hausbesitzer, Grundeigenthuemer, wie wollte ich dass meinen Herrn Papa ganz deutlich machen."

22 Letters from Bitter to George Emerson, datelined Geneva, Dec. 14, 1895, and Rome, Jan. 3, 1896. These are in the possession of Dr. Francis Bitter.

23 Scrapbook-diary, June 8, 1899.

24 *Ibid.,* April 29, 1899.

CHAPTER II

1 The *World,* Dec. 10, 1890; see souvenir supplement entitled "Pulitzer Building."

2 *Ibid.*

3 Hans Kestranek, "Karl Bitter," *Kunst and Kunsthandwerk,* XXIII (Vienna, 1920), 81.

4 Albums of photographs taken of Bitter's sculpture are in the possession of his daughter, Mrs. Walter Abel, New York City.

5 Exactly when and why the four bronze female figures disappeared so soon after the completion of the building, no one has yet discovered.

6 *A History of the Parish of Trinity Church in the City of New York,* ed. Leicester C. Lewis (New York, 1950), pp. 188–90.

7 Bitter did one relief for a tympanum above the main entrance of Post's Manufactures and Liberal Arts Building. The entrance was inside a porch based on the triumphal Arch of Constantine, and the relief consisted of an enthroned female figure accompanied by an allegorical figure on either side. This relief is illustrated in *Century Illustrated Monthly Magazine,* XLIV (May, 1892), 398.

8 Henry Van Brunt, "Architecture at the Columbian Exposition," *Century Illustrated Monthly Magazine,* XLIV (May, 1892), 94.

9 *Ibid.,* pp. 92–93.

10 For a picture of Permoser's Prince Eugene of Dresden as a Feldherr with Hercules, Victory, Fame, and a fallen Turk, see Bruno Grimschitz, *Ars Austriae* (Vienna, 1960), plate 147.

11 For well-photographed examples of the groups on the Administration Building, see illustrations in J. B. Campbell, *Campbell's Illustrated History of the World's Columbian Exposition* (Philadelphia, 1894), I, 116, 121, 139, 153, 160, 182. See also Figure 108.

12 Homer Saint-Gaudens, ed., *The Reminiscences of August Saint-Gaudens* (New York, 1913), II, 75.

13 The quotations in this paragraph are from Van Brunt, in *Century Illustrated Monthly Magazine,* XLIV, 88.

Fig. 108.—Completion of a group in staff, Administration Building, Columbian Exposition, Chicago, 1892.

14 Ferdinand Schevill, *Karl Bitter: A Biography* (University of Chicago Press, 1917), p. 25.

15 Kestranek, in *Kunst und Kunsthandwerk,* XXIII, 82.

16 An invitation was printed for a viewing of the finished doors to be held on June 25–30, 1894, at Henry-Bonnard Bronze Co., New York City. (A copy is in the files of the National Sculpture Society, New York.)

17 Bitter provided recognition to this antecedent on a menu printed for a dinner party given to celebrate the completion of the doors. One of the dishes served was prepared "ala Ghiberti."

CHAPTER III

1 J. Elfreth Watkins, *History of the Pennsylvania Railroad Company, 1864–1896* (Philadelphia, 1896), II, 52. The Broad Street Station was closed on April 27, 1952, and torn down immediately.

2 William Campbell, "Frank Furness: An American Pioneer," *Architectural Review,* CX (July–Dec., 1951), 312.

3 Watkins, II, 53.

4 The *Philadelphia Bulletin,* July 30, 1923, reported the removal of the panels after a fire destroyed the shed.

5 Watkins, II, 52.

6 *New York Times,* quoted by Campbell, in *Architectural Review,* CX, 312.

7 Campbell, p. 312.

8 Quoted in Watkins, II, 52; source unspecified.

9 Watkins, II, 52.

10 Quoted in Watkins, II, 52; source unspecified.

11 Quoted in Watkins, II, 52; source unspecified.

12 *Philadelphia Evening Bulletin,* Jan. 11, 1933, reports that this panel was moved to the new Thirtieth Street Station in 1933.

13 William Bender Wilson, *From the Hudson to the Ohio and Other Sketches* (New York, 1902), p. 157.

14 Anna Raster-Hercz, "Karl Bitter, Ein Deutsch-Amerikanischer Bildhauer," *Die Glocke,* II (June, 1907), 148–49.

15 The original owner of the building was H. O. Havemeyer, the art-collecting founder and controller of the sugar trust, The American Sugar Refining Company.

16 The atlantes were given to the City of Indianapolis in 1958 when the St. Paul Building was demolished to make way for the new Western Electric Building. Several years later the figures were placed on an artificial ruins constructed for them in Holiday Park.

17 Russell Sturgis, "A Review of the Work of George B. Post," *Architectural Record,* Great American Architects Series, No. 4 (June, 1898), p. 22.

18 The bank building is the main office of the Cleveland Trust, Cleveland, Ohio. While the pediment is modest, its sculpture is an important work in Bitter's career and is discussed in Chapter VII.

CHAPTER IV

1 Karl Bitter's scrapbook-diary, entry dated Jan. 28, 1898.

2 Ferdinand Schevill, *Karl Bitter: A Biography* (University of Chicago Press, 1917), p. 39.

3 Bitter's first portrait monument is of Dr. William Pepper, president of the University of Pennsylvania. It is discussed in Chapter V.

4 Scrapbook-diary entries during September, 1897, and August, 1898.

5 See Henry Hope Reed, Jr., *The Appellate Division of the Supreme Court of the State of New York, First Judicial Department* (New York, 1957), a pamphlet published by the Municipal Art Society of New York. Of the $633,768 allocated for the building, $422,468 was for construction; $157,000 for statuary; and $54,300 for mural painting.

6 "Public Art in New York," *Municipal Affairs,* III (Sept.–Dec., 1899), 758: "The architect, Mr. James Brown Lord, of New York City, is to be credited not merely with all architectural features, but also with the general scheme of decoration, interior and exterior, all of which was included in his original plan for the building, and which, to her great good fortune, the City of New York, under authority of the legislature, permitted him to carry out, leaving him full freedom in the choice of the other art workers who cooperated."

7 Scrapbook-diary, June 26, 1899.

8 Lorado Taft, *The History of American Sculpture* (New York, 1924), p. 421.

9 *Municipal Affairs,* III, 755–58.

10 The ground plan of the arch was 70 feet in length across Fifth Avenue, 35 feet in breadth over the axis of Twenty-fourth Street, and 85 feet to the top of the attic story.

11 Scrapbook-diary, July 27, 1899. Bitter, who was a member of the National Sculpture Society committee appointed to approach the city officials concerning the Society's desire to contribute something sculptural to the Dewey Reception, reports that for a while the prospects for their project were not very bright. This was changed, however, when General Butterfield, chairman of the Dewey Reception Committee; Mr. Clausen, president of the Park Commission; Mr. Guggenheimer, president of the Borough of Manhattan; and members of the National Sculpture Society committee held a meeting on the yacht of Lewis Nixon. Nixon was a right-hand man to Richard Croker, the boss of Tammany and therefore of the machine's man in office, Mayor Van Wyck. After this meeting on July 27 the project no longer had any difficulty in being supported by the city.

12 *Municipal Affairs,* III, 755–58. The hurried erection of the Dewey Arch was a popular attraction for New Yorkers, and the continuous crowds were reported to have numbered in the tens of thousands—enough to fill large portions of Madison Square and to make it almost impossible at times for the trolley cars and other vehicles to make their way through the area.

13 The other three pier groups were designed by Daniel Chester French, Philip Martiny, and Charles B. Niehaus.

14 The Dewey Arch came close to being remade in stone as a permanent monument. A private committee was organized for this purpose, but when it failed to raise enough money the remnant of the temporary arch was declared a public nuisance by the New York Board of Health in December, 1900, and torn down. Fragments were shipped to Charleston for the South Carolina Interstate and West Indian Exposition. In January, 1901, a second attempt was made by the United States Naval Academy Alumni Association to have the arch reconstructed in marble on Battery Park as a monument to the Navy. This plan was also abandoned, and finally a wealthy banker named J. Kennedy Tod bought whatever remained of the arch for his summer estate at Sound Beach near Stamford, Conn. See New York newspapers for Dec. 5–22, 1900; Jan. 12–20, 1901; and March 1–18, 1901.

15 Winifred E. Howe, *A History of the Metropolitan Museum of Art* (New York, 1913), II, 276.

16 Albert Ten Eyck Gardner, "Those Blocks," *Metropolitan Museum of Art Bulletin,* XI, (May, 1953), 254. Gardner quotes from a letter written by Hunt.

17 *Ibid.*

18 Scrapbook-diary, Feb. 6, 1899.

19 Illustrated in the Gardner article in *Metropolitan Museum of Art Bulletin,* XI, 256. The head is most likely meant to be that of Minerva, Goddess of the City and protector of civilized life.

20 Bitter finished the caryatid sketches on June 27, 1899 (scrapbook-diary).

21 Oliver W. Larkin, *Art and Life in America* (New York, 1949), p. 392. This does not justify the dismissal of Bitter's figures by Oliver Larkin as "four quotations from Goujon," for they bear only an incidental resemblance to anything the French Mannerist is known to have produced, including the famous relief figures on the *Fontaine des Innocents.* Even the armless caryatids on Goujon's *Tribune des Caryatides* in the Louvre are Mannerist adaptations of the Erechtheion figures, and they consequently support an entablature on their heads.

22 These works by Giambologna are now in the Palazzo dell' Universita in Genoa.

23 William Walton, "An Alliance of Architecture and Sculpture," *The Outlook,* XCII (June 26, 1909), 463.

24 *Ibid.,* p. 464.

CHAPTER V

1 "The New Museum Buildings," *University of Pennsylvania Bulletin,* III, No. 9 (June 1, 1899), p. 378. With the construction of a new intersection, the Pepper monument was removed several years ago and for a long time sat beneath the bleachers of Franklin Stadium. It has now been reinstated to the campus, and stands in front of the University Museum.

2 Karl Bitter's scrapbook-diary of the 1890's, entry dated June 12, 1899.

Fig. 109.—Sketch model for Soldiers' monument competition, for Albany, New York, 1909.

3 Edward P. Cheyney, *History of University of Pennsylvania* (Philadelphia, 1940), p. 354.

4 *New York Mail & Express,* March 12, 1900.

5 *Ibid.,* March 14, 1900.

6 Scrapbook-diary, Feb. 17, 1899.

7 *Ibid.,* Feb. 18, 1899.

8 *Ibid.,* Feb. 20, 1899.

9 The sketch is pasted into the scrapbook-diary, and underneath it Bitter has written, "My first sketch for Lafayette Monument," Feb 28, 1899.

10 The deceased were Thomas W., Frank A., and Albert Cornell, respectively.

11 Just before his death in 1900 Hubbard had secured the gratitude of his townsmen by providing the capitol city with a public library on land contributed from his extensive real estate holdings.

12 Letters from Bitter to Hans Kestranek, Nov. 29, 1901, and April 13, 1902.

13 Letter from Bitter to Kestranek, Feb. 10, 1902.

14 *Proceedings upon the Unveiling of the Statue of Baron von Steuben,* ed. George H. Carter (Washington: U.S. Printing Office, 1912), p. 170.

15 *Ibid.,* p. 9.

16 Letter from Bitter to his wife, May 6, 1909. That Bitter would mention his disappointment over the Steuben monument three years after losing the competition does not necessarily suggest sour grapes. In fact he was very objective about such decisions when he considered the winning design a good one. Only a day before, he had written to Mrs. Bitter about a competition for a Soldiers' monument in Albany, New York. His entry, in the form of a small sketch, represented a return from battle with two wounded men riding a horse accompanied by six tattered foot soldiers (see Fig. 109). The group

was designed for a high pedestal to be placed in the center of a platform flanked by circular benches. Without mentioning his proposal, however, Bitter praised the design of Hermon MacNeil which he thought should win and harshly criticized a design by Adolph A. Weinman for its contradictions of the real and the ideal: "In the center a woman on horseback, astride in the saddle—na, hoeren Sie! Alongside a baby boy with his military father, in front some other Greek lady, etc., a regular fritto misto of goddesses and soldiers and what seems their offspring. Einfach laecherlich, and I told him so, which made him quite hot."—Bitter to his wife, May 5, 1909.

17 For photograph see *Proceedings,* ed. Carter.

18 In a letter to his wife written in St. Louis and dated Feb. 13, 1904, Bitter refers to a proposal for a monument to General Sigel in that city. Monuments were also planned in Cincinnati, Milwaukee, Philadelphia, Baltimore, and Washington.

19 *New York Daily Tribune,* Oct. 26, 1902.

20 *Monumental News* (Madison, Wis.; Feb., 1904).

21 *New York Times,* March 17, 1907.

22 *New York Herald,* June 4, 1905. The committee left the choice of a site somewhere in New York City completely up to Bitter.

23 To get the horse to pose in this position, Bitter is said to have tied an apple around the animal's neck.

CHAPTER VI

1 John M. Carrere, "The Architectural Scheme," *Art Hand Book: Official Handbook to the Pan-American Exposition* (Buffalo, 1901), pp. 12–17.

2 *Ibid.,* p.13.

3 *New York Evening Post,* July 6, 1907.

4 Karl Bitter, "The Sculpture Plan," *Art Hand Book,* p. 49.

5 For a list of the architects, see "Catalogue of Buildings," *Art Hand Book,* p. 34.

6 Bitter, *Art Hand Book,* pp. 51–52.

7 For a list of the sculptors of each work, see "Catalogue of Sculpture," *Art Hand Book,* pp. 55–80.

8 Delaware Park was a picturesque landscape consisting of an irregularly shaped lake in the middle of a naturalistic woods designed several years before by Frederick Law Olmsted.

9 Bitter, *Art Hand Book,* p. 53.

10 *Ibid.,* p.58.

11 Letter from Bitter to his wife, May 19, 1901. Bitter wrote this on the day the first of the standard-bearers was unveiled.

12 Charles M. Kurtz, *Saint Louis World's Fair* (St. Louis, 1903), pp. 17–19. The over-all cost of the buildings and exhibitions as appropriated by the participating states and countries was at least four times the initiating amount of $15 million.

13 *Congressional Record,* 56th Cong., 2d Sess., 1901, XXXIV, part 3, 2585.

14 Kurtz, p. 18.
15 *Ibid.*, p. 20.
16 *Ibid.*, p. 39. While Isaac Taylor, a local architect, was appointed Director of Works, Masqueray was the Chief of Design.
17 For a drawing of the Festival Hall, Terrace of the States, and Cascade Gardens by Masqueray, see *ibid.*, p. 28.
18 Ruckstuhl, one of the founders of the National Sculpture Society, had placed an early bid for the position of Chief of Sculpture and his appointment was made official in September, 1902. It was not long, however, before he and Isaac Taylor suffered a falling out. Their difficulty came to a climax when Taylor ordered Ruckstuhl to reduce the amount of sculpture that he had planned for the exposition buildings without informing the architects. Ruckstuhl was also accused of allotting too much of the sculpture to himself. When Bitter took over, no contracts had as yet been let to any sculptor and he was free to introduce a new scheme. (Statement by Ruckstuhl, addressed to the members of the Board of Directors for the St. Louis Exposition on Dec. 3, 1902, Missouri Historical Society, St. Louis.)
19 "Report of the Chief of the Department of Sculpture, Louisiana Purchase Exposition Company, St. Louis, Missouri," one of three typewritten statements by Bitter concerning his role at the St. Louis Fair, included in three bound albums of photographs entitled *St. Louis Louisiana Purchase Exposition, 1904,* Art Division, New York Public Library.
20 America's new status as an imperial power was also a keynote of the Fair as indicated by the space devoted to the display of her newly acquired possessions. For example, the Philippine exhibit alone covered forty acres.
21 Sadakichi Hartmann, the art critic and historian, offered an outline for the sculpture of the Fair that called exclusively for historical subjects ranging from the patriotic to the provincial. Hartmann seemed to be obsessed with scenes of outdoor sports and battle. An entrance group of Yankee Doodle and the Star Spangled Banner was as allegorical as he could get. (Five-page handwritten draft now in Frick Art Reference Library, New York City.)
22 See typewritten report dated Feb. 19, 1903, in which Bitter outlines his scheme of sculpture for the Advisory Board of Sculpture made up of John Quincy Adams Ward, Augustus Saint-Gaudens, and Daniel Chester French. Included in albums mentioned in n. 19, above.
23 Karl Bitter, "Sculpture at the Fair," *Harper's Weekly* (April 23, 1904), p. 16.

CHAPTER VII

1 Letter dated Oct. 1, 1905.
2 Bitter was overjoyed to meet Sullivan and immediately wrote to his wife from Chicago about the experience on Aug. 6, 1903:

"The real event of the day was my meeting the famous architect Sullivan, a most remarkable character, better known perhaps in Europe than in his native town of Chicago. An accidental introduction in the street developing into a friendly drink at a nearby place and also bringing about better acquaintance resulted in my visit at Sullivan's office this P.M. at the sixteenth floor of the Auditorium Tower high above this mercantile city. This interesting man read to me aloud and with splendid pathos his prose poems on art and architecture, which, compelling the most serious and admiring attention, were a rare treat to me. The man fairly fascinated me; I confess that I was surrendering to him in ecstasy. I hope my impressions will not pale too much before I can give you a better and more detailed description of the incident."

3 See minutes of the March 16, 1911, Council Meeting, National Sculpture Society, New York City.

4 Letter from Bitter to his wife, May 6, 1907.

5 *The Cleveland Trust Company* (Cleveland, 1908), pp. 15–16.

6 During the depression of the 1930's the old Bank of Pittsburgh failed and the building on Fourth Avenue was left vacant. A few years after World War II it was all but demolished to make room for a parking lot. Only the six Corinthian columns and the entablature with its sculptured pediment were preserved. In 1953 the façade was dismantled and removed piece by piece to Jefferson Memorial Park, a suburban cemetery, where the columns now stand in a circle as part of a mausoleum. As for the pedimental figures by Bitter, they disappeared in the process and were presumably destroyed in the name of the Pittsburgh Renaissance.

7 Letter from Bitter to his wife, May 6, 1907.

8 *Ohio Architect and Builder,* II (June, 1908), 40.

9 *Ibid.;* $12,000 was to be spent on sculpture.

10 In 1920 the First National Bank was merged with five other local banks to become the Union Trust Company. As a consequence the First National Bank building was abandoned and razed. Most of the marble and decorative fixtures of the building were purchased by the Rev. John M. Powers, who eventually used them to build St. Ann's Church in Cleveland Heights. Unfortunately, Bitter's sculpture was not considered appropriate for a church and no trace of it remains. Apparently it was destroyed after having graced Euclid Avenue for only a dozen years or so.

11 The marble used for the Chamber of Commerce group turned out to be faulty, and the figures were removed in 1926. See New York Chamber of Commerce, *Monthly Bulletin,* XVIII (1926–27).

12 For a well-illustrated article on the Haus Rheingold see Hans Schliepmann, "Haus Rheingold—Berlin, Eine Meisterschoepfung von Bruno Schmitz," *Deutsche Kunst und Dekoration,* XX (April–Sept., 1907), 1–45.

CHAPTER VIII

1 The Wisconsin Legislature of 1903 appointed a Building Commission to consider the construction of a larger capitol building after a large portion of the old one was destroyed by fire on Feb. 27, 1904. *Wisconsin Blue Book* (Madison, 1917), p. 452.

2 Letter from Burnham to the Wisconsin Capitol Commission, July 11, 1906. Official documents dealing with this commission and the new capitol building are collected in the State Historical Society, Archives Division, Madison, Wis.

3 *Ibid.*

4 Letter from Bitter to his wife, Aug. 6, 1906.

5 Letter dated March 12, 1909, from Bitter to Lew Porter, Secretary of the Capitol Commission. All correspondence between these two men which is referred to in this chapter is in the Capitol Commission Files of the State Historical Society, Madison, Wis.

6 The Woodbury Granite Company, Hardwick, Vermont.

7 Letter from Bitter to John Grignola, Aug. 11, 1909, Capitol Commission Files, State Historical Society, Madison, Wis.

8 Letter from Bitter to Porter, Dec. 20, 1909. The carvers must have protested about their discomfort actively enough to cause some embarrassment for Bitter. He wrote: "Meanwhile please accept my apologies; I suppose the poor fellows felt rather chilly (coming from sunny Italy) and took what they considered the most direct route to obtain relief. I will see that a stove is provided for them at once."

9 Letter from Bitter to Porter, Dec. 5, 1908.

10 Letter to Porter, Jan. 26, 1909.

11 Letter from Bitter to Porter, Dec. 5, 1908.

12 *Ibid.*

13 Letter to Porter, Feb. 15, 1911. The quotations in the following three paragraphs are also from this letter.

14 Letter from Bitter to Kestranek, Oct. 30, 1910.

15 Letter from Bitter to Porter, April 12, 1910.

16 Letter dated May 16, 1910.

17 Letter to Kestranek, Jan. 2, 1910.

18 The central figure of the "Wisdom" group is posed in the *contrapposto* of late Greek and later Roman Apollo figures.

19 That Bitter was innovating a new style of conservative sculpture is indicated by comparing his contributions with the more conventional, academic works produced by three of his contemporaries for the Wisconsin capitol building. The south pediment relief by Adolf A. Weinman, the north pediment by Attilio Piccirilli, and the gilded bronze statue of "Forward," surmounting the lantern of the dome, by Daniel Chester French conform to the traditional naturalism prescribed for "idealistic" sculpture by the academy in the late nineteenth century.

CHAPTER IX

1 The building specifications are available in the Office of the Custodian at the Cuyahoga County Courthouse, Cleveland, Ohio. The architects were Lehman & Schmidt, a local firm.

2 A building commission consisting of three County Commissioners and four

private citizens was appointed by the Common Pleas Judges of Cuyahoga County. *Cuyahoga County Board of Commissioners Journal,* No. 26 (1910), Office of the Custodian, Cuyahoga County Courthouse, Cleveland, Ohio.

3 *Cleveland Plain Dealer,* July 16, 1909.

4 "The County Court House" (undated, mimeographed pamphlet, Office of the Custodian, Cuyahoga County Courthouse, Cleveland, Ohio), p. 8.

5 It was finally finished in the thirties, on the basis of Bitter's model, by his student Karl Gruppe (interview with Karl Gruppe, summer, 1961).

6 In several letters written to his wife while away on trips Bitter requests that she send books to him.

7 "James Burrill Angell Papers," Vol. 31, Michigan Historical Collections, Univ. of Mich. Letter of Nov. 27, 1909, from A. H. Fisch, secretary to Arthur Hill who sponsored the monument, to President Angell acknowledging photographs of Bitter's studies.

8 *Ibid.,* letter of Jan. 21, 1910, from Gilbert M. Stark to President Angell. Stark was an attorney and close friend of the patron, Arthur Hill. He wrote from New York saying that he had seen the finished model and was much pleased with it.

9 *The University of Michigan: An Encyclopedic Survey,* ed. Walter A. Donnelly (Ann Arbor, 1958), IV, 1570–73.

10 Jesse Siddall Reeves in *DAB* s.v. "Angell, James Burrill."

11 Letter from Bitter to Hans Kestranek, Nov. 17, 1909. The adjective he used was *umstaendlich.*

12 Letter to his wife, May 6, 1909.

13 For photographs of Saint-Gaudens' McCosh see *American Sculptors Series,* Vol. VIII: *Augustus Saint-Gaudens* (New York: W. W. Norton & Co., under the auspices of the National Sculpture Society, 1948), p. 33.

14 The money for this portrait had also been provided by Arthur Hill, the philanthropic Saginaw lumberman.

15 Frank J. Klingberg in *DAB* s.v. "Tappan, Henry Philip."

16 Bitter apologized for the dog as it originally appeared, saying he had no model (letter to Kestranek, June 25, 1913). However, Karl Gruppe relates that Bitter finally sent for a mastiff which he used for two or three days (interview with Karl Gruppe, summer, 1961).

17 Letter to Kestranek, July 8, 1902.

18 Letter from Bitter to Kestranek, Nov. 21, 1912.

19 See photograph of the Quay statue being carved that accompanies an editorial against the senator and Pennsylvania's big business politics in general in *Colliers,* XL (Jan. 18, 1908), 7.

20 Letter to Kestranek, Nov. 21, 1912, On Nov. 26, 1912, Bitter delivered a report to the Park Board of Kansas City concerning the erection of a monument to Thomas H. Swope, who had once donated the land for the city's largest park. Bitter very emphatically disapproved of any suggestion leading to portrait sculpture in Swope Park. Instead, he recommended a "symbolic memorial," to be situated on an ellipse in the middle of a boulevard that formed the park entrance (*Kansas City Times,* Nov. 27, 1912).

21 Letter from Bitter to his wife, April 25, 1911.

22 Letter from Bitter to Kestranek, June 14, 1912.
23 This title was used for the plaster cast when it was exhibited at the Albright Gallery in 1916.

CHAPTER X

1 *St. Louis Globe-Democrat,* Nov. 3, 1912.
2 *Ibid.*
3 Letter from Bitter to his wife, July 18, 1909.
4 The quotations are from a letter from Bitter to D. R. Francis, July 23, 1909. All correspondence cited in this chapter between these two men is in the Missouri Historical Society, St. Louis.

While this scheme was vastly more ambitious than anything Bitter had in mind before he went to St. Louis, he was certain that it would not be beyond the funds available and he included a rough estimate of the costs, totaling $250,000: temple and terrace for sculpture, $130,000; statue of Jefferson and "The Signing of the Treaty," historical reliefs, and all other sculpture, $70,000; landscape gardening, stairways, etc., $50,000.

Bitter closed his letter by assuring Francis that the above outline for the Jefferson monument was the result of careful consideration and he believed that if it were carried out it would be the most impressive structure of its kind on this hemisphere.

5 Letter from Bitter to Francis, July 23, 1909.
6 Letter to the commission, Oct. 12, 1909, Missouri Historical Society, St. Louis.
7 The firms were Barnett, Haynes & Barnett; Eams & Young; Widman & Walsh; and Theodore C. Link.
8 Minutes of Executive Committee of the Exposition Company, Dec. 29, 1910, Missouri Historical Society, St. Louis.
9 Letter dated Jan. 3, 1911. This letter was presented to the Executive Committee meeting on Jan. 6, 1911, and entered into the minutes in full.
10 Contract for Jefferson Memorial sculpture, May 3, 1911, Missouri Historical Society, St. Louis. Drawn up by Bitter himself, the contract was signed by all concerned without delay.
11 Executive Committee Minutes, May 3, 1911, Missouri Historical Society, St. Louis.
12 Bitter reported progress on the statue in letters to Hans Kestranek, Nov. 21, 1912, Jan. 5 and April 17, 1913.
13 William Curtis, *The True Thomas Jefferson* (Philadelphia, 1901), p. 134.
14 Undated letter from Bitter to D. R. Francis.
15 See Fiske Kimball, *The Life Portraits of Jefferson and Their Replicas* (Philadelphia, 1944).
16 When Bitter finished his portrait monument of Jefferson for St. Louis he wrote that his Jefferson period had come to an end (Bitter to Kestranek, Jan. 5, 1913). President Alderman of the University of Virginia, however, liked the St. Louis statue so much that he expressed a wish to have a replica

erected on the campus opposite the Washington statue by Houdon. Charles R. Crane, the philanthropic progressive, heard of this desire and commissioned his close friend, Karl Bitter, to furnish the replica. The figure was reduced in size to a height of approximately five feet and was cast in bronze. The position of the right arm was changed, but otherwise it is essentially a small reproduction of the St. Louis statue (letter from Bitter to D. R. Francis, Dec. 15, 1914).

17 Merrill D. Peterson, *The Jefferson Image in the American Mind* (New York, 1960), p. 9.

CHAPTER XI

1 Claude Moore Fuess, *Carl Schurz, Reformer, 1829–1906* (New York, 1932), pp. 382–83.

2 Hans Kestranek, "Karl Bitter," *Kunst und Kunsthandwerk,* XXIII (Feb., 1920), 94.

3 Letter to Kestranek, Jan. 5, 1913.

4 As in the case of the two earlier commemorative monuments to Baron von Steuben and General Sigel with which Bitter was associated, the erection of the Carl Schurz monument was an important event among German-American citizens and was dedicated as a symbol of ever-increasing friendship between Germany and the United States. Although it was a cold, windy day, the Schurz monument was unveiled with pomp and ceremony before a crowd of 50,000. In addition to a two-hour long military parade, the United German Singing Societies sang their tribute from a stand built especially for them. Joseph H. Choate, who soon afterward was to work so hard for America's entry into World War I against Germany, read a letter from President Wilson. George McAneny, President of the Borough of Manhattan and Schurz's associate on the National Civil Service Reform League, delivered a biographical address. Count von Bernstorff, longtime German ambassador to the United States, ironically gave Schurz credit for anticipating in 1848 the German unity realized by Bismarck. Richard Bartholdt, the congressman from Missouri whose bill had resulted in the erection of the Steuben monument, represented all German-Americans. Finally, Mayor Gaynor accepted the monument on behalf of New York City, referring to "this work of art—great in a way that I do not fully understand, but which I suppose I shall hereafter fully understand." After the speeches, Bitter, who had predicted in a letter to Kestranek on April 17 that the speakers would not know what they should say regarding the event, helped Agathe, the spinster daughter of Schurz, remove the American flag from the statue. When that was accomplished, the German contingent accompanied the German ambassador to the Deutsches Haus, a memorial building to Schurz at Columbia University, where a portrait of the Emperor was presented as a gift from the Kaiser himself. See *The New York Times,* May 11, 1913.

5 Bitter's visit to the Vienna Secession on June 14, 1909, is recorded in a journal he kept during a month-long trip to Austria where he returned to receive

a long awaited amnesty as a deserter from Emperor Franz Joseph's army. This journal is now in the possession of Mrs. Walter Abel, New York City.

6 According to Karl Gruppe and Mrs. R. McAneny Loud, daughter of George McAneny and business partner for many years of Mrs. Bitter, the bronze statue now standing on the Morningside monument is not the one originally dedicated. When the first figure was cast in bronze by the lost-wax process at the Roman Bronze Foundry it shrank more than was expected, and Schurz, who was a tall thin man in real life, became short and squat in sculpture. Bitter was so unhappy with the original bronze cast when it was installed that after the unveiling ceremonies he immediately set to work to do something about it. At his own expense he and his student-assistant, Karl Gruppe, added several inches to the original plaster model by cutting it into three sections and building it up in between. This lengthened figure was then cast in bronze and the exchange of statues is said to have been made in the middle of the night. (Interviews with Mrs. R. McAneny Loud and Karl Gruppe, April, 1961.)

7 Fuess, p. 381.

8 *New York Herald,* June 6, 1909.

9 Each of the end panels of the Schurz monument measures approximately three and one-half feet in height, while the relief panel for the pedestal is about four and one-half feet square.

10 Letter to Kestranek, March 11, 1911.

11 Interview with Karl Gruppe, April, 1961. The line drawing of a female head in profile (Fig. 91) is owned by Mr. Gruppe and hangs in his New York City studio.

CHAPTER XII

1 Proceedings of the Board of Park Commissioners, June 19, 1911, City Hall, Minneapolis, Minn.

2 Letter to Kestranek, Sept. 11, 1911.

3 *Ibid.*

4 Subscription lists were opened at the Northwestern National Bank, a Lowry-controlled business, and any sum from one dollar was acceptable. Each subscriber received a life membership in the Thomas Lowry Memorial Association and every name was to be listed in the press.

5 Letter from Bitter to Kestranek, Aug. 24, 1911.

6 Letter dated June 14, 1912.

7 Letter from Bitter to Kestranek, June 29, 1912.

8 Letter to Kestranek, July 17, 1912.

9 Letter from Bitter to Kestranek, Nov. 21, 1912.

10 Proceedings of the Board of Park Commissioners, Aug. 6, 1913, City Hall, Minneapolis, Minn.

11 Letter dated Oct. 26, 1913.

12 Letter to Kestranek dated Dec. 26, 1913.

13 *Ibid.*

14 Letter from Bitter to Kestranek, Nov. 26, 1914.
15 Letter from Bitter to his wife, July 29, 1913.
16 Letters from Bitter to Kestranek, Sept. 8 and Oct. 26, 1913.
17 The plaster models of the Lowry statue and one of the allegorical figures were exhibited at the annual exhibition of the Architectural League of New York in February, 1914. See Index of Exhibits, 29th Annual Exhibition, Feb. 8–28, 1914.
18 Letter from Bitter to Kestranek, June 25, 1913.
19 Letter from Bitter to Kestranek, Sept. 11, 1911.
20 Letter from Bitter to Kestranek, Nov, 17, 1909.
21 Letter from Bitter to Kestranek, Sept. 11, 1911.
22 Letter from Bitter to Kestranek, June 25, 1913. Included in the letter is a small sketch of one of the figures.

CHAPTER XIII

1 Each of the speakers at a memorial meeting held in New York's Ethical Culture Hall on May 5, 1915, a month after Bitter's death, emphasized his service to the community in general as well as to the community of sculptors. The moralist, social worker, and reformer, Dr. Felix Adler, who founded the Society for Ethical Culture, praised Bitter for his rectitude and selflessness. Representing the National Sculpture Society, Herbert Adams spoke of Bitter as a "natural commander" with rare executive ability and a strong public spirit. George McAneny, President of the Board of Aldermen, praised Bitter for working to make New York City more beautiful and serviceable. Finally, Oswald Garrison Villard, speaking as a close personal friend, considered Bitter a democrat who recognized the obligations of citizenship by serving in the public interest. See *Proceedings at the Meeting in Memory of Karl Bitter* (New York, 1915). The meeting was held under the auspices of the National Academy of Design, National Sculpture Society, Architectural League of New York, National Institute of Arts and Letters, Art Commission Associates, and Century Association, with Dr. Felix Adler presiding.
2 *Karl Bitter: A Biography* (University of Chicago Press, 1917).
3 *New York Evening Post,* June 23, 1917, Book Section, p. 1.
4 Bitter's scrapbook-diary, entry dated Jan. 25, 1898.
5 In *Municipal Affairs,* II (March, 1898), 73–97. The *Municipal Affairs* was published under the auspices of the New York Reform Club, Committee on Municipal Administration.
6 A bronze by Henry Kirke Brown erected in 1870. See critical editorial in *The New York Times,* Sept. 21, 1870, which describes the Lincoln as "a hideous nightmare which people have after supping on roast beef and lobster salad."
7 "Public Art, the Test of Greatness," *Municipal Affairs,* V (Dec., 1901), 810–17.
8 *Ibid.,* p. 812.

9 *Ibid.*, p. 816.
10 See John Burchard and Albert Bush-Brown, *The Architecture of America: A Social and Cultural History* (Boston, 1961), pp. 274–75.

CHAPTER XIV

1 *Municipal Affairs,* III (Dec., 1899), 616–50.
2 Typical of the other speakers, the architect Charles R. Lamb limited his proposals for City Hall Park to a huge new municipal building of many stories. It would have had intersecting arcades crossing underneath like those eventually used in the skyscraper designed for this purpose by McKim, Mead, and White.
3 Bitter, in *Municipal Affairs,* III, 633.
4 *Ibid.*, p. 636.
5 *Ibid.*, p. 634.
6 *Ibid.*
7 Henry James thought the monument did more for the place than all of its other elements put together because it introduced refinement to a "medley of accidents." See *The American Scene* (New York, 1946), p. 166.
8 Quoted from Joseph Pulitzer's will by his son, Ralph, in a letter to the Secretary of the Art Commission of New York City, June 4, 1912, Correspondence Files, Office of the Art Commission, City Hall, New York.
9 Letter from George L. Rives to Hermon MacNeil, March 21, 1912, Correspondence Files of the National Sculpture Society, New York City.
10 Minutes of the April 9, 1912, Council Meeting, National Sculpture Society, New York City.
11 Minutes of the May 14, 1912, Special Sculptors' Meeting, National Sculpture Society, New York City.
12 Letter dated June 4, 1912, Correspondence Files, Office of the Art Commission, City Hall, New York City.
13 Francis C. Jones and I. N. Phelps Stokes were Bitter's fellow committeemen. The latter was later to compile the comprehensive *Iconography of Manhattan* (6 vols.; New York, 1915–1928).
14 Letter from Bitter to Herbert Adams, June 14, 1912, Correspondence Files, National Sculpture Society, New York City.
15 Copy of letter from Adams to Bitter, June 19, 1912, Correspondence Files, National Sculpture Society, New York City.
16 Minutes of the Art Commission, July 2, 1912, Office of the Art Commission, City Hall, New York City.
17 The first draft of this letter was composed by Robert W. de Forest, Vice President of the Metropolitan Museum, who was also an art commissioner. It was then redrafted by John Quincy Adams, Assistant Secretary of the Art Commission, before it was sent to Bitter for his final approval on July 9, 1912. (See letter from Adams to Bitter, July 9, 1912, Correspondence Files, Office of the Art Commission, City Hall, New York.) Bitter made revisions which clearly stated that his subcommittee approved the type of fountain

proposed by Pulitzer, that is, one similar to those on the Place de la Concorde, but it could not see how a work of that character could be constructed properly for the amount of the bequest. (See letter from Bitter to Adams, July 13, 1912, Correspondence Files, Art Commission Office, City Hall, New York City.)

18 Letter from Ralph Pulitzer to John Quincy Adams, July 29, 1912, Correspondence Files, Office of the Art Commission, City Hall, New York City.

19 Copy of letter from Ralph Pulitzer to Park Commissioner Stover, Oct. 14, 1912, Correspondence Files, Office of the Art Commission, City Hall, New York. Copies were also sent to Bitter; George McAneny, Borough President; and Mr. Wilcox, President of the Public Service Commission of the First District.

20 *Ibid.*

21 The *World,* Dec. 22, 1912. The competing firms were Carrere & Hastings; McKim, Mead, and White; Arnold W. Brunner; H. Van Buren Magonigle; and John Russell Pope. The jury consisted of George B. Post, representing the executors; Whitney Warren, a landscape architect representing the Park Commission; the architects Paul P. Cret and Charles A. Platte; and the sculptor Herbert Adams.

22 The *World,* Jan. 21, 1913.

23 *Ibid.* Fortunately Bitter was wrong about the Fifty-ninth Street trolley line, which was replaced by a subway. Hastings' plans called for inconspicuous iron and glass entrances to the station below.

24 *New York Tribune,* Jan. 21, 1913.

25 Nothing so large as the restaurant proposed in 1961 by Huntington Hartford would have been tolerated however.

26 Of course the replacement of the Cornelius Vanderbilt house with the Bergdorf-Goodman Building, the multiplication of skyscrapers, and the growth of trees at either end of the Plaza have altered the general setting of the Pulitzer Fountain considerably.

27 These accessories were designed and executed by Orazio Piccirilli. See the photograph in the Year Book of the Architectural League of New York and Catalogue of the Thirteenth Annual Exhibition (New York, 1915).

28 The estimates for building the fountain amounted to $27,000 and the figure cost $10,000. The balance of the bequest was used for the architect's fee and all further detail work. See the *World,* Jan. 21, 1913.

29 Letter from Bitter to Hans Kestranek, Nov. 11, 1914.

30 Although Konti is credited with carrying out Bitter's design for the Pulitzer Fountain figure in Ferdinand Schevill's biography of Bitter, in Helen Henderson's account of the Plaza in *A Loiterer in New York* (New York, 1917), and in Beatrice Proske's discussion of Bitter for *Brookgreen Gardens* (Brookgreen, S.C., 1943), Karl Gruppe maintains that he was the one who actually did the greatest part of the work on the full-scale version. According to him, Konti merely visited the studio and touched up a few minor details on the finished figure in order that he should be associated with such an important occasion as Bitter's final work. The notion, among those who

have written about the fountain figure, that Bitter and Konti were close friends is not borne out in Bitter's letters. Even though both were from Vienna and were well acquainted from the time they arrived in the United States, Bitter wrote of losing his respect for Konti and his work (letter from Bitter to Kestranek, March 15, 1914).

31 See John Pope-Hennessy, *Italian High Renaissance and Baroque Sculpture* (London, 1963), Fig. 93, p. 73.

32 The original scale model in plaster for the Plaza figure is owned by Karl Gruppe of New York City, while a bronze cast made from it is in the possession of Dr. Francis Bitter of Centerville, Mass., and another is on display in the outdoor museum of American sculpture, Brookgreen Gardens, near Charleston, S.C.

33 Entry in Bitter's scrapbook-diary on April 16, 1899.

34 Several editions of this statuette were reproduced for sale under the auspices of the National Sculpture Society, and for this reason each is marked with the copyright date of 1910. The Metropolitan Museum has one in storage, another is owned by Mrs. Walter Abel of New York City, and still another one is on display at the Carnegie Institute in Pittsburgh, Pa.

35 While the Plaza and its fountain figure may be considered Bitter's last work, he was actually engaged on another public fountain at the time of his death. By sheer coincidence, Indianapolis had received a bequest in 1913 that was quite similar to the Pulitzer gift to New York City. Emma Ely Depew bequeathed $50,000 to the city for a fountain to be erected on University Square in downtown Indianapolis in memory of her husband, Dr. Richard J. Depew. At the end of the year the Park Board contracted Bitter to design and execute a fountain with a granite basin and bronze figures. During the following year he constructed a sketch model composed of eight early-adolescent figures dancing hand in hand around an elevated basin that supported a female figure playing cymbals; see the photograph reproduced in Ferdinand Schevill, *Karl Bitter: A Biography* (University of Chicago Press, 1917). Early in 1915 Bitter started to develop his design with a large number of figure studies in pencil. (These sketches have been bound and are now in the possession of Mrs. Walter Abel of New York City.) After his death the project was turned over to Alexander Stirling Calder, who used Bitter's basic design for the fountain, including a circle of dancers and a cymbalist (see Fig. 110). On Jan. 20, 1916, a viewing took place at Calder's New York studio on West Tenth Street, at which his scale model for the fountain was displayed alongside Bitter's sketch. Present were members of the Indianapolis Board of Park Commissioners, Henry Bacon, the architect, the executors of Bitter's will, Mrs. Bitter, and Carl H. Lieber, who was invited by the Indianapolis authorities to report on Calder's design. He wrote that Calder had preserved and developed Bitter's original conception, but added that the substitute sculptor should be encouraged to carry out the figures and their accessories in his own style. See Carl H. Lieber's report to the Board of Park Commissioners, Jan. 26, 1916, Correspondence Files, Board of Park Commissioners, City Hall, Indianapolis, Indiana.

Fig. 110.—Depew Fountain, Indianapolis, Indiana, 1915–1916, begun by Bitter and finished by Alexander Calder.

CHAPTER XV

1 Members of the National Sculpture Society exhibited at the exhibitions of the Architectural League during the winter of 1893/1894, in May, 1895, and in May, 1898. An undated letter from the exhibition committee of the National Sculpture Society, consisting of F. W. Ruckstuhl, Thomas Hastings, and Daniel Chester French informs the members of the refusal of the Architectural League to permit the sculptors to participate in their exhibition from Dec. 18, 1893, to Jan. 9, 1894, as a society. See Correspondence Files, National Sculpture Society, New York City.

2 A two-page printed report written by Bitter and his committee concerning the exhibition difficulties of the Society was distributed among its members at the Oct. 18, 1904, meeting. See Minutes, National Sculpture Society, New York City.

3 Minutes of the Regular Meeting, Jan. 10, 1905, National Sculpture Society, New York City.

4 *New York Tribune,* March 22, 1906.

5 *New York Herald,* April 8, 1907.

6 Bitter's inquiry and the replies to it are in the Correspondence Files of the National Sculpture Society, New York City. See letters from W. M. R. French, Director of the Art Institute of Chicago, May 31, 1907; Charles M. Kurtz, Director of the Buffalo Fine Arts Academy and Albright Gallery, June 1, 1907; and Frederick B. McGuire, Secretary and Director of the Corcoran Gallery, June 1, 1907.

7 Correspondence between Bitter and William M. Ellicott from June 5, 1907, to July 12, 1907, is in the Correspondence Files of the National Sculpture Society, New York City.

8 Minutes of the Baltimore Exhibition Committee Meeting, March 18, 1908, National Sculpture Society, New York City.

9 Official Bulletin of the National Sculpture Society, May 5, 1908, Correspondence Files of the National Sculpture Society, New York City.

10 Minutes of the meetings of the jury for the Toledo Exhibition, Oct. 20 and 24, 1911, National Sculpture Society, New York City. Bitter served on this jury.

11 Minutes of the Regular Meeting, Nov. 10, 1914, National Sculpture Society, New York City.

12 Minutes of the Council Meeting and the Regular Meeting, Dec. 8, 1914, National Sculpture Society, New York City.

13 Minutes of the Council Meeting, Feb. 9, 1915, National Sculpture Society, New York City.

14 *Ibid.* The letter from Bitter to Cortissoz was entered into the minutes.

15 Minutes of the Council Meeting, March 9, 1915, National Sculpture Society, New York City.

16 Correspondence between Bitter and Lewis M. Starr, president of Theodore B. Starr, Inc., Jewelers and Silversmiths, concerning the sale of the illegal reproductions manufactured by the Electric Fountain Co. of New York City,

March 17–22, 1915. See Correspondence Files of the National Sculpture Society, New York City.

17 Minutes of the Council Meeting, March 9, 1915, National Sculpture Society, New York City.

18 Minutes of the Council Meeting, Feb. 19, 1904, National Sculpture Society, New York City.

19 Minutes of the Special Council Meeting, April 7, 1909, National Sculpture Society, New York City.

20 See Article II, Section XI, of the National Sculpture Society Bylaws, and the "Code Governing the Conduct of Members of the National Sculpture Society Taking Part in Competitions." The Bylaws and the Code were last published in pamphlet form along with the Constitution and a brief history of the Society in 1960.

21 *Evening Star,* Washington, D.C., Nov. 10, 1897.

22 Minutes of the regular meeting, Feb. 14, 1908, National Sculpture Society, New York City.

23 The Art Commission charter was written by Elihu Root, who as senator in 1910 also sponsored the creation of a National Commission of Fine Arts to advise on and approve future developments in the District of Columbia.

24 Letter from Hermon A. MacNeil, President of the National Sculpture Society, to Charles B. Stover, Park Commissioner of New York City, April 8, 1910, Correspondence Files, National Sculpture Society, New York City.

25 Minutes of the Regular Meeting, April 9, 1912, National Sculpture Society, New York City.

26 Minutes of the Regular Meeting, Jan. 12, 1915, National Sculpture Society, New York City.

27 Minutes of the Regular Meeting, March 9, 1915, National Sculpture Society, New York City.

28 Minutes of the special Council Meeting, March 20, 1915, National Sculpture Society, New York City.

29 The letter from Bitter to George W. McAneny was written into the minutes of the special Council Meeting, March 20, 1915, National Sculpture Society, New York City.

CHAPTER XVI

1 Bitter's contract with the Panama-Pacific Exposition, Sept. 21, 1912. This document is now in the possession of Dr. Francis Bitter, Centerville, Mass.

2 Bitter's journal of his return to Austria, entry dated June 15, 1909.

3 *Ibid.,* June 28, 1909.

4 *Ibid.,* June 30, 1909.

5 Letter to Kestranek, Oct. 30, 1910.

6 Letter to Kestranek, Nov. 17, 1909.

7 Letter dated Jan. 20, 1907. "Ich gehoere meiner sehnsucht nach, meinen Geistesleben nach (wenn ich von dem ueberhaupt reden darf) den Modernen an, meiner Erziehung aber und meiner Entwicklung nach nicht."

8 Letter to Kestranek, June 29, 1912.

9 Quotations in this paragraph are from a letter to Kestranek, Jan. 2, 1910. "Die Einfachheit der archaeischen Formen ist nicht Willkuer, sondern Zwang des Materiales. Die Ueberlieferung bringt Technik; Technik allein ermoeglicht reichere Formengebung. So sehen wir von Stufe zu Stufe die Vervollkommung eines Motives, zaghaft blos fuegen sich neue Themes, neue Motive hinzu. Aber wieder entwickeln sie sich und blos naturgemaess, wie das groessere Beherrschen des Materials es ermoeglicht. So weit ich die Antike kenne, erscheint kein Ding in derselben unvermittelt, ploetzlich in grosser Vollendung."

10 The original draft of this lecture was provided by Mrs. Walter Abel, New York City.

11 Quoted by Edwin Murtha, *Paul Manship* (New York, 1957), pp. 11–12.

12 When Konti first came to the United States from Vienna in 1892 he worked as an assistant in Bitter's studio, and Bitter mentioned him repeatedly throughout his correspondence with Kestranek.

13 Walter Raymond Agard, *The New Architectural Sculpture* (New York, 1935), p. 34.

A Note On Unpublished Sources

THE UNPUBLISHED SOURCES which I cite most frequently are a collection of letters written by Karl Bitter to his wife, Marie, and to a close friend, Hans Kestranek, of Vienna. This collection is in the possession of Bitter's son, Dr. Francis Bitter, Centerville, Massachusetts. Bitter wrote to Mrs. Bitter about his work in a very relaxed and fluent English, which I could use as a guide while translating from his German script the letters to Austria. Both languages appear in a scrapbook-diary kept sporadically by Bitter from the spring of 1896 to early 1900. This document is in the possession of his daughter, Mrs. Walter Abel, New York City. My translation of German into English was imposed upon four extensive entries, written at long intervals between June, 1896, and January, 1898. In them Bitter reminisces about his childhood and youth, and records certain of his experiences as a successful young artist in New York. He made day-by-day entries in English throughout 1899 which provide useful information about his projects of that year. Sketches and photographs are an integral part of the scrapbook-diary and serve as a supplement to the several albums of photographs Bitter kept of his sculpture throughout his career. These too are in the possession of his children.

Two journals (written in English) of trips to Europe are among Bitter's personal effects now in the care of Mrs. Abel. The first is a light-hearted record of the Bitters' wedding trip through France and northern Italy from July to October, 1901. The second is a much more introspective account of his return home to Vienna in June and July, 1909. He had just received an amnesty for his desertion from the Austrian army twenty years earlier, a situation that contributed to the depth of his reflections en route.

Of a professional nature are three typewritten statements written by Bitter in 1903 and 1904 to explain his role as chief of sculpture at the Louisiana

Purchase Exposition. They are included as a text for three bound albums of photographs labeled "St. Louis Louisiana Purchase Exposition, 1904" deposited in the Art Division of the New York Public Library. In them Bitter discusses his plan for the World's Fair sculpture, the techniques and expenses of carrying it out, and the success he had in overcoming labor difficulties. Further documents and letters dealing with the sculpture for the St. Louis World's Fair are found in the D. R. Francis Papers in the Missouri Historical Society, St. Louis. This collection also includes correspondence between Bitter and Francis, and other officials, concerning the design and construction of the Jefferson Memorial in St. Louis, from 1909 to 1913.

Letters exchanged by Bitter and Lew Porter, Secretary of the Wisconsin Capitol Building Commission, dated 1906 through 1912, were a great aid in tracing the development of sculpture for the new capitol in Madison. These and related documents were made available through the State Historical Society, Archives Division, Madison, Wisconsin.

Correspondence of 1909 and 1910, concerning Bitter's relief portraits of University of Michigan presidents Tappan and Angell is located in the James Burrill Angell Papers, Vol. XXXI, Michigan Historical Collections, University of Michigan, Ann Arbor. Of similar importance for the Thomas Lowry monument in Minneapolis are the proceedings of the Minneapolis Board of Park Commissioners, 1911–1913, at City Hall, Minneapolis, Minnesota.

The correspondence files of the City Art Commission at City Hall, New York City, provided valuable information concerning Bitter's role on the Commission, and were especially helpful in following the progress of his plans for the Plaza and its sculpture during the years 1912 and 1913. Finally, of crucial importance to this study were the minutes and correspondence of the National Sculpture Society, New York City. From the late 1890's to 1915 they revealed much information and many insights toward an understanding of Bitter as an artist and aesthetically motivated administrator.

Index